VICO'S
Science of Imagination

VICO'S
Science of Imagination

Donald Phillip Verene

Cornell University Press

ITHACA AND LONDON

First published 1981 by Cornell University Press.
First printing, Cornell Paperbacks, 1991.

International Standard Book Number 0-8014-1391-5 (cloth)
International Standard Book Number 0-8014-9972-0 (paper)
Library of Congress Catalog Card Number 80-69828

*Librarians: Library of Congress cataloging information appears
on the last page of the book.*

Printed in the United States of America

⊗ The paper in this book meets the minimum requirements
of the American National Standard for Information Sciences—
Permanence of Paper for Printed Library Materials, ANSI Z39.48-1984.

To
Giorgio Tagliacozzo

We wander ignorant of the men and the places.
—Virgil, *Aeneid*

Contents

Preface

Giambattista Vico (1668-1744) was throughout his mature years professor of Latin Eloquence at the University of Naples. His works, first written in Latin and later in Italian, were not understood in his lifetime and have not been widely known or understood since. Vico wrote in his *Autobiography*: "Among the caitiff semi-learned or pseudo-learned, the more shameless called him a fool, or in somewhat more courteous terms they said that he was obscure or eccentric and had odd ideas." Vico's "odd ideas" are concentrated in his extraordinary work, the *Scienza nuova,* which he thought to contain the total meaning of his philosophy. Vico has remained an obscure and eccentric thinker. His philosophical interpreters have too frequently bent his ideas to conform to their own. My aim is to allow Vico's ideas to speak for themselves, to see them as fundamental sources of philosophical understanding.

What can be learned from Vico's thought? This question has led me to this book and my purpose is to answer it. Over a ten-year period my views of Vico's thought have developed from an early perception of Vico as the founder of the philosophy of culture and philosophy of myth to an appreciation of the basic significance of all his ideas. I began with a regard for Vico's importance for these special areas and find myself now an *appassionato* of Vico. I wish to consider him as an original thinker without attaching his ideas to any contemporary doctrine or philosophical school.

The translations of Vico's *Autobiography* (1944) and *New Science* (1948/1968) by Thomas Goddard Bergin and Max Harold Fisch have provided the basis for the development of a literature on Vico in English. The translation of these two key works makes access to Vico's ideas possible for English readers. Any scholar who knows both Italian and English will find these excellent translations useful in approaching the texts. Fisch's introductions to these editions and his essays on various aspects of the background of Vico's thought are indispensable to the study of Vico. I have made repeated use of them. Fisch's introductory essay to the *Autobiography* remains the best general introduction to Vico in English.

Two book-length studies on Vico have appeared in English in recent years: Leon Pompa, *Vico: A Study of the 'New Science'* (1975), and Isaiah Berlin, *Vico and Herder: Two Studies in the History of Ideas* (1976). The Vico portion of Berlin's work is an expansion and revision of his earlier study, "The Philosophical Ideas of Giambattista Vico" (1960). My book follows a different course from Pompa's in that I take the imaginative universal and imagination (*fantasia*) as the basis of Vico's *New Science*. This emphasis on the importance of the imagination places my work closer to that of Berlin. It differs from Berlin's in its focus on the meaning of Vico's philosophical ideas considered apart from the problem of their significance for the history of ideas.

The present book originated in a telephone call from Giorgio Tagliacozzo in late spring 1969. This became one of many calls, the beginning of an association, a collaboration on our volume *Giambattista Vico's Science of Humanity,* and a friendship that has continued throughout my study of Vico. Giorgio Tagliacozzo, who founded the Institute for Vico Studies in New York in 1974, is singlehandedly responsible for the current activity in Vico studies among English-speaking scholars. Were it not for

PREFACE

his initial prodding of my own interest in Vico, the present book would not have come about.

The particular idea for this book began with my view, advanced at the 1976 New York conference on Vico and Contemporary Thought, that there are two kinds of *fantasia* in the *New Science*—poetic or mythic *fantasia* and recollective or philosophic *fantasia*. In fulfilling his duty as the commentator on my paper, Isaiah Berlin advanced sympathetic questions and remarks that led me to pursue the possibility of developing this view into a full interpretation of the *New Science*. The present study has taken my idea in various unforeseen directions.

The final stage in my thinking on Vico owes a debt to Ernesto Grassi of the University of Munich, to our friendship and the stimulating conversations I have had with him at various times in the past several years. These have led me to see the philosophical significance of rhetoric and have suggested to me a sense of rhetoric coming from Renaissance humanist thinkers which has enabled me to understand the role of rhetoric in Vico. Without these insights I would have been unable to connect *fantasia* with a type of speech through which philosophical thought can ground itself in more than conceptual criticism. Professor Grassi has kindly read the manuscript and raised many helpful points.

Molly Black Verene, in this as in other Vichian projects, has given valuable help. I am most grateful for her attention and careful suggestions.

I wish to thank the American Council of Learned Societies for support of travel to Venice to the Vico/Venezia conference in August 1978, which allowed me opportunity to discuss my thesis of Vico's originality with a number of Italian scholars. I thank the Institute for the Arts and Humanistic Studies of The Pennsylvania State University for a research grant for fall term 1978 given in support of this project. I also thank the Central Fund for Research of the College of Liberal Arts for several occasions of support. Finally, I thank The Pennsylvania

11

State University for a period of sabbatical leave spent in Italy on the writing of this work.

D. P. V.

Florence, Italy

Chronology of Vico's Principal Writings

Inaugural Orations 1699–1707

De nostri temporis studiorum ratione 1709
  (On the Study Methods of Our Time)

De antiquissima Italorum sapientia 1710
  (On the Ancient Wisdom of the Italians)

Il diritto universale 1720–22
  (Universal Law)
    De uno universi iuris principio et fine uno 1720
      (On the One Principle and the One End of Universal Law)
    De constantia iurisprudentis 1721
      (On the Constancy of the Jurisprudent)
    Notae in duos libros 1722
      (Notes on the above two works)

Scienza nuova 1725
  (First New Science)

Vita di Giambattista Vico scritta da se medesimo 1725–28
  (Autobiography)

Scienza nuova seconda 1730/1744
  (New Science)

Supplement to the Autobiography 1731

De mente heroica 1732
  (On the Heroic Mind)

VICO'S
Science of Imagination

Frontispiece to Vico's *New Science*, 1730/1744

CHAPTER 1

Introduction: Vico's Originality

At the beginning of Vico's *New Science* is a frontispiece that depicts the relation of the divine to the world. God appears in the sky as an eye within a triangle, reflecting his vision onto the breast of a female figure of metaphysic who surmounts a globe representing the world of nature. In addition to this abstract symbol of nature we see thick clouds and forest surrounding a clearing in which are spread out various objects of the world of civil society, prominent among which is a fasces representing the origin of civil law. To the left, illuminated by a ray reflected from the breast of metaphysic, is a statue of Homer, the first known poet of Western tradition. In the middle, separating the earth from the sky and the forest from the clearing, and by one of its corners supporting metaphysic and the globe of nature, is a stone altar, upon which, among other objects, is placed a lituus for taking auguries, signifying divination. The picture distinguishes the divine from the world and, within the world, the natural from the human. In the framework of these two separations appear the oppositions of darkness and light, earth and sky, forest and clearing, divination and civil practice, metaphysics and poetry.

In the opening sentence of the *New Science* Vico says that this engraving is to serve the reader as a conception of the idea of the work before he reads it, and as an aid to his imagination and memory to recall the work once read. Vico included the frontispiece and its explanation at the last minute during the printing of the second version of the *New Science*. They were substituted for an advertisement of this second version accompanied by correspondence showing the difficulties Vico encountered in bringing out the edition in Venice and his decision to recast the contents and bring the work out himself in Naples. In the final hour Vico deleted this undistinguished material and produced a master image, a seal of his thought. This picture, which is the origin point for the reader, itself depicts an origin; it is the coat of arms, the heroic hieroglyph, or mute sign of the truth of the *New Science*.[1]

My aim in this work is the act of recall of which Vico speaks. I have before me not only the frontispiece, but the *New Science* itself and other of Vico's works that surround it and make up its genesis.[2] The center point, the middle term for my analysis, is

---

[1]The frontispiece and its explanation first appeared in the second edition of the *New Science* in 1730; see *The Autobiography of Giambattista Vico*, trans. Max Harold Fisch and Thomas Goddard Bergin (Ithaca: Cornell University Press, 1944; Cornell Paperbacks ed., 1975), p. 194. Fisch indicates that Vico's withdrawal of the material was probably due to a conciliatory letter from Lodoli in Venice (ibid., p. 221, n. 198). Fisch suggests that Vico may have been influenced by Shaftesbury's employment of a frontispiece in his *Second Characters* (ibid., pp. 81–82). Fausto Nicolini suggests that Vico also may have seen the frontispiece of the original edition of Hobbes's *Leviathan* of 1651 and conceived the figure of metaphysic as an allegory of spiritual values in contraposition to the materialistic significance of the figure of Hobbes's work. See Nicolini, *Commento storico alla seconda Scienza nuova*, 2 vols. (Rome: Edizioni di Storia e Letteratura, 1949–50), I, sec. 1. Paolo Rossi remarks that the female figure of metaphysic was probably inspired by Ripa's *Iconologia* (ed. of Padova, 1611). See Rossi, *Le sterminate antichità: Studi vichiani* (Pisa: Nistri-Lischi, 1969), pp. 184–85. The engraving for the *New Science* was designed at Vico's direction by Domenico Antonio Vaccaro.

[2]Throughout this book, the title *New Science* denotes the *Scienza nuova seconda*, the title coined by Vico for the second edition of 1730 and commonly used since Nicolini to designate this and the third edition of 1744. The first edition of the *New Science*, the *Scienza nuova prima* of 1725, will be referred to as the first *New Science*. By the term "new science," I will mean Vico's doctrine itself rather than

the framework of the divine, natural, and human worlds as illuminated by these works. Their crossings and oppositions are the *topoi* of my account. Many minds have applied their ingenuity to Vico's work, and it is the nature of great thinkers such as Vico to present many sides for interpretation. My approach to Vico is philosophical.[3] Most study of Vico has been preoccupied with sources, influences, and comparisons. My concern is to consider the philosophical truth of Vico's ideas themselves, rather than to examine their historical character. The historical context is of great importance for understanding the meaning of Vico's terms and the general sense of his thought, but a great deal has been done on this and I wish to presuppose much of it.

My approach is twofold: to interpret the central theses of Vico's thought and at the same time to develop the problems of Vico's philosophy themselves. In this sense the present book is intended as both an examination of Vico and a work of Vichian philosophy. I hold that Vico's ideas constitute a philosophy of recollective universals which generates philosophical understanding from the image, not from the rational category. This approach regards imagination as a method of philosophical thought, rather than as a subject matter to which philosophical thought can be directed. I believe the approach to Vico's thought through these two levels—the textual interpretation of his ideas and the apperception of their unity in the conception

---

the work that contains it, i.e., rather than the *New Science* of 1730/1744. References to the *New Science* are to the paragraph enumeration common to the *Scienza nuova seconda* of the Laterza edition and the Bergin and Fisch revised English translation: *Opere di G. B. Vico*, 8 vols. in 11 (Bari: Laterza, 1911–41), 4, and *The New Science of Giambattista Vico*, rev. trans. of the third edition, Thomas Goddard Bergin and Max Harold Fisch (Ithaca: Cornell University Press, 1968; 2d printing 1975).

[3]Recent book-length studies of Vico's philosophical ideas are: Leon Pompa, *Vico: A Study of the 'New Science'* (Cambridge: Cambridge University Press, 1975); Isaiah Berlin, *Vico and Herder: Two Studies in the History of Ideas* (New York: Viking Press, 1976); Ferdinand Fellmann, *Das Vico-Axiom: Der Mensch macht die Geschichte* (Freiburg/Munich: Verlag Karl Alber, 1976). The relationship of my views to Pompa's and Berlin's are noted above in the Preface. See my review of Fellmann's work in *Journal of the History of Philosophy*, 17 (1979), 471–74.

of philosophy as a special kind of recollective imagination—is the application to Vico of his own method of philological and philosophical understanding. His texts are the philological particulars or "certains" of my account, and their truth as recollective imagination is the philosophical universal.

Vico's thought must be understood from the inside. The act of recalling Vico's science is not the examination of its elements as externals. Memory and imagination, at least as Vico understood them, are powers that give us an inside perspective, an internal relation to the thing known. Understanding requires that we enter into the mental place of Vico's *New Science* and its internal motions. This process in turn presupposes that it is possible to recirculate the elements of the *New Science,* not precisely in the way Vico circulated them, but in a manner so that certain aspects of his work can be reflected in different words. Behind these reflections, as if they are an image on glass, should be seen Vico's own work, and behind its transparency, the real motions of the divine, natural, and human worlds.

In his last important work, the oration "On the Heroic Mind" (1732), Vico urges his listeners to seek to manifest the heroic mind we all possess,[4] to lead ourselves beyond our believed capacities, to enter areas of thought for which we do not think ourselves prepared. The heroic mind is the basis for true education. It seeks the sublime. It seeks the sublime first, Vico says, in the divine and then in nature. Finally, it has as its goal the wisdom of the human world oriented toward the good of the human race. This wisdom is the spirit of the whole which pervades and informs all the parts of true knowledge.

Vico's view of the importance of the vision of the whole is reflected in his later address to the Academy of Oziosi on the connection between philosophy and eloquence (1737), in which

---

[4]*De mente heroica, Opere* 7: 3–20; English trans. "On the Heroic Mind," trans. Elizabeth Sewell and Anthony C. Sirignano, in *Vico and Contemporary Thought,* ed. Giorgio Tagliacozzo, Michael Mooney, and Donald Phillip Verene (Atlantic Highlands, N.J. and London: Humanities Press and Macmillan, 1979), pt. 2, pp. 228–45.

he speaks of the grace with which Socrates reasoned about all parts of knowledge human and divine.[5] These late views relate back to Vico's first work of original philosophy, his oration *On the Study Methods of Our Time* (1708–9).[6] The subject of this oration is the contrast between the ancients and the moderns. What is lacking in modern education, Vico says, is the perspective of the whole. The grasp of the whole through specific study is the flower of wisdom.[7] These orations teach that the whole is the flower of wisdom, the true heroism of the mind, and the eloquence of thought. To approach Vico's work in less than the spirit of the whole is counter to his advice and his understanding of the education of the soul. The heroic age is the middle age of Vico's ideal eternal history, his *storia ideale eterna*, which comprises the ages of the divine, heroic, and human. The heroic is the basis of his thought, and the sense of tragedy characteristic of the heroic pervades and informs the *New Science* as a whole.

In his section on method in the *New Science* Vico indicates that the proof of his science is that the reader make the science for himself.[8] The reader is to narrate the science to himself. In so doing, Vico says, the reader will experience in his mortal body a divine pleasure. This divine pleasure flows from the reader's power to cause the ideal eternal history of humanity to arise within himself, to grasp the necessities of the divine ideas that guide it. My recall of Vico's thought is motivated by this divine pleasure. My aim is to reflect the place and motion of the *New Science*. My account does not meditate fully all the aspects of Vico's narration, and in my recall the divine pleasure is incomplete, but it is aimed in the direction of completeness. Like Dante at the beginning of the *Divina commedia*, I wish to attain the *dilettoso monte*, with Vico, not Virgil, as my guide. I wish to see Vico as a guide to the ideas of wisdom, heroism, tragedy, barba-

---

[5]"Le accademie e i rapporti tra la filosofia e l'eloquenza," *Opere* 7: 33–37.

[6]*On the Study Methods of Our Time*, trans. Elio Gianturco (Indianapolis: Library of Liberal Arts, Bobbs-Merrill, 1965), sec. 14.

[7]Ibid., p. 77.

[8]*New Science*, §§342–50.

rism, memory, providence, imagination, and ingenuity—ideas that have fallen by the wayside in modern philosophy.

Vico is described in histories of philosophy as the founder of the philosophy of history. This common view is not an adequate conception of his philosophy since it presents Vico as a specialized thinker. Vico is the author of a complete philosophy that can hold its own in terms of the level of critical examination commonly associated with the study of such figures as Descartes, Locke, Leibniz, Hume, Kant, and Hegel. Vico's philosophy contains principles of mind and reality which are as basic as any found among the well-known works that have actively shaped modern humanistic thought. Vico's ideas are of universal value. His ideas are not simply interesting for his time or primarily valuable for the comprehension of the background of some special field of thought.

Vico has, in fact, had no serious effect on the development of modern thought or society. The scholarship concerning Vico's influence on French thinkers and the nineteenth-century German Romantics, in addition to the circulation of his thought in Great Britain, and the use of his ideas by early Italian nationalists does not show that Vico has had any decisive influence on the course of Western thought and life in the two and one-half centuries since the publication of his definitive version of the *New Science*. Vico's ideas have been endorsed and, in some cases, directly used by famous figures such as Foscolo, Jacobi, Goethe, Herder, Michelet, Cousin, Coleridge, Marx, Croce, Sorel, Joyce, and W. B. Yeats. His ideas were strongly promoted by Michelet in the nineteenth century and by Croce in the twentieth century. They figure in some of the most important literary work of the twentieth century, that of Joyce. There are references to Vico in influential works, as in Marx's footnote to Vico in *Capital*.[9] Vico has not been a force in shaping the modern mind in any way

[9]See Fisch's remarks on Vico and the Marxist tradition, *Autobiography*, pp. 104–7. For Marx's footnote to Vico see *Capital*, vol. 1, ch. 13.

comparable to the classic thinkers of continental rationalism, British empiricism, or German idealism.

The primary danger in interpreting Vico, a danger perhaps common to the study of obscure but original thinkers, is placing his thought in the service of a position not his own. Both Michelet and Croce, through the brilliance of their own minds, bent Vico's thought in their own directions as they attempted to promote his ideas. Michelet made an abridged translation of the *New Science* and concentrated on those aspects of Vico's conception of history that most fit his own. Croce's interest in seeing Vico as the Italian Hegel is the basis for his study *La filosofia di Giambattista Vico* (1911), translated by the British idealist R. G. Collingwood (*The Philosophy of Giambattista Vico*). Croce's interest in connecting Vico to Hegel led him to create an imaginary conversation set during Hegel's last days, in which Hegel is introduced to Vico's thought by a visiting Neapolitan scholar.[10] The connection of Vico with Hegelianism opened Vico studies to the twentieth century, but it began a period in which Vico was seen only through the eyes of a philosophy of the idea. Many of Vico's most brilliant interpreters hang like albatrosses around his neck, inhibiting open readings of his views. The practice of turning Vico's thought to one's own is a danger to which a great number of his commentators have succumbed, and Vico's ship has been sailed under many flags—absolute idealism, Catholicism, Marxism, historicism, particular conceptions of contemporary epistemology, and the methodologies of various contemporary schools of philosophy. Although Vico's thought can be found through such approaches, it is soon lost in the security of their shores.

One area of Vico scholarship has emphasized the lines of Vico's influence on others. This research originated in the learned and indispensable *Bibliografia vichiana* of Croce and

---

[10]Benedetto Croce, "An Unknown Page from the Last Months of Hegel's Life," trans. James W. Hillesheim and Ernesto Caserta, *The Personalist*, 45 (1964), 344–45, 351.

Nicolini,[11] and is summarized and extended by Fisch in his expert introduction to the English edition of Vico's *Autobiography*.[12] Vico's effect on various intellectual traditions has also been the subject of numerous particular studies.[13] Vico himself hoped to be an influential thinker. In the *Autobiography* he calls attention to the favorable response of Jean Le Clerc, who received and reviewed the first two volumes of Vico's *Universal Law*.[14] Although Le Clerc never understood the true meaning of this work, his was the only significant response Vico received from the thinkers of northern Europe during his career. In *Vici vindiciae*, his defense against a false description of the first *New Science* (1725) placed in the book notices of the Leipzig *Acta Eruditorum*, Vico could point only to this recognition by Le Clerc, and to the invitation to write his *Autobiography* which he had had from Gian Artico Porcìa of Venice, as evidence that he was a scholar.[15] In a letter to Abbé Esperti early in 1726,[16] Vico laments the reception of the first *New Science* in terms that remind one of Hume's remark that his *A Treatise of Human Nature* fell "deadborn from the press."

It is possible to reason here, as Vico himself appears to have reasoned: if the ideas and discoveries of these works are of the first magnitude, and they are, then they should produce effects similar to those of the works of great authors. I include in this area not only studies that seek out Vico's lines of historical influence, but also those that in a comparative fashion seek to demonstrate that Vico expressed certain ideas in advance of later thinkers, not directly influenced by him. It is difficult to

[11]Benedetto Croce, *Bibliografia vichiana*, rev. and enlg. by Fausto Nicolini, 2 vols. (Naples: Ricciardi, 1947–48).

[12]"Vico's Reputation and Influence," *Autobiography*, pp. 61–107.

[13]E.g., various of the essays in: *Omaggio a Vico* (Naples: Morano, 1968); *Forum Italicum*, vol. 2, no. 4 (1968); *Giambattista Vico: An International Symposium*, ed. Giorgio Tagliacozzo and Hayden V. White (Baltimore: The Johns Hopkins University Press, 1969); and *Archives de Philosophie*, 40 (Jan.-Mar. 1977), no. 1.

[14]*Autobiography*, pp. 158–59, 164–65.

[15]*Vici vindiciae, Opere* 3, sec. 7.

[16]"All'Abate Esperti in Roma," *Autobiografia, seguita da una scelta di lettere, orazioni e rime*, ed. Mario Fubini, 2d ed. (Turin: Einaudi, 1970), pp. 109–12.

explain why Vico's ideas have influenced only particular individuals and enjoyed only limited periodic revivals, seeming to
follow Vico's own principle of course and recourse, of *corso e
ricorso.*

In his still valuable study on Vico published in 1884, Robert
Flint says of Vico: "The more the sciences of history, of society,
and of law are cultivated, the more will his reputation grow."[17]
Despite considerable cultivation of these fields, this has not
happened.[18] Perhaps Vico's explanation in his letter to Esperti
still holds true, that a book that displeases the many cannot
achieve universal applause, and that his idea of providence as
the true justice of the human race is too challenging an idea in a
world of letters dominated by the fluctuation between the
"chance" of Epicurus and the "necessity" of Descartes' rationalism. I will shortly add my own answer to the question of why
Vico has not been better understood, in terms of Vico's emphasis on the image as the primary source of philosophizing.

Another area of concentrated investigation of Vico concerns
the sources of his thought, with considerable recent interest in
the relationship of Vico's ideas to the culture and thought of his
own time. In this context it is possible to reason: if Vico's ideas
are to be understood, they must be seen in relation to certain
precedent ideas in classical and Christian thought, or in relation
to certain currents of modern thought in the Naples of Vico's
day. In the *Autobiography* Vico describes his schooling and pro-
grams of reading in classical and scholastic thought and places
the basis of his thought in his "four authors"—Plato, Tacitus,
Bacon, and Grotius.[19] Much more than he reports, Vico was involved in the intellectual atmosphere of Naples, even during
his early years while outside Naples at Vatolla.[2] It is rare that

[17]Robert Flint, *Vico* (Edinburgh and London: William Blackwood, 1884), p. 3.
[18]See Fisch's remarks, "What Has Vico to Say to Philosophers of Today?" in
Vico and Contemporary Thought, pt. 1, pp. 9–19.
[19]*Autobiography*, pp. 138–39, 154–55.
[20]Paolo Rossi, Introduzione, in *La scienza nuova*, ed. Paolo Rossi (Milan: Rizzoli,
1977), pp. 5–13. See also Fisch, Introduction, *Autobiography*, pp. 34–37.

an author gives as much information on the genesis of his own thought as does Vico in the *Autobiography,* but he never explains how he generated his most original ideas from his study or associations.

His conception that "the true is the made," *verum et factum convertuntur,* around which so much of his thought turns, is an example. Whether it is derived from the Thomistic saying that "truth and reality are convertible," *ens et verum convertuntur,* connected with the Augustinian doctrine that God creates by knowing (a view that Croce argues against),[21] or is derived from orthodox Catholic thought (as Löwith holds),[22] or is best approached through its precursors in ancient thought and its roots in the Renaissance Platonism of Marsilio Ficino and the mathematical and experimental method of Galileo (as Mondolfo suggests in his book on this principle),[23] is by no means clear. Even less clear is how Vico moved from this idea as a metaphysical doctrine of truth, in *On the Ancient Wisdom of the Italians,* to it as a principle of history as made by humans, in the *New Science.* Vico gives no account of the transference of this principle from his early to his later thought.[24]

Karl-Otto Apel in *Die Idee der Sprache in der Tradition des Humanismus von Dante bis Vico* (The Idea of Language in the Tradition of Humanism from Dante to Vico) has called Vico the owl of Minerva of Renaissance humanistic culture.[25] Ernesto Grassi in

[21]Benedetto Croce, "The Sources of Vico's Theory of Knowledge," Appendix III of *The Philosophy of Giambattista Vico,* trans. R. G. Collingwood (New York: Russell and Russell, 1964).

[22]Karl Löwith, "Geschichte und Natur in Vicos 'Scienza nuova,'" *Quaderni Contemporanei,* 2 (1969), 135–69.

[23]Rodolfo Mondolfo, *Il "verum-factum" prima di Vico* (Naples: Guida, 1969). See further the exchange between M. Reale and Rodolfo Mondolfo in *La Cultura,* 9 (1971), 61–96; 392–96, and Eugenio Garin, "Ancora sul 'verum-factum' prima di Vico," *Bollettino del Centro di Studi Vichiani,* 2 (1972), 59–61.

[24]A translation of *De antiquissima Italorum sapientia* (On the Ancient Wisdom of the Italians) is currently being prepared by Lucia Palmer (Cornell University Press). A translation of this work (but omitting the chapters on metaphysical points) and portions of other of Vico's early works is forthcoming by Leon Pompa, *Vico: Selected Writings* (Cambridge University Press).

[25]Karl-Otto Apel, *Die Idee der Sprache in der Tradition des Humanismus von Dante bis Vico,* 2d ed. (Bonn: Bouvier Verlag Herbert Grundmann, 1975), pp. 320–21.

Macht des Bildes (Power of the Image) has made a similar observation.[26] Here and in other works he has emphasized the importance of the connection of Vico's thought to the views of rhetoric and imagination involved in the works of such thinkers as Pico della Mirandola, Gianfrancesco Pico, Petrarch, Salutati, Landino, Poliziano, and Valla.[27] The ideas of these thinkers are generally regarded as literary in nature and given very little philosophical study. Vico's thought is close in form to the forgotten humanistic thinkers of the Renaissance, although this connection is not a simple one. Much could be learned from examination of the relation of Vico's doctrines to the thought of Giordano Bruno and the Hermetic tradition.[28]

Although the Renaissance seems quite important for understanding the form of Vico's thought, the attitudes of scientific and theoretical inquiry that surrounded Vico in his own age are also of great importance. Vico's conception of a "new science" cannot be understood apart from the intellectual atmosphere of his time, to which, for example, Fisch[29] and Garin[30] have in different ways called attention. Vico can be rightly understood only if

[26]Ernesto Grassi, *Macht des Bildes: Ohnmacht der rationalen Sprache, Zur Rettung des Rhetorischen* (Cologne: M. DuMont Schauberg, 1970), p. 194.

[27]Ernesto Grassi, *Humanismus und Marxismus: Zur Kritik der Verselbständigung von Wissenschaft. Mit einem Anhang "Texte Italienischer Humanisten"* (Hamburg: Rowohlt, 1973); and *Die Macht der Phantasie: Zur Geschichte abendländischen Denkens* (köingstein/Ts.: Athenäum, 1979).

[28]Frances A. Yates, *Giordano Bruno and the Hermetic Tradition* (London: Routledge and Kegan Paul, 1964) when read in connection with the *New Science*, is most suggestive, as is her work *The Art of Memory* (Chicago: University of Chicago Press, 1966). In a recent review Isaiah Berlin has remarked concerning the possible connection of Vico and the Renaissance Hermetic tradition: "if only Dame Frances Yates could be interested in turning her learning and imagination to this rich and relatively unplowed field!" See Berlin, "Corsi e Ricorsi," *Journal of Modern History*, 50 (1978), 484. See also A. Corsano, "Vico e la tradizione ermetica," in *Omaggio a Vico*, pp. 7–24; and Paolo Rossi, *Le sterminate antichità*, pp. 197–202 et passim.

[29]Max H. Fisch, "The Academy of the Investigators," in *Science, Medicine, and History: Essays on the Evolution of Scientific Thought and Medical Practice Written in Honour of Charles Singer*, ed. E. Ashworth Underwood, 2 vols. (London: Oxford University Press, 1953), I, 521–63.

[30]Eugenio Garin, "Vico e l'eredità del pensiero del Rinascimento," in *Vico oggi*, ed. Andrea Battistini (Rome: Armando Armando, 1979), pp. 69–93.

both his sense of rhetoric and his sense of scientific inquiry are kept in mind.

Another trend of research on Vico aims to establish the importance of his ideas for contemporary thought. Here there is an attempt to make Flint's above-mentioned reasoning actually come true: if Vico's ideas have not in the past been agents shaping the development of modern knowledge, they can now become so by their relevance for the social sciences and the humanities. Studies in this area have concentrated on the connection of Vico's ideas with those of seminal thinkers in phenomenology, structuralism, semiotics, literary criticism, genetic psychology, myth analysis, and linguistics. More generally Vico's *New Science* has been regarded as a basis for confronting the fragmentation of contemporary thought, a fragmentation characterized by the increasing lack of a common culture within which the divisions of knowledge can be formed. The concern to seek the foundations of knowledge through Vico's thought has provided the background for recent attempts to bring Vico's thought to the attention of English-speaking scholars.[31]

The importance of Vico's conception of barbarism for understanding present society is a central concern of this book. The fragmentation of contemporary knowledge is not simply a conceptual problem of understanding the process of specialization of mental activity. It is a symptom of the "deep solitude of spirit and will," the *somma solitudine d'animi e di voleri,* of which Vico speaks and which he associated with the third age of a sequence of ideal eternal history, the decadence in which men "finally go mad and waste their substance," in which *finalmente impazzano in istrapazzar le sostanze.*[32] This is the barbarism of reflective thought, of the intellect that has lost its connection with the imagination of the whole, which is the flower of wisdom.

Such barbarism indicates a loss of the human's image of itself, the inability of the thinker to reflect his own wholeness into the

[31]Giorgio Tagliacozzo, "Introductory Remarks," in *Vico and Contemporary Thought,* pt. 1, pp. 1–8.
[32]*New Science,* §§241 and 1106.

products and divisions of his own thought. This barbarism of thought is a reflection of the barbarism of technological life, the life of procedures of action and social organization which give increasing definiteness to human experience without cultural center or perspective of mind. At the beginning of his edition of Vico's *On the Study Methods of Our Time,* Elio Gianturco rightly remarks: "We live in a Cartesian world, a world of scientific research, technology, and gadgets, which invade and condition our lives."[33] The use of Vico's thought to seek the foundations of social and humanistic knowledge fits his concerns, stated in the early and late orations, to connect knowledge with wisdom, heroism, and eloquence.

The danger involved in each of the approaches mentioned above is that expressed in the second axiom of Vico's *New Science.*[34] Broadly stated, it claims that the mind has a propensity to reduce the unfamiliar, the distant and obscure, to what is familiar. If Vico's ideas are not examined with great sensitivity to this principle, their meanings are easily merged with those developed more fully and with more familiarity by later thinkers, or are seen as transformations of better-understood earlier ideas, or attain life only through their importance for issues in contemporary thought. The movement from the unfamiliar to the familiar does not always take place in obvious fashion. As I have mentioned, Vico's Achilles' heel is the ease with which his thoughts have been transformed into viewpoints not his own, viewpoints that are more easily understood.

In his early work, *De antiquissima Italorum sapientia* (On the Ancient Wisdom of the Italians) (1710), Vico says that he is not a follower of any school.[35] This can profitably be used as a principle for the interpretation of his ideas. I am not a follower of any school, nor am I attempting to apply some given doctrine of method to the interpretation of Vico's texts. Three authors and

[33]Elio Gianturco, "Introduction," *Study Methods,* p. ix.
[34]*New Science,* §122.
[35]*De antiquissima Italorum sapientia, Opere* 1: Prooemium. See also *Autobiography,* p. 133.

three particular works have especially affected my thought: Kant's *Critique of Judgment,* Hegel's *Phenomenology of Spirit,* and Cassirer's *Philosophy of Symbolic Forms.* What I have understood from these works has led me to understand things about Vico's work. They are the background from which I have read Vico and against which in large part I wish to place his ideas.

Vico should be approached as an unfamiliar other, whose thought teaches doctrines much less close to us than we may wish to think. My claim that Vico's philosophy is a philosophy of recollective imagination, of recollective universals, is not an attempt to familiarize Vico's thought in terms of an existing philosophical perspective or method. Vico is the originator of a new orientation for philosophical thought. This philosophy places the image over the concept, the speech over the argument, and the mythic divination over the fact.

It is a truism to say that the Western philosophical tradition is dominated by reason.[36] Western philosophical thought begins with the notion of reason and attempts to have reason come to terms with the concreteness of experience as it is perceived and lived. The Platonic quarrel with poetic images and Aristotle's concern to conceive man as rational are each in their own way evidence of this. I think that Vico stands outside the Western tradition of philosophical thought, despite Croce's efforts to integrate him into it through the philosophy of Hegel.

Cassirer, a thinker in many ways quite close to Vico, saw the problem of modern philosophy in terms of a difference between the philosophy of spirit or *Geist* and the philosophy of life or *Leben.* This distinction was so fundamental for him that he planned a fourth volume of *The Philosophy of Symbolic Forms* to treat it.[37] The distinction between philosophies of *Geist* and those

[36]My remarks here follow my paper "Vico's Philosophical Originality," in *Vico: Past and Present,* ed. Giorgio Tagliacozzo (Atlantic Highlands, N.J.: Humanities Press, 1981), pt. 1, pp. 127–43; Italian trans.: "L'originalità filosofica di Vico," trans. Andrea Battistini, in *Vico oggi,* pp. 95–120.

[37]Donald Phillip Verene, ed., *Symbol, Myth, and Culture: Essays and Lectures of Ernst Cassirer 1935–1945* (New Haven: Yale University Press, 1979), Introduction and Appendix; and Ernst Cassirer, *The Philosophy of Symbolic Forms,* trans.

of *Leben* is useful for understanding Vico's position in relation to modern philosophy set against the tradition of reason in Western philosophy.

Cassirer sees philosophical idealism as a development of the philosophy of *Geist,* moving from Descartes and Leibniz to Kant and Hegel and on to his own conception of the symbol.[38] Cassirer was aware that Kant's understanding of the concept must move from its basis in scientific understanding in the *Critique of Pure Reason* toward connections with other concrete frameworks of cultural life. Cassirer sees the roles of the imagination in the schematism of the first *Critique* and in the *Critique of Judgment* as important centers of Kant's thought. Kant's interest in the bond between the intuition and the concept (as developed in the theory of the schematism of the first *Critique*) and in the existence of the "reflective judgment" (*reflektierende Urteilskraft*) and organic form (as analyzed in the third *Critique*) points in the direction of a concrete philosophy of all areas of human culture. The direction of thought here is from conceptual reason to the concrete.

Hegel's effort within the philosophy of *Geist* to revise our ordinary understanding of the concept as something abstracted from experience, and to create by means of his doctrine of the speculative proposition (*spekulative Satz*) a new sense of the concept as "concrete universal" (*Begriff*), is an act of philosophical heroism on behalf of the Western tradition of reason. Hegel was a genius of reason. His transformation of reason as simple understanding, or *Verstand,* into reason as the inner form and movement of experience, or *Vernunft,* is a monumental work of thought. As Cassirer points out, this attempt, which takes place in the *Phenomenology of Spirit,* ends in the reduction of the idea to the single form of logic in the *Science of Logic,* even though Hegel claims this to be a logic of the concrete idea.[39]

Ralph Manheim, 3 vols. (New Haven: Yale University Press, 1953–57), III, Preface.

[38]*Philosophy of Symbolic Forms,* I, Introduction.

[39]Ibid.

Cassirer's attempt to advance the philosophy of *Geist* by finding in the symbol the phenomenal analogue to Kant's schematism, while at the same time joining Hegel's sense of the self-movement of consciousness with specific research into human culture, is philosophical genius. Cassirer, with his understanding of Kant and Hegel, is a hero of the symbol, but the fundamental model of the symbol in Cassirer's thought is cognitive. It is this basically cognitive model of thought which he attempts to extend to other forms of experience, to language, art, history, and especially myth. Although Cassirer calls Vico the true discoverer of the myth, "der eigentliche *Entdecker des Mythos*,"[40] Cassirer, unlike Vico, discovers the myth through the rational concept. Cassirer identifies Vico with the philosophy of *Geist*,[41] but Vico's thought is in fact different from both the philosophy of *Geist* and that of *Leben*.

Opposed to the philosophy of *Geist* is the philosophy of the irrational, the philosophy of *Leben*, of life and existence. The philosophy of life in Cassirer's terms is a reaction to the systematic impetus of the philosophy of *Geist*. It attempts to come to terms directly with the immediate. We see this in the thought of Nietzsche and Kierkegaard and in the philosophies of Scheler and Heidegger. Our fatigue with the rational concept and its promises makes *Existenzialphilosophie* attractive. The promise of the possible appearance of Being is an invitation to prepare vitally for its arrival. This is especially true in contemporary life, which confronts us with the meaningless conditions of technologically ordered existence, conditions which have their philosophical basis in the method of Cartesian thought, in the clarity and distinctness of the Cartesian world. The Cartesian philosophy that Vico, in his mature thought, so forcefully opposed

[40]Ernst Cassirer, *Das Erkenntnisproblem in der Philosophie und Wissenschaft der neuern Zeit*, 4 vols. (Darmstadt: Wissenschaftliche Buchgesellschaft, 1973), IV, 300; English trans.: *The Problem of Knowledge*, trans. William H. Woglom and Charles W. Hendel (New Haven: Yale University Press, 1950), p. 296.

[41]Cf. Cassirer's remarks on Vico in *Leibniz' System in seinen wissenschaftlichen Grundlagen* (Marburg: N. G. Elwert, 1902), pp. 447–49; and Cassirer's lecture "Descartes, Leibniz, and Vico (1941–42)" in *Symbol, Myth, and Culture*, pp. 95–107.

produces a reaction on behalf of life. This is so even when the Cartesian idea is filtered and revised through a full philosophy of the concrete universal and the symbol. Spirit is seen not as a transformation of life, but as an alienation of it, an inauthentic relationship to Being.

Western philosophy in its modern period presents us with a disjunct. We are asked to pursue philosophical understanding either in terms of the principles of evidence, the concept, and the argument, or to reject these and think directly from the situation of life, to "transvaluate values," introspect, or await Being. Vico offers us another possibility. His thought begins outside this disjunct. It begins neither with *Geist* nor with *Leben*. It begins instead with the imagination, with *fantasia,* as an original and independent power of mind. In Vico's thought, images are not images of something; they are themselves manifestations of an original power of spirit which gives fundamental form to mind and life. Images or *universali fantastici* are not, in Vico's terms, simply concepts in poetic cloaks. The image is not to be understood in relation to the concept. The image is to be understood on its own terms.

How does Vico build a philosophy on the image, the *universale fantastico,* as a starting point and develop his thought so that his perspective never dissolves into that of the concept or the rational category? This is the question I propose to answer. It is from this perspective, by building his philosophy on *fantasia,* that Vico creates a position outside Western philosophy as traditionally understood. Vico's thought teaches the art of memory, the art of recovery; it recalls a capacity of mind that has been left behind in Western philosophy. It is an art in which many of the ancients and figures of the Renaissance excelled. Philosophies of memory have no solid place in histories of philosophy. They are always seen as literary and rhetorical in nature. Because they are not conceptual, they are regarded as not philosophical.[42]

Traditionally in philosophy the imagination has been the

---

[42]Works that do recognize the importance of the history of the art of memory are, e.g.: Paolo Rossi, *Clavis universalis* (Milan-Naples: Ricciardi, 1960), and Frances A. Yates, *The Art of Memory.*

handmaiden of the concept. The imagination has occupied one of two standard places in philosophical thought: either it has been regarded as an element of mind subject to investigation by theory of knowledge or it has been viewed as part of the theory of art and aesthetics. In theory of knowledge imagination has usually been understood as an element of mental activity standing between the perception and the concept. The product of the imagination is seen as the image that induces sufficient form into sensation to permit conceptual comprehension of the object. The imagination gives sensations their immediate shape. When the imagination is considered as part of artistic creation, it is seen as something apart from the concerns of theory of knowledge proper.[43] The image is given its own realm of freedom apart from the concept. Imagination is seen as having various special functions, as based in pleasure or in the human impetus toward valuation.

By considering imagination either as part of theory of knowledge or as part of theory of art, philosophy handles imagination as a subject matter. The imagination never truly enters into the mode of philosophical thought itself. At most the image and the metaphor become devices for illustrating philosophical meanings that are conceptual at base. The image remains outside the form of philosophical thought, to be used only at a point when conceptual reasoning rises toward a view of the whole, or as a simple instrument of communication to enliven thought. Plato's discussion of the ancient quarrel between philosophy and poetry in the tenth book of the *Republic* sets the tone for the traditional understanding of the image. In it the rational idea is separated from the wisdom of Homer. Both of the traditional philosophical understandings of the image—that it serves sensation and that it serves art—arise from the terms of this quarrel.

Vico's philosophy offers a new starting point, not simply by siding with the wisdom of Homer against the rational wisdom of

[43]Cassirer's approach to art and that of Susanne Langer, which owes much to Cassirer, are exceptions to this. See Cassirer's papers on art in *Symbol, Myth, and Culture*, pp. 145–215.

Plato, but by interpreting the wisdom of Homer in a new way. This interpretation is centered in Vico's theory of poetic wisdom, *sapienza poetica,* through which we come to a new understanding of the image and the rational idea. By means of his concept of memory, Vico works his way back to the world of original thought, to the myth. Through his discovery of the imaginative universal, of *fantasia* as a way of thinking and acting, Vico finds a new origin for philosophical thought.

Vico makes a new route for the comprehension of both the idea and the image. He creates a new place for philosophical thought outside the modern disjunct between spirit and life and the ancient disjunct between idea and image. The basis of Vico's originality is his conception of *fantasia.* It is the conception on which his new place for Western philosophy is based.

CHAPTER 2

Truth

In the first chapter of his work *On the Ancient Wisdom of the Italians,* Vico says: "divine truth is a solid image of things, a kind of plastic art; human truth is a monogram, a flat image, a kind of painting."[1] The difference between a divine truth and a human truth is like that between sculpting an object and painting an object. In the plastic making of an object reality is represented by an ingenious combination of the elements of its own medium. Nature is actually reshaped; a new specific form is instantiated alongside the specific forms of objects in nature. In painting the third dimension, the solidness of the object is not actually present. It can be simulated only by perspective. Painting can achieve only indirectly the dimension that is immediately there in the medium of plastic form. Vico is not proposing here a theory of art, but a device to differentiate between divine and human truth on the level of the image. Both divine and human truth are made, but they differ in terms of the way each is made.

In the conclusion of this work Vico says he has intended to advance: "a metaphysics commensurate to the weakness of human thought. It does not concede to man the possibility of knowing all truths, nor does it deny to him the faculty of being

[1]*De Italorum sapientia,* ch. 1, sec. 1.

36

able to know them; but it concedes to him alone to apprehend some of them."[2] Human thought is weak in that it cannot know all truths, but this is not due to a defect of the faculty of knowing. There are some truths that are specific to man. Metaphysics stems from the weakness, not from the superiority of human thought. Its concern is to learn the difference between divine and human truth. When this difference is understood, it can be seen that some truths pertain to the human alone and stand only in analogical relationship to the divinely made truths. Human truth is comprehensible in terms of a comparison with divine making.

The divine has an inside relationship to what it makes. It makes the specific forms of nature. Humans are not the makers of these forms and we have only an outside relation to things of divine creation. In a world of images our truths are those of the plane. We are painters who through our ingenuity, our own genius, can more and more approximate the plastic through perspective, but our making is still that of the flat surface. To this flat making we have an inside relationship. It is this relationship that approximates the truth of our making to the divine. We must, like the Renaissance painter Paolo Uccello, spend our nights mastering perspective.

Although Vico's final doctrine appears only in the *New Science* (1730/1744), understanding of his ideas as developed in the *Ancient Wisdom* (1710) is important for discovering the basis of his mature position. The *Ancient Wisdom* contains two of Vico's most original doctrines: (1) his principle of *verum-factum,* the identity of the true and the made; and (2) his doctrine of "metaphysical points," *puncta metaphysica,* the conception of the real that he reaches through his conception of knowledge. Although this interesting work deserves study in itself, I wish to consider only these two doctrines. Vico's metaphysics and his conception of truth, as developed in the *Ancient Wisdom,* are not definitive.

[2]Ibid., Conclusio.

In his oration *On the Study Methods of Our Time* (1709), published the year before the *Ancient Wisdom,* Vico says that every method of study involves three things: instruments, aids, and aims, *instrumenta, adiumenta et fines.*[3] The aim "should circulate, like a blood-stream, through the entire body of the learning process."[4] The aim, he says, of all intellectual pursuits is truth. In this work Vico invokes truth as the goal of all study and knowledge, but he says very little about it, and instead concentrates his discussion on the first two elements of study. At one point he says: "We demonstrate geometrical propositions because we make them, if we could demonstrate the propositions of physics, we would make them."[5] Here Vico states his principle of *verum-factum* without directly naming it. In his explanation of the principle in the *Ancient Wisdom* he refers the reader back to this statement.[6] How are we to understand this principle upon which Vico's conception of truth is based? How does Vico derive or support the truth of this principle itself?

Vico claims that in Latin *verum* and *factum* have a reciprocal meaning, which, he says, can be put in scholastic terms as *verum et factum convertuntur.*[7] In the *Risposte,* Vico's answers to criticism of his work in the *Giornale de' Letterati d'Italia* (1711–12), he says that this interconnection of the true and the made can also be seen in translation from Latin to Italian, in that *factum* (when used as an affirmative answer to a question) is equivalent in Italian to *È vero* ("It is true.").[8]

God is the true maker and the true knower, the creator of all things and the perfect knower of truth. His knowledge is perfect because that which He creates is not outside his being. God contains the things of his making. God is the sculptor of the solids of the world, and as their cause He is the knower of their

---

[3]*De nostri temporis studiorum ratione, Opere* 1, sec. 1; *Study Methods,* p. 6.
[4]*Study Methods,* p. 6.
[5]*De studiorum ratione,* sec. 4 (my trans.); *Study Methods,* p. 23.
[6]*De Italorum sapientia,* ch. 3.
[7]Ibid., ch. 1.
[8]*Risposta* (1711), *Opere* 1, sec. 1 and *Risposta* (1712), *Opere* 1, sec. 3.

truth. There is no outer and inner nature of things for Him. No dimension of the being of things in nature is closed to God as their complete and full cause of being. These are well-known metaphysical ideas. Vico accepts them and shows little interest in the traditional problems of metaphysics that surround the question of God as first and perfect cause.

Vico does not advance proofs of this conception of God as maker and knower to justify his beginning point, although he does offer statements in defense of his views in the *Risposte*. Vico accepts this conception of divine creation and knowledge as an inheritance of Western metaphysical imagination and asks whether any of the human sciences offer images of this reciprocity of the true and the made. He concludes that mathematics does. For Vico mathematics is a divine science, not because it discovers the principles by which God created nature, but because it imitates the divine act. In producing the science of geometry man makes his own truth. He creates the point, the line, and the plane out of his own mental ingenuity. The truths of geometry are truths because the human mind is their maker, their cause. The mind creates such objects, Vico says, as if it created them from nothing, ex nihilo.[9] In mathematical thought something is true only if we can make it from the fundamentals or elements that are themselves directly made by the mind.

There is a fundamental difference between physics and geometry. In mathematical thought the true and the made are identical because there is no outside to mathematical objects. In such thought mind is thinking itself. The truths of physics involve the relation of the mind to the event in nature that is to be understood. The object of physics is a given, and the success of physics is due to its ability to approximate the making of its object through experiment.[10] In experiment a truth is made, but it cannot be wholly made, since what is made must still be connected to an other in nature on which its truth depends. This

[9]*De Italorum sapientia*, ch. 1, sec. 2.
[10]Ibid.

outside relation of the mind to its object is only mediated in experiment; it is not converted into a relationship inside the mind. The convertibility of *verum* and *factum* is not possible in principle for physical knowledge.

Morals, Vico says, is a less certain study than mechanics or physics because it concerns not just physical motions, but motions of minds as they relate to desire.[11] Perhaps Vico is thinking here of the difficulty of employing experiment in questions of morals. Vico's application of the *verum-factum* principle to the motions of the human world in the *New Science* may seem a reversal of this earlier view of the uncertainty of morals, but it need not be regarded as such. Morals, or even the social scientific investigation of custom and habit, has never successfully taken up experiment. The *verum-factum* principle is not inductive. Induction is an analogue to it, practiced when the object under investigation is in principle external to the mind. The inductive investigation of the human places the mind in an external relation to itself. If experiment became successful in morals, its success would be no greater than that which now exists in physics. The perfection of induction would not generate the identity of the true and the made. Even perfect induction is different from the principle of convertibility, because the logical idea of perfect induction does not entail the creation of the objects known.

In the *Study Methods* Vico advocates the value of imagination and memory as the basis of education. He maintains that early training in logic and criticism is unnatural and damages young minds. The young should instead be trained in common sense, in *sensus communis*—the sensibilities, feelings, metaphors, and memories upon which human culture rests. Conceptual reason, the logical criticism of concepts upon which modern science rests, is appropriate to the activity of mature minds. Such reasoning presupposes background training in the imaginative and rhetorical arts. The intellectually mature mind is defective

[11]Ibid.

in the process of conceptual reasoning, Vico claims, if it has failed to learn the art of topics, the power of eloquence.

Topics is the art of locating the connecting link between concepts, the art of the "middle term."[12] A mind trained in conceptual clarity is flat and inelegant because it lacks the perspective possible through metaphor. The conceptually trained mind regards metaphors as composed of elements to be taken apart, mechanisms held together by the springs of particular proportionalities. The logical mind always believes metaphors are analogies.

Vico knows that any inference done by the mind at the conceptual level presupposes the powers of imagination and memory to create topics. In the widest sense this requires the creation of the *sensus communis,* the ultimate context within which any piece of conceptual reasoning is meaningful. Logic does not create the meanings of its terms; it uses them. In the narrower sense this means that the "middle term" of an inference through which the mind can pass from one proposition to another is created by something other than the mind's logical powers. A specific topic is necessary to support the conceptual connection. The mind must see a unity-in-difference, something it learns by the early metaphorical exercise of its powers of imagination and memory. The metaphor is always a unity-in-difference, which is different from an analogical combination of elements. On the conceptual level of thought the metaphor can be transformed into an analogy. But to make an inference and a process of reasoning that can follow from it, the mind must have the power to create the point where two concepts touch, their locus in a middle term. It must produce the *topos* as a concrete from which conceptual discretes can emerge as an inferential structure.

In the *Study Methods* Vico is arguing against the model of education based on the Port-Royal *Logic* and the Cartesian conception of education. In the *Discourse on Method* Descartes describes his own education in just those subjects that Vico advo-

---

[12]*Study Methods,* p. 15.

cates for the early training of the mind: languages, histories, literature, and fables. Descartes argues that these subjects are a kind of ignorance that can cause one to lose touch with one's own time, become unprogressive, and fall back into the world of the ancients. Such study can lead to extravagance of mind: "those who regulate their conduct by examples which they derive from such a source, are liable to fall into the extravagances of knights-errant of Romance, and form projects beyond their power of performance."[13] For Descartes eloquence and poetry are talents, not types of knowledge or elements in the attainment of truth. Logic is sufficient in itself such that: "those who have the strongest power of reasoning, and who most skillfully arrange their thoughts in order to render them clear and intelligible, have the best power of persuasion even if they can but speak the language of Lower Brittany and have never learned Rhetoric."[14] In Descartes' view, to dream of projects beyond one's performance is dangerous, and truth is truth in any language, even *bas breton*.

Vico's conception of education includes what Descartes excludes. Vico maintains that Descartes misses the connection in his own education between the study of imaginative, historical, and rhetorical forms of thought and his later mastery of conceptual criticism and methodology. Descartes cuts himself off from time; the rational truth that he seeks is eternal, without basis in history. In Vico's view the ingenuity Descartes seeks in his fourfold method of truth, of beginning with what is evidently true, dividing difficulties into parts, moving from simple to complex, and continual review and enumeration,[15] presupposes the ingenuity of mind trained in the metaphor to produce the middle term, the locus within which such a conceptual process can take place. Descartes misses the sense of eloquence wherein language is used to arrive at insight. He sees rhetoric simply as an activity

[13]*The Philosophical Works of Descartes*, trans. Elizabeth Haldane and G. R. T. Ross, 2 vols. (Cambridge: Cambridge University Press, 1931), I, 85.
[14]Ibid.
[15]Ibid., p. 92.

of persuasion; when rightly used it is the power to persuade someone of a truth already known. Rhetoric, in Descartes' view, is something outside rather than inside the process of truth. Yet despite his rejection of such forms of thought, Descartes says that the *Discourse* can be read as a *histoire* or *fable*.[16] In the "Author's Letter" to the *Principles of Philosophy* he says that the work should be read through first as a *roman*.[17]

In the *Study Methods* Vico does not mention Descartes by name and cites Cartesianism only once, in a list of general viewpoints with which modern students are confronted.[18] In the *Ancient Wisdom*, published the following year, Vico criticizes Descartes' philosophy fully and by name. Descartes fails to understand the relationship between the topic and the logical inference. He also fails to understand the relationship between making and truth; he fails to grasp the mind's relationship to itself. Vico points out that Descartes' first truth, the *cogito ergo sum*, is the same as that of Plautus' Sosia, whose image is taken on by Mercury and who appears as Sosia's double to the extent of making Sosia doubt his existence. Mercury has all the external signs of Sosia's existence but not the internal sign Sosia has of himself: "when I think, I am certainly the same one who has always been."[19] This internal sign that the thinker has of himself is a certain, a point beyond doubt, but it is not a criterion for the true and it is not an answer to skepticism.

Descartes, in Vico's view, has failed to distinguish between what is true, *verum,* and what is certain, *certum*; and he thus fails to distinguish between scientific knowledge, *scientia,* and consciousness, *conscientia. Scientia,* whose object is the true, requires a knowledge of causes. Such knowledge would require the mind to possess the form from which to make itself. In the *cogito* the thinker discovers himself as a *certum*; he encounters himself as a certain of which he is indubitably aware. The *conscientia* of the

[16]Ibid., p. 83.
[17]Ibid., p. 209.
[18]*Study Methods*, p. 77.
[19]*De Italorum sapientia*, ch. 1, sec. 3.

sign of his being is not a *scientia* of its truth. The criterion of the true requires no productive moment. The *cogito* is simply an extraordinary presentation of something certain. From this extraordinary *certum*, this exceptionally powerful act of consciousness, it is not possible to generate *verum*, true knowledge of causes.

Certum always involves an outside relation between knower and object because it is not convertible with *factum*. The *cogito* is an external that appears as the ultimate internal. In Vico's view Descartes' "evil genius," with its ability to reverse the world, is not left behind when Descartes moves from the first to the second of his *Meditations*. This external character of the certain sign, of an object of consciousness but not a cause, suggests a reason for Vico's abrupt treatment of proofs for God's existence. He calls such proofs matters of impiety and curiosity and dismisses them in a sentence.[20] Neither the proofs for the existence of the *I* nor for the existence of God offer a criterion of the true.

Vico's meaning might be seen this way: if we take, for example, the ontological proof to be sound, it would yield for us only a sign, perhaps a certain sign, of God's existence. It would give us no knowledge of God, no *scientia* of his cause, the divine self-cause. In the ontological argument as traditionally understood (not regarded in the broad sense as the presupposition of the rationality of experience, as it has at times been in modern idealistic interpretation), God remains outside our finitude. Our finitude does not contain the form through which we could be producers of God's being or truth. Like the *certum* of the *cogito*, God remains an object of *conscientia* in the ontological argument. What is Vico's justification of the truth of the *verum-factum* principle? What supports Vico in saying that the true is the made?

The *Ancient Wisdom* is written in the style of a traditional metaphysical system. Vico planned that it would contain an appendix on logic and be followed by volumes on physics and ethics, but none of these were published. In the *Risposte* Vico

[20]Ibid., ch. 3.

44

claims that his work is in principle a complete metaphysical system and not simply an essay proposing some metaphysical ideas.[21] Vico never claims that the *verum-factum* principle is justified by self-evidence or by some procedure of logical undeniability, the two common means by which rationalistic metaphysics affirms such first principles.

In several pages of remarks on the meaning of the *verum-factum* principle, Fisch suggests that it is associated with the traditional notion of "transcendentals" in metaphysics.[22] *Verum* is one of the transcendentals in the medieval conception of metaphysics and is "convertible" with the others on the traditional list: *ens, unum, verum, bonum*—being, one, true, good. As Fisch points out, the transcendentals are above categories, apply to every category, and refer to the truth of things, not to propositions. Fisch claims *verum* means true in this sense of transcendentals and, more precisely, it means "intelligible." The reciprocal identification of *verum* and *factum* is not part of the traditional list, but has a basis in the medieval doctrine of God as Maker. *Factum*, the made, enters the list because of its convertibility with *ens*, the *ens-factum* principle of God's being, and it follows that what is made is the true or intelligible. What is true or intelligible is intelligible to its maker.

These are powerful suggestions of how to understand Vico's principle of *verum-factum*, a notion that is at once very simple but very difficult to understand. Fisch locates a basis for its understanding in the concern of first philosophy to understand universal being. Vico's justification for the *verum-factum* would involve the more general justification of the traditional transcendentals. I wish to connect this view concerning transcendentals to Vico's claim to have derived the *verum-factum* principle from the origins of the Latin language.[23] The one feature of Vico's

[21]*Risposta* (1711), sec. 2.

[22]Max H. Fisch, "Vico and Pragmatism," in *Giambattista Vico: An International Symposium*, ed. Giorgio Tagliacozzo and Hayden V. White (Baltimore: The Johns Hopkins University Press, 1969), pp. 403, 407–8.

[23]*De Italorum sapientia*, ch. 1, sec. 1.

work which differentiates it from a more traditional metaphysical system is Vico's insistence on the connection of his ideas with the origins of Latin—a point made clear even in the title of the work, *De antiquissima Italorum sapientia ex linguae latinae originibus eruenda* (On the Ancient Wisdom of the Italians Recoverable from the Origins of the Latin Language). I think that Vico's connection of his ideas with their origin in Latin is more than a stylistic or presentational eccentricity and is in fact an essential justification of the principles of his "first philosophy."

In the preface to this work Vico says that the learned phrases present in Latin could not have come from the Romans, who were a practical and not a speculative people, but could have entered Roman speech from the Ionians and the Etruscans.[24] It is known that the Ionians excelled in learned thought and the Etruscans in the knowledge of sacred rites. He says in the first chapter that the proposition that the true is reciprocal with the made was the principle of truth held by the "ancient thinkers of Italy."[25] Vico claims that this principle is Ionian or Etruscan in origin. What is Vico claiming by this?

Vico is claiming that the first principle of *verum-factum* is present in the thought of an original Western people—if we consider the Etruscans such, for their origin is not known, nor is the meaning of their language. Unlike Descartes and rationalistic metaphysics generally, Vico does not derive his first principle from conceptual intuition or the law of contradiction. Instead, he sees it issuing from the *sensus communis* as present in an ancient mentality, from the *archai* or first human understandings upon which any subsequent reasoning about the nature of things is based. Ernesto Grassi suggests that *archai* come from original forms of speech which are not part of the process of rational inference.[26] I do not agree with those readers who think

[24]Ibid., Prooemium.
[25]Ibid., ch. 1, sec. 1.
[26]Ernesto Grassi, "Rhetoric and Philosophy," *Philosophy and Rhetoric*, 9 (1976), 201–3. See also Ernesto Grassi, *Rhetoric as Philosophy: The Humanist Tradition* (University Park: The Pennsylvania State University Press, 1980).

that Vico's presentation of his metaphysics in terms of an investigation into the origin of the wisdom of the ancient Italians is superfluous to his thought. It is instead the clue to the justification of his first truth of the *verum-factum*.

It makes no difference whether Vico's etymologies are open to question. The philosophical point remains that his first truth is not logically derived; there is no proof for it.

Vico's first principles are traced back to that first kind of speech which Grassi discusses. Such truths are presented by Vico as tied to an older metaphysical wisdom preserved only in the philology of Latin. The beginning point of metaphysical truth is a reflection of the speech by which thought or *sapienza* itself begins. This way of approaching the problems of philosophy at a point behind the logical concept is mixed with Vico's style of rationalistic metaphysics in the *Ancient Wisdom*. It is a way of thinking Vico develops further in *Universal Law* and fully in the *New Science*, leaving behind the rationalistic elements of this first treatise. Vico takes up the traditional metaphysical doctrine of transcendentals, modifies it by the introduction of *factum*, and grounds it rhetorically in Latin speech. In the various terms of this speech lives the wisdom of two earlier cultures, the reflective Ionian and the religious Etruscan.

To grasp how the *verum-factum* is a first truth it is also necessary to keep in mind Vico's conception of the art of topics, the art of generating the middle term, which Vico sees as missing in the mind educated only in logic and criticism. The *verum-factum* is the middle term of middle terms. The middle term makes possible any particular line of reasoning; the *verum-factum* permits the making of any truth. The middle term is the term held in common by the two premises of a syllogism; it is the basis for the connection between the other two terms of the syllogism asserted in the conclusion. The middle term is a product of the fact that the Aristotelian syllogism is built on the notion of threes—three terms, one being the middle term, contained within three propositions, one of which being the conclusion.

The middle term can be viewed not only as a feature of the

syllogism as already made, but also as the element necessary to bring a syllogism into existence. Considered in this way the middle term refers to the self-coherence of thought, the ability to connect thoughts conceptually. The syllogism is not just a framework for the expression of truths in correct form, but a process through which probable truths can be formed. Produced by ingenuity, the middle term is a conception of the mind's ability to make a thought intelligible by placing it into a proper or new arrangement with other thoughts. In terms of the classical syllogism the middle term is the ability to make a proposition, held as a conclusion, intelligible by bringing forth a further proposition as a first premise and, by means of a common middle term, connecting this through another premise back to the conclusion.

Seen as the medium of thought, the middle term is a manifestation of the *verum-factum* principle. In the process of the middle term the mind makes an intelligibility; it makes a *verum*. Behind any middle term is the *verum-factum* as the middle term of thought itself, the ability of thought to connect itself to itself, to create intelligibility. This power of ingenuity on which the coherence of the mind depends is present in any act of reasoning. Whether it is expressed in the syllogism or in wider logical forms, the middle term is the medium of thought. In its general idea it is the notion that rational thought requires a topical basis of meaning from which to construct a proof in language. The ability of the mind to bring forth the middle term and successfully employ the *verum-factum* principle in the act of thought rests on the rhetorical art of topics which is the subject of the sixth chapter of this book.

The real basis for Vico's counter to Descartes' philosophy and to Cartesian rationalism in general is not the arguments with which he formulates his position, but that he derives a first principle from that part of the mind which Descartes leaves behind. Vico says in the *Study Methods* that great achievements such as the machines of Archimedes and the dome of the church of Santa Maria del Fiore designed by Filippo Brunelleschi, the great Renaissance architect and inventor of linear perspective, are done not by geometrical method but by the faculty of ingenuity (*ingenium*) which makes such applications of thought possible.[27] Even though there are many Cartesian statements in Vico's Inaugural Orations (1699–1707), those before the *Study Methods*, Vico and Descartes have different senses of human experience. Unlike Descartes, Vico never renounces the rhetorical and imaginative sources of mentality which date from his early years. These sensibilities inform Vico's metaphysics in the *Ancient Wisdom*.

Vico begins his explanation of "metaphysical points" with the assertion that in Latin *punctum* and *momentum*, point and momentum, have the same significance.[28] This is not as philosophically arresting a union of terms as the reciprocal identity of *verum* and *factum*, but Vico introduces this second fundamental idea of his metaphysics in the same way. The doctrine of metaphysical points is a truth made from the principle of *verum-factum*. The point is a real, intelligible to metaphysical thought and made by it through reflection on geometrical thought. Geometry is a divine science of the finite mind because geometry makes its objects and their truth directly from the nature of the mind. There are no externals to the objects of geometry. They are inside the mind. Geometrical thought is an analogue to creation ex nihilo, the mode of divine creation. The fundamental object of geometry is the point, the notion of an indivisible, unextended unit from which particular points, lines, and planes can be made, from which extension can be generated.[29]

Metaphysics is a study that underlies all other sciences, including geometry. Metaphysics directs its attention to the notion of the point not as a basis for the principles of extension, but as the notion of an ultimate real that lies between divine making in nature and geometrical making in finite mind. Metaphysics is concerned with the notion of the point as such, as a middle

[27]*Study Methods*, p. 29.
[28]*De Italorum sapientia*, ch. 4, sec. 2.
[29]Ibid., ch. 1., sec. 2.

ground between divine making ex nihilo and the reflection of this in geometric making in which man is in some way God.[30]

The metaphysical point lies midway between the divine and the human act of making and between God and nature. The extended bodies of which nature consists are in motion, while God in Himself is at rest. Conatus, the power to cause motion but itself not a motion, is midway between rest and motion. The metaphysical point is related through conatus to the motion of bodies in nature. Metaphysical points are endowed with conatus. The metaphysical point thus combines in itself the powers of extension and of movement. Vico maintains that the unlimited power of extension of metaphysical points equally underlies unequal extensions, and that the unlimited power of causing motion equally causes unequal motions. He also maintains that extended bodies are capable of motion, but not conatus.

Fisch points out that Vico's doctrine of metaphysical points explains the existence of the physical world; it does not take the physical world as a brute fact.[31] Vico intends his doctrine of metaphysical points to oppose the Cartesian dualism of thought and extension. The metaphysical point is the motionless cause of motion and the incorporeal substance of body. Vico does not attempt to prove the existence of the physical world on the basis of metaphysical points, nor does he attempt to prove the existence of metaphysical points themselves. Such points are intelligible to the metaphysical mentality because it makes them. Metaphysics is a kind of painting at the limits of perspective. It is not the true plastic art of the divine, the working in the solids of nature. The finite flat surface upon which metaphysics works is illuminated from behind not from the front.

In Vico's view, metaphysics is not knowing things clearly and distinctly. To know clearly and distinctly is a liability of the mind because it involves seeing things in their limits. To know clearly and distinctly, Vico says, is to see as if by night with lamplight; the object can be seen but its background is cut off. The meta-

[30]Ibid., ch. 4, sec. 2.
[31]Fisch, "Vico and Pragmatism," p. 410.

physician, Vico says, attempts to see the daylight of the divine through the opacity of the bodies of the world.[32] One is reminded here of the ray of light shining from the eye of God onto the breast of metaphysic in Vico's frontispiece of the *New Science*. This light, at least in its metaphysical reflection, can be seen only by attention to the whole, not by concentration on the part which uses the mind like a lamp. We might speak of Descartes' lamp and Vico's sun-vision, of Descartes creating a science of parts and of Vico risking his vision on a direct look at the sun. What is Vico's proof of his doctrine of metaphysical points?

As Fisch points out, Vico claims that his metaphysics of the *verum-factum* principle and the doctrine of metaphysical points fit with inductive and experimental physics, rather than with the conception of physics as deductive, which regards experiment as a secondary and less proper form of its activity.[33] Galileo could have appreciated the hypothesis of metaphysical points. Vico's claim that his doctrine of points fits with experimental physics, a science that discovers the actual extensions and motions of bodies in nature, is not a proof that would satisfy the rationalist mentality. In addition to the justification that the doctrine of points fits with physical investigation as actually practiced, Vico's view has a rhetorical ground that is the full answer to the rationalist notion of proof in metaphysics.

Vico introduces his rhetorical view through his discussion of the Latin meaning of point. His metaphysical principle of intelligibility, of *verum-factum*, is also a principle of metaphysical knowledge itself. Metaphysical intelligibility, or the true in metaphysics, is itself something made. This making involves the recovery of the original forms of human wisdom, of the ancient apprehension of the real. Such a procedure confronts the rationalistic interest in proof with the interest in origin. It confronts first proof with first speech.

In the *Risposte* Vico says that to profit from metaphysical

[32]*De Italorum sapientia*, ch. 4, sec. 2.
[33]Fisch, "Vico and Pragmatism," p. 411.

meditation one must lose oneself in it.[34] In the *Ancient Wisdom* Vico offers arguments and specific replies to possible objections to his views. His specific answers to the criticisms of the review in the *Giornale de' Letterati d'Italia* are done in the same argumentative manner. Yet while doing this he indicates that there is more to metaphysical knowledge than what can be attained through the traditional procedures of argument. His comment that one must lose oneself in metaphysical meditation is very like his point in the section on method in the *New Science* that the reader must make the science for himself.[35] He even associates this activity of self-making with the notion of proof. This conception of the reader making the new science for himself goes back to the *verum-factum* principle of the *Ancient Wisdom*. The *Ancient Wisdom* and the *New Science* have points of connection although, as Vico also rightly claims in the *Autobiography*, his later work depends upon a change in philosophical understanding from his earlier work.[36]

Metaphysics is inside knowing, in which what is known is intelligible as an internal, not as an external, as is the object known in physical experiment. The illumination of the intelligible metaphysical object is of external source and comes from behind the canvas of the finite mind. But how do we know what we are understanding is true? Why is the *verum-factum* principle when applied to metaphysical knowledge not just as easily a principle of solipsism as of objective truth?

For Vico the beginning point of philosophical thought is not a logical truth. It is an element derived from the *sensus communis* of early human wisdom and speech. This is the basis on which, he says in the *Study Methods*, the young are first to be educated. This grasp of the common sense contains the power of the middle term that is based on the nature of metaphor learned when young. The *sensus communis* is created not by logic but by original, archaic human speech which bursts forth from the human

[34]*Risposta* (1711), sec. 3.
[35]*New Science*, §349.
[36]*Autobiography*, p. 153.

52

condition itself. The forms taken by archaic human speech are the primary representations of the real; they are original makings of the true, original modes of intelligibility. In Vico's view, common sense, or *sensus communis,* is not a proto-scientific form of knowledge, but the common way of experiencing the world present in the life of a people. It is not a set of consciously formed cognitive or empirical beliefs. The *sensus communis* of a people is rooted in a common way of feeling, speaking, and symbolizing meaning in the world.

Vico claims that his principles of *verum-factum* and *puncta metaphysica* are true because they are taken from the wisdom that grew from a particular embodiment of the *sensus communis,* the learning of the Ionians and the piety of the Etruscans. Vico joins these elements present in Latin speech to the *sensus communis* as refracted in Christianity, with its notion of making ex nihilo and knowing by making. Vico's own metaphysical speech is the voice of these *archai.* It is the art of perspective introduced into metaphysical speech. The "proof" of Vico's metaphysical doctrines lies in his rhetorical power to recall for us the elements of this original speech. The *verum-factum* sounds so familiar that it sends us searching for its basis in Western philosophy, the principles of which are only reflections of more ancient original forms of wisdom and speech, apprehensions of the reality of the whole. We are not accustomed to hearing such a voice.

I doubt that Vico himself saw the implications of his procedure in the *Ancient Wisdom.* Often his etymologies seem merely tacked on to his arguments, rather than being the basis of them. In making my analysis I have gone beyond his text and have drawn on his later orientation in the *New Science.* Vico's criticism of the *cogito* and of Descartes' dualism of thought and extension does not constitute the whole of his attack on Cartesianism in the *Ancient Wisdom.* Ultimately, that criticism lies in Vico's understanding reality from a position Descartes and most modern philosophers, including most contemporary schools of philosophy, know nothing about—the ability to think from origins, from the forms of an original *sensus communis* of humanity. Vico reveals this ability in the traditional terms of his study of rhetoric in the *Study Methods*, and again, perhaps almost unconsciously, in the Latin etymology of the *Ancient Wisdom*. In the *New Science* this ability to think from origins becomes the basis of a new conception of philosophy.

In his discussion of method in the *New Science*, Vico refers indirectly to the convertibility of the true and the made, but he does not mention this principle by name. He draws a parallel between the concept of *storia ideale eterna*, ideal eternal history, the course of events traversed in time by the nations, and the science of geometry. The human is the maker of history and he can thus be its knower. In the *Ancient Wisdom* Vico regards geometry as the prime example of the conversion of the true and the made. In his discussion of method in the *New Science*, Vico says that we as the makers of the human world can be the knowers of it, can have a science of its truth. Knowledge of history in Vico's view differs from knowledge of nature because there can be no inside knowledge of the physical object for the finite mind, only for the divine creator. In this section of the *New Science* Vico claims that the science of human institutions treats of a reality greater than that of geometry. The science of human things has "a reality greater by just so much as the institutions having to do with human affairs are more real than points, lines, surfaces, and figures are."[37] Although this science has a reality greater than geometric science, it has a divine character similar to that which he attributes to geometric making in the *Ancient Wisdom*.

In the *New Science* the middle-ground position of the metaphysical points, halfway between the divine and natural extensions and motions, is replaced by the providential structure of history with its three eternal stages. Ideal eternal history is halfway between the true eternal of the divine and history as the immediate, changeable, and unequal motions of the human world. The important relationship here is that of God to history, rather

[37]*New Science*, §349; cf. §331.

than of God to the natural world. Through the concept of the *verum-factum* we are in the *New Science* to come to an understanding of the eternals of the motions of institutions by a "metaphysical art of criticism."[38] Vico's claim that the science of human activity has a greater reality than that of geometry points to the fact that the objects of geometry are more abstract, more wholly mental, than the objects of human activity. This claim signifies that geometry and metaphysics as conceived in the *Ancient Wisdom* presuppose a more fundamental science. Geometry and metaphysics of natural processes are human activities and must be understood in terms of their ground in the human. This finally requires a new science based on a "metaphysical art of criticism."

In the science of human institutions or nations the object under investigation does not have the immediacy of the object which is made intelligible in the process of geometrical or metaphysical reasoning about the reals of the natural world. When the mind wishes to have knowledge of what has been made in human institutions, to gain a picture of its own truth, it faces the problem of temporal distance. Time introduces a factor of externality within the mind's relation to its own creation, to human thought and action. Time is not present as such a factor in divine creation, divine knowing. Geometry and metaphysical thought are divine in their denials of time. Although they are not temporal in relation to their own objects, they do exist as forms of knowledge within the ideal eternal history and are subject to its providential course, to its time.

In the science of the human world the powers of memory and imagination permit us to overcome the externality introduced by time, to enter into the origin and its first making of intelligibility in the primary *sensus communis* of human institutions. Memory and imagination must remake the original immediacy so that the mind can find its own inside and learn to know in a way counter to time. Geometry is a divine science when compared to physical, experimental science. But when

---

[38]*New Science*, §348.

geometry is compared to the science of the human world, it is not the fundamental model of divine human making. In the science of the human world, the science of ideal eternal history, what is made are not fictions, like the point, line, and plane. What is made is not an analogue of divine activity, but the true story of the presence of the divine as providence in human institutions.

Providence along with time represents an element of externality in this conversion of making and the true (or intelligible) in the human world. Providence is not an external which is opaque in the sense that the external object of the physical investigation of nature is opaque. By looking for the furthest point of perspective on the canvas of ideal eternal history, by looking closely at the dimensions of its human field, the illumination of the plastic form, the solidity of providence can be seen. This illumination is the cause of the "divine pleasure" of which Vico speaks.[39] In principle this pleasure can be only partially experienced in the making of geometric truth since this activity is only like the divine, only analogic of it. The meditating of ideal eternal history is the presence of the divine in thought, the true story of the workings of the divine in time. Only metaphysical vision can approach the illumination of the *topos* of providence behind the *sensus communis* of the human world and grasp this world as a middle term between the divine and the natural.

The second term besides *factum* that Vico associates with *verum* is *certum*. The association of these terms is not a principle of the *Ancient Wisdom,* although *certum,* the certain, is mentioned in this work.[40] Vico first treats the connection of *verum* and *certum* in the first book of his *Universal Law,* published in 1720, ten years after the *Ancient Wisdom.* In his chapter on the relation of the true and the certain in law Vico states: *certum est pars veri.*[41] This notion that the certain is part of the true is fundamental to Vico's view of the relationship between philosophy and philology as de-

[39]*New Science,* §349.
[40]*De Italorum sapientia,* ch. 2.
[41]*De uno universi iuris principio et fine uno, Opere* 2, ch. 82.

veloped in the *New Science*. In this subsequent view the certain is not seen as part of the true as such. Instead they are joined as poles within the form of thought which makes up the science of the human world. In this form of thought philosophy, identified with *il vero*, is linked with philology, identified with *il certo*. In his explanation of the idea of the *New Science*, Vico says that "philosophy undertakes to examine philology" and that philology is "the doctrine of all the institutions that depend on human choice; for example, all histories of the languages, customs, and deeds of peoples in war and peace."[42] These are the certains or particulars of the human world. In the form of thought of the *New Science*, philosophy, which by its nature and past history inclines toward the universal, is to join its mode of understanding to the philological understandings of these particulars.

The *verum-factum* principle, the convertibility of the true and the made, and the *verum/certum* principle, the connectibility of the true and the certain, have a mutual involvement in the *New Science*. The certainties of the human world are made in human action; they are truths or "intelligibilities" of human choice. The intelligibility of these truths of human action is made in philological investigation. When these philological truths of particular languages, customs, and deeds are comprehended as elements that fit with the truth of the providential structure of history, the ideal eternal history, a juncture of philology and philosophy is achieved. The *verum/certum* relationship can be placed within the *verum-factum* equation.

Both of these principles are fundamental to the conception of the *New Science*. The commonly held view of the *verum-factum* principle is that Vico discovered it in the *Ancient Wisdom* (1710) and made it the basis of his criticism of Descartes there. He then realized that this was a principle applicable not only to theoretical and mathematical knowledge, but also to historical knowledge. Through a gradual understanding of the implications of this principle he moved to his later thought of the *New*

[42]*New Science*, §7.

Science. But how did Vico actually come to apply the *verum-factum* principle to history and the institutions of humanity? In his *Autobiography* (1725, 1728, 1731), in which he discusses the development of thought leading to the *New Science,* he makes no reference to the *verum-factum* principle. He does not even mention this principle in commenting on the *Ancient Wisdom,* nor is there any mention of it in the first *New Science* (1725). In fact there is no mention of the *verum-factum* principle between 1710, in the *Ancient Wisdom* and 1730, the date of the second edition of the *New Science.*

Guido Fassò in his essay "The Problem of Law and the Historical Origin of the *New Science,*"[43] based on his earlier study, *I "quattro auttori" del Vico* (Vico's "Four Authors"),[44] has argued that: "It is the principle of the identity of the true and the certain, and not of the true and the made, which, historically, generates the new science."[45] Fassò's view allows us to place Vico's *Universal Law* within the genesis of the *New Science* and it focuses attention generally on the importance of law for understanding Vico's conception of truth.

Vico's interest in law is a most important key to understanding his thought. He devotes the longest section of his first work of original philosophy, the *Study Methods,* to an analysis of law as an example of his thesis on the education of the young and the relationship between the ancients and the moderns. The work on *Universal Law,* consisting of *De uno universi iuris principio et fine uno* (On the One Principle and the One End of Universal Law), *De constantia iurisprudentis* (On the Constancy of the Jurisprudent), and a third book of notes and additions, is a work of greater size than the *New Science.* Fisch in his essay, "Vico on Roman Law," has indicated the central importance of Roman

[43]Guido Fassò, "The Problem of Law and the Historical Origin of the *New Science,*" in *Giambattista Vico's Science of Humanity,* ed. Giorgio Tagliacozzo and Donald Phillip Verene (Baltimore: The Johns Hopkins University Press, 1976), pp. 3–14.

[44]Guido Fassò, *I "quattro auttori" del Vico: Saggio sulla genesi della "Scienza nuova"* (Milan: Giuffré, 1949).

[45]Fassò, "The Problem of Law," p. 8.

law for Vico's thought.[46] Roman law was Vico's chief source of example for his views in *Universal Law* and is the fundamental source of his own philology in the *New Science*. Vico regarded his interpretation of the Roman Law of the Twelve Tables, which he frequently mentions in the *New Science*, as one of his most important discoveries.[47] The distinction between philosophy and philology, which is the basis for the general division of the general axioms of the *New Science*,[48] follows the two divisions of Vico's earlier *De constantia iurisprudentis*, that is, *De constantia philosophiae* and *De constantia philologiae*.

Fassò maintains that Vico's concern with the problem of the relationship between ideal law, valid for all times, and positive historical law, present in a particular time, leads Vico to the form of thought of the *New Science*, its union between the philosophical and the philological. Vico's concern with rational law and its connection to law as made by human will, by *auctoritas*, goes back to the beginning of his legal studies, even before his discussion of law in the *Study Methods*.[49] The relationship between these two types of law is developed specifically in the direction of the *New Science* from the first book of *Universal Law*, *De uno principio* (1720), forward. In this work Vico speaks of the importance of the relationship of reason and authority, of *ratio* and *auctoritas*, and makes the statement that *certum est pars veri*. This idea that the *certum*, produced by *auctoritas*, is part of *verum* is developed one year later in the second book of Vico's *Universal Law*, *De constantia iurisprudentis*, in which the principle of *certum est pars veri* is extended to all of philology and history. The second part of *De constantia iurisprudentis* begins with a chapter containing Vico's first sketch of his *New Science*, entitled "Nova scientia tentatur" (A New Science Is Essayed).[50] From this point forward

---

[46]Max H. Fisch, "Vico on Roman Law," in *Essays in Political Theory, Presented to George H. Sabine*, ed. Milton R. Konvitz and Arthur E. Murphy (Ithaca, N.Y.: Cornell University Press, 1948), pp. 62–88.

[47]*Autobiography*, p. 193.

[48]*New Science*, §163.

[49]Fassò, "The Problem of Law," p. 10.

[50]*De constantia iurisprudentis, pars posterior, Opere* 2, ch. 1.

Vico develops his thought on the problem of the certain and the true toward a conception of a natural law for all of humanity understood through the providential pattern of history.

That the certain is a part of the true can be understood in terms of Vico's conception of the "natural law of the gentes" (*diritto naturale delle genti*) which was part of the title of the first *New Science* and is maintained as a basic notion of the *New Science*. The "natural law of the gentes" contains Vico's solution to the problem of the relation of rational law and positive historical law. Vico's view is developed against those of the seventeenth-century natural-law theorists, Hugo Grotius, John Selden, and Samuel Pufendorf. In an early chapter of the first *New Science* Vico holds that none of these thinkers has given proper regard to providence as the basis of what is immutable. It is not possible to derive the immutable from the human condition. Yet, as Vico remarks, "the hypotheses of Grotius and Pufendorf are just to establish natural law as immutable!"[51] In the *New Science* Vico says that Grotius, Selden, and Pufendorf "should have taken their start from the beginnings of the gentes, where their subject matter begins. But all three of them err together in this respect, by beginning in the middle."[52] In Vico's view the conception of natural law in Grotius, Selden, and Pufendorf is based on an inadequate understanding of providence and reflects a failure to understand the origin of society.

Fisch points out that the conception of the natural law of the gentes advanced in the *New Science* is based on the distinction between public and private law originating in late and possibly classical Roman law.[53] Under private law a distinction was made between civil law and *ius gentium*. Civil law was that part of private law peculiar to each state. *Ius gentium* meant universal law in the sense of that part of private law that was found in all states. It was universal law in the sense that it was dictated by natural reason. It was *ius gentium* because it was *ius naturale*. This is a

[51]*Scienza nuova prima, Opere* 3, bk. 1, ch. 5.
[52]*New Science*, §394.
[53]Fisch, Introduction, *New Science*, E3.

notion of universal law as that which underlies the life of every society. It is not universal in the sense of international law between countries, nor is it universal in the sense of the rational ideal principles upon which actual law is based.

Ius gentium conceived as the natural law of the gentes is established by custom and is a reflection of the *sensus communis* upon which any human society, in Vico's view, is based. This *sensus communis* is formed from the appearance of Jove, the primordial experience common to all nations. *Diritto,* or law in the sense of natural law, the *diritto naturale delle genti,* is not formed as a rational ideal in terms of which men attempt to constitute the laws of human society. *Diritto* instead emerges from the conditions of primordial existence and the unvarying pattern of responses they elicit from all societies. *Diritto* is a direct expression of human nature in its original social state; it emerges as the form of society itself and is the basis from which law is subsequently formed. *Legge* is law in the more standard sense of law formed by the authority of a lawmaking body, law that is enacted.

In Vico's view, Grotius, Selden, and Pufendorf have an untenable conception of natural law because they have a defective conception of the origin of society. They begin "in the middle," attributing the rationality they find in their own age of thought to the beginnings of society. Their view cannot account for the rise of rationality in human society. They first conceive of an original barbarous state in which men were like beasts and then posit that men crossed from this state into the beginning of human society by an act of rational intelligence. In this way rationality is brought into human society as a *deus ex machina.*

In Vico's view society was formed neither by any single act of prudent agreement between men nor by foresight. Human rationality grew within the providential structure of history as human social action grew. This social action was not originally based on acts of reflective judgment but on the formation of the world through the powers of memory and imagination. The "natural law of the gentes" was formed by custom and the "natu-

61

VICO'S SCIENCE OF IMAGINATION

ral law of the philosophers" was formed by reason.[54] The natural
law of the philosophers was possible only when men came to
think in abstract sentences, when they could form meanings of
words and thoughts by their powers of reason apart from their
imagination and senses. The natural law of the philosophers,
which is natural law conceived as a rational ideal of law, is a late
development in the history of a nation. Grotius, Selden, and
Pufendorf were mistaken to attribute this late development of
mind to the beginning of humanity which, in fact, acted by
custom and thought in images, not rational concepts.

Vico conceived human society as developing through three
ages—that in which men lived and thought in terms of gods, that
in which they lived and thought in terms of heroes, and that in
which they lived and thought in wholly human terms. This
three-part structure of human society, which Vico derives from
the Egyptians, is the great truth of the natural law of the gentes.
Its archetypal divisions must be kept in mind at all times when
attempting to comprehend the *New Science*. Vico says: "These
are: (1) The age of the gods, in which the gentiles believed they
lived under divine governments, and everything was commanded them by auspices and oracles, which are the oldest institutions in profane history. (2) The age of the heroes, in which they
reigned everywhere in aristocratic commonwealths, on account
of a certain superiority of nature which they held themselves to
have over the plebs. (3) The age of men, in which all men recog-
nized themselves as equal in human nature, and therefore there
were established first the popular commonwealths and then the
monarchies, both of which are forms of human government."[55]
According to Vico in Book IV of the *New Science*, humanity
manifests a particular nature in each of these three ages, and
arising from this there are, particular to each age, kinds of customs, natural law, governments, languages, characters or modes
of symbolization, jurisprudence, authority, reason, and judg-

[54]*New Science*, §313.
[55]*New Science*, §31.

62

ments of social rights. In addition there are three sects of times (*tre sètte di tempi*), or types of cultural spirit.

The philosophical concept of natural law that ushers in the third age is possible only because the more fundamental sense of universal law as universal custom is already realized in society. Since providence is the ideal eternal history actually present in a society as its three ages of thought and life, it is the natural law, in the sense of divine natural law, of its total course of development. Providence is not an ideal of human society. Providence is the fundamental form of a society and is a conception of the divine that reflects the natural law of the gentes as a conception of the human.

Within Vico's conception of the natural law of the gentes is a conception of how the certain is part of the true. The natural law of the gentes is a *verum/certum*. The *ius gentium* is true because it is universal, like the natural law of the philosophers which presupposes it. It is true for all peoples at all times and all places. The *ius gentium* is not the invention of an original people who, as the true founders of the human race, communicated it to all other nations. It arises naturally as the basis of each nation in its separate primordial existence. Unlike the natural law of the philosophers the *ius gentium* is also *certum*. The natural law of the gentes is not an abstract principle but is present as the actual life of any society. It is true not as a rational ideal but as the actual basis of social practice. Vico's notion of the natural law of the gentes is a realization of what is originally implied in *certum est pars veri* as it moves from the *Universal Law* to the notion of *verum/certum* in the *New Science*. This notion of natural law is the fundamental context in which to understand the association of philosophical and philological ways of thinking.

The importance of the relationship of *verum* and *certum* for the historical genesis of the *New Science* does not in any way deny the importance of the *verum-factum* principle for the development of Vico's thought seen as a progression of philosophical ideas. In logical terms a line can be traced from the idea of the *verum-factum* principle in the *Ancient Wisdom* to Vico's later work, but in the history of Vico's thought the relation of the certain and the true is the dominant problem. These two senses of the true come together in the *New Science*. The *verum-factum* principle allows Vico to pass beyond the conception of truth in Cartesianism, and the *verum/certum* principle allows Vico to develop his interpretation of law into an understanding of all human activity. Both of these principles are necessary to the *New Science*; that is, that men make their world, and that this world can be understood only when *ratio* and *auctoritas* are brought together, when philosophy masters its fear of the particular and "undertakes to examine philology."

The principle of *verum-factum* accomplishes a distinction between the divine and the worlds of nature and of man. The principle of *verum/certum* projects this distinction into the basis for understanding the total motions of the human world.

CHAPTER 3

Imaginative Universals

In his explanation of the frontispiece of the *New Science,* Vico describes the one principle upon which this science and all his thought depends, and what it has cost him to discover it. The principle is both a conception of origin and what we would today call mythic mentality but what Vico calls "poetic wisdom," *sapienza poetica.* The beginning of the human world is tied to the beginning of languages and letters. "We find," Vico says, "that the principle of these origins both of languages and of letters lies in the fact that the first gentile peoples, by a demonstrated necessity of nature, were poets who spoke in poetic characters. This discovery, which is the master key of this Science, has cost us the persistent research of almost all our literary life, because with our civilized nature we [moderns] cannot at all imagine and can understand only by great toil the poetic nature of these first men."[1]

Vico goes on to state that "poetic characters" are certain "imaginative genera." Later in his discussion of the "Elements," he connects these two terms with "imaginative universals."[2] Vico variously uses the three terms *caratteri poetici, generi fantastici,* and

[1] *New Science,* §34.
[2] *New Science,* §209.

65

universali fantastici to designate this principle of the origin of human mentality.[3] I will use the third of these terms to refer to the conception expressed in all three of them. Vico contrasts the idea of imaginative universals with "intelligible universals," *generi intelligibili* or *universali intelligibili*.[4] The first two ages of the *storia ideale eterna*, the age of gods and the age of heroes, are typified by the thought of imaginative universals, by the thought of *fantasia*. The third age, that of men, is typified by the abstract thought of intelligible universals, the logical concepts of genus and species.

This conception of an original mentality that ordered experience in terms of imaginative universals is the "master key" (*la chiave maestra*) of this new science. At the beginning of the section on method Vico states that the period of work required for this discovery was "a good twenty years" (*ben venti anni*).[5] In his discussion of poetic characters in the first *New Science* (1725) Vico more precisely says that it took twenty-five years for this discovery.[6] The period Vico assigns in the *New Science*, originally published in 1730, would locate the beginning of this conception in his first works of systematic thought, the *Study Methods* (1708/1709) and the *Ancient Wisdom* (1710). The statement in the first *New Science* would place the origin of the conception at the be-

[3]The passages that make up the core of Vico's theory of imaginative universals in the *New Science* are: §§34, 204–210 (axioms 47–49), 403, 809, and 933–34. The term Vico most frequently uses is *caratteri poetici*. He occasionally uses a variation of one of the three main terms for this concept, as indicated in parentheses in the following list. On Vico's use of *caratteri poetici* see, e.g.: §§34, 68, 81, 209, 381, 416, 429, 431 (*caratteri fantastici*), 562, 762, 772, 783, 808, 809, 816, and 818. On *generi fantastici* see, e.g.: §§34, 209, 403, 495 (*generi poetici*), 809, and 819. On *universali fantastici* see, e.g.: §§209, 381, 460, 933 (*universali poetici*), 934, and 1033. Cf. *De constantia iurisprudentis, pars posterior, Opere* 2, ch. 12 and *Scienza nuova prima, Opere* 3, bk. 3, chs. 5–6.

[4]E.g., *New Science*, §§34, 209, and 934–35. In relation to *generi intelligibili* and Vico's variations on this term see, e.g.: §§34, 209, 460, 501 (*universali intelligibili*), 934–35, 1033 (*universali intelligibili*), and 1040 (*universali astratti*). Relevant to this term are Vico's remarks on philosophic or abstract sentences, e.g.: §§219, 704, and 821.

[5]*New Science*, §338.

[6]*Scienza nuova prima*, bk. 3, ch. 5.

ginning of his professional literary production itself, at the time of the first or second Inaugural Oration (1699 or 1700), and before Vico's break with Cartesian thought.[7] The point is not whether Vico's thought began to turn toward the conception of the imaginative universal at the beginning of his mature thought, which seems unlikely, or whether this development dates from the first works of his systematic thought. The force of Vico's remarks is that he intends us to regard all his thought as pointing not only to his conception of a new science, but specifically to the conception of the imaginative universal that makes it possible.

It is rare that an author gives such a direct statement of the central premise of his thought, and surprising that he provides such clear guidance for its interpretation. More surprising is the fact that none of the commentators who have written book-length studies of Vico's thought have made the imaginative universal the basis of their interpretation.[8] Few articles take it up as a particular topic. When they do discuss this conception, as for example in analyses of Vico's theory of language, scholars tend simply to echo Vico's remarks on poetic characters and make little attempt to penetrate the imaginative universal as a key to his conception of knowledge.

One reason for this lack of study of the *universale fantastico* is that there is little mention of it in the text. Although it is constantly in the background of the *New Science,* there is no particular chapter or section devoted to it and there are not a great

---

[7]Fisch, Introduction, *Autobiography,* p. 37. Cf. *Autobiography,* p. 117, but also Fubini's remark, *Autobiografia,* p. 9, note.

[8]Isaiah Berlin, in *Vico and Herder: Two Studies in the History of Ideas* (New York: Viking, 1976), emphasizes Vico's conception of imagination and the fact that a new type of knowledge is involved in Vico's philosophy. He does not discuss at length the logic of the imaginative universal itself. Ferdinand Fellmann, *Das Vico-Axiom: Der Mensch macht die Geschichte* (Freiburg/Munich: Verlag Karl Alber, 1976) gives attention to the imaginative universal, but the central focus of this work is on Vico's conception of historical knowledge. Leon Pompa, *Vico: A Study of the 'New Science'* (Cambridge: Cambridge University Press, 1975), discusses the imaginative universal only briefly.

number of passages where Vico directly explains its nature.[9] Perhaps another and deeper explanation of this neglect is that the *universale fantastico* renders very problematic the assimilation of Vico's thought into a traditional or contemporary system of reason or theory of history. While only vaguely aware of this difficulty, many commentators instinctively pass over or minimize these passages of the *New Science*. Since the imaginative universal is ultimately a theory of the image and not of the concept in any traditional sense, it causes great difficulties for standard philosophical interpretation.

Croce regards the imaginative universal as the great error of Vico's thought. Although he carefully presents many features of the imaginative universal in an illuminating analysis he believes that the imaginative universal contains an unmediated contradiction in which the imaginatively intuited particular and the rationally universalizing concept are not brought together.[10] Neither does Vico's conception of poetic wisdom, in Croce's view, offer an adequate theory of the aesthetic, as he regards Vico as basing both the mythic and the poetic proper, that is, the aesthetic and the artistic, on this same model of imaginative thought. Croce regards this conception as inadequate to both these functions of mind, more or less for the above reason.[11]

Behind Croce's view is Hegel. Simply put, the system of Hegel, including the *Phenomenology of Spirit,* has no theory of the mythical consciousness as a stage of primitive mentality out of which consciousness itself first develops. Hegel's phenomenology of spirit begins with the world of sensory consciousness. Cassirer claims that in Hegel's philosophy this world of sense qualities and perception remains ungrounded in the more primordial form of the mythical apprehension of the object wherein the

[9]See above, n. 3.

[10]Benedetto Croce, *The Philosophy of Giambattista Vico,* trans. R. G. Collingwood (New York: Russell and Russell, 1964), pp. 57–59.

[11]Ibid., pp. 65–67.

object is grasped in terms of the potencies and powers, the demons and gods found in primitive life.[12]

To the extent that Hegel discusses mythology, he connects it to art and religion, advanced sensuous forms of reason, moments of absolute spirit, which embody the rational concrete universal. Although Hegel in his early period had a special interest in myth and in the significance of *Phantasie,* his mature system begins and ends in the rational concept. This is so even though the concept is seen as concrete, the *Begriff* that is mediated in the activity of consciousness in the development of the forms of spirit. Croce criticizes Vico's *universale fantastico* for failing as a concrete form of the concept such as can be found in Hegel's system or in Croce's own idealism. An approach that understands reason more abstractly, that regards the concept and principles of rational explanation in a standard logical or scientific sense, has even more difficulty interpreting Vico's imaginative universal and probably must ignore it altogether.

I wish to discuss the imaginative universal from three perspectives: (1) as a theory of concept formation, (2) as a theory of the metaphor, and (3) as a theory of the existential conditions of thought. Vico himself speaks about the imaginative universal in these ways. I wish to draw out the implications of what he puts in a condensed, but precise way.[13]

Vico's discussion of poetic wisdom, which together with his discussion of the principles of his science takes up most of the *New Science,* contains a theory of knowledge not to be found elsewhere in Western philosophy. The theory of poetic wisdom is the prime illustration and demonstration of the correctness of two of Vico's central methodological doctrines: that "doctrines

---

[12]See Ernst Cassirer, *The Philosophy of Symbolic Forms,* 3 vols., trans. Ralph Manheim (New Haven: Yale University Press, 1953–57), II, pp. xv–xvii.

[13]My discussion of the first point above follows in part my essay, "Vico's Science of Imaginative Universals and the Philosophy of Symbolic Forms," in *Giambattista Vico's Science of Humanity,* ed. Giorgio Tagliacozzo and Donald Phillip Verene (Baltimore: The Johns Hopkins University Press, 1976), pp. 320ff.

must take their beginning from that of the matters of which they treat"[14] and that "philosophy undertakes to examine philology"[15] which, as discussed in the preceding chapter, is grounded in the *verum/certum* principle.

Vico's theory of poetic wisdom is based on an idea generally held in the eighteenth century: that ancient primitives, contemporary savages, children, and peasants share a common form of mentality.[16] Vico associates this mentality with the "speech" of mutes and various pathological defects in normal speech; he also stresses the importance of these phenomena for understanding the origin and basis of language.[17] For Vico, "the first science to be learned should be mythology or the interpretation of fables."[18] In this way the understanding of human mentality can begin where human mentality itself begins. The means for having such a science of origins involves the combination of the propensity of philosophical thought to uncover the universal principles of order which are inherent in particulars and the power of philological thought to present particulars in the human world in their true particularity. For Vico, the science of origins, upon which all true understanding of the human world depends, requires a new method of thought, one which is at once: philosophical-philological.

Vico's theory of myth is not euhemeristic, nor does it constitute a kind of modified or neo-euhemerism, as some of his com-

[14]*New Science*, §314.

[15]*New Science*, §7.

[16]See Frank E. Manuel, *The Eighteenth Century Confronts the Gods* (Cambridge: Harvard University Press, 1959), p. 156. In the *New Science* see §§206–17, 375–76, 437, 470, 498, 517, 658, 708, 841, and 1095, esp. 206–17.

[17]On mutes see *New Science*, §§225–30, 434, and 461. On the similarities of speech defects and first speech see §§453 and 462. Vico also connects poetic speech with the mentality of women, see §457. Cf. Vico's attention to speech defects with Cassirer's "Toward a Pathology of the Symbolic Consciousness," *The Philosophy of Symbolic Forms*, III, pt. 2, ch. 6, especially his concept of the importance of the theory of aphasia for knowledge of the symbolic process, speech, and representational thought.

[18]*New Science*, §51.

mentators have maintained.[19] Although euhemerism—that is, that myths are to be interpreted as traditional accounts of real incidents in human history—was a commonly held view in Vico's age, and although Vico frequently expresses the view that fables "were the first histories of the gentile nations,"[20] to interpret his view of myth as euhemeristic is to overlook what Vico means by "fable." Vico defines fables as "imaginative class concepts" (*generi fantastici*).[21] For Vico, fables are not embellishments of actual events or historical figures. There is not present epistemologically for the poetic or mythic mind: (1) an empirical or historical order of events which the mind (2) subsequently renders into fabulous form. Events themselves are given form through fables.

This notion of the mind's activity as giving form to experience goes back to the *verum-factum* principle of the *Ancient Wisdom*. The *universale fantastico* is a way of making intelligibility. It is a conception of how intelligibility takes place at the origin of human mentality, at the beginning of the human world. The fable, which depends upon the mind's power of *fantasia,* is the means by which the world first takes on a shape for the human. Imaginative universals are the form of thought for the first two of Vico's three ages—the age of gods, the age in which men ordered their world in terms of gods, and the age of heroes, the age in which men ordered their world in terms of heroic figures. The imaginative universals of the first age are formations of the immediately experienced forces of nature, such as Jove's pres-

---

[19]E.g., see Richard Chase, *Quest for Myth* (Baton Rouge: Louisiana State University Press, 1949), pp. 22–27; Manuel, *Eighteenth Century Confronts the Gods,* p. 160; and David Bidney, "Vico's New Science of Myth," in *Giambattista Vico: An International Symposium,* ed. Giorgio Tagliacozzo and Hayden V. White (Baltimore: The Johns Hopkins University Press, 1969), pp. 269–70 (see my criticisms of Bidney's view in my review in *Man and World,* 4 [1971], 347–50). Croce is quite correct in maintaining that Vico's view is not neo-euhemeristic; see *Philosophy of Giambattista Vico,* p. 65.

[20]*New Science,* §51.

[21]*New Science,* §403.

71

ence as the thunderous sky, or transformations of physiological bases of human existence, such as Juno, the form of everything relating to marriage, the social ordering of sexual actions.[22] The heroes of the second age give form to human qualities. Thus Achilles represents "all the deeds of valiant fighters" and Ulysses embodies "all the devices of clever men."[23]

The intelligible universal, the form of thought characteristic of Vico's third age, the age of men, is that of the generic concept of Aristotelian logic. In this age men think thoughts that have no figurative presence about them. The generic concepts of traditional Aristotelian logic are formed by the mind's power to select from a multiplicity of particular things those features that are common to all. Objects are collected into classes in terms of their possession of some common property. The essential function of thought in this regard is that of comparing and differentiating the features of particular objects. The essential features of these objects are abstracted through reflection. As the mind rises from the perception of individual objects to the essential properties that constitute them as species and to the generic ordering of the species by omitting sensuous content from the original perceptions, so the mind can descend from genus to species to individual object by adding elements of specific content. According to this view, the universal is that which can be conceived as a property common to the members of a given class and which can be predicated commonly to all members of the class.

In the development of human culture the formation of human experience in terms of imaginative universals gives way to the intelligible universal. For Vico, this process does not occur simply by internally modifying the imaginative universal to produce the intelligible universal in thought. The process involves the alteration of social forms of life, specifically the movement from the age of heroes to that of men. In Vico's work thought and society can be seen as co-determinative structures, wherein

---

[22]*New Science,* §933.
[23]*New Science,* §934; cf. §§403 and 809.

a certain type of thought is inconceivable without a certain social structure, and vice versa. The relationships between social conditions and forms of thought are more structural than causal. It is not that social conditions cause ideas, nor that thought causes certain social or political conditions; certain social conditions and certain forms of thought necessarily go together and arise as co-determinative forces of history.[24]

If the relationship between imaginative universals and intelligible universals is seen in purely logical terms, the terms in which Vico in fact frequently presents it, the elements of the imaginative universal can be isolated. Vico's method here, like his method of constructing the *New Science* as a whole, can be conceived as one of asking the question: if we as modern thinkers form concepts in terms of intelligible genera, how did the first men think such that our manner of concept formation can be understood as developing from a first form of thought? This question can be regarded as stating the philosophical side of Vico's philosophical-philological method.

The philological side of the method is that Vico has before him both his knowledge of the mythology of ancient Greece and Rome and the eighteenth-century insight that there is a common way of thinking among ancients, primitives, peasants, children, and those who suffer certain pathologies of speech. Vico's philology includes an awareness of other cultural areas, such as China and Africa, and specific primitive peoples, such as the American Indians, whom he mentions with some frequency. Vico wishes to see a difference in form in the productions of these cultures and mentalities, a difference that will reflect in structural terms the difference that myths and fables more obviously have in subject matter from the thought and writings of modern men. In this way Vico intends to associate the *certum* of the human world with its *verum*.

The first men, for Vico, created order in experience, not by

---

[24]See Fisch's description of the generation of Vico's three ages, *Autobiography*, pp. 49–54.

abstracting a property held in common by a collection of particular entities, but by creating an ideal portrait. This portrait took the form of the fable, a description of a particular reality. The first men were not capable of ordering or conceiving of the perceived unities of the human world or nature through a single property abstracted from them. The first men did not encounter the world as a world of clear-cut objects and persons, but instead as a world of forces and emotional qualities.[25] For Vico the poetic character, or fable, occupies the same central position in poetic (mythic) thought which the generic concept occupies in rational (modern) thought.

In the intelligible universal discrete particulars can be ordered into classes in terms of properties which can be abstracted from them and formulated in language apart from any representation of their unique properties. The intelligible universal, for Vico, is tied to the power of language to form abstract words. In the imaginative universal, language always operates metaphorically. It always preserves in its own symbolism or manner of statement something of the particulars it orders. For Vico, the movement from imaginative class concepts to intelligible class concepts is not simply an alteration of thought, but it is accomplished through an alteration of the type of linguistic symbolism involved.[26] This idea of the connection of the form of thought with the form of symbolism is an idea of considerable significance in contemporary semiotic science. This idea, which Vico had in advance of contemporary semiotical research, allows him to show that the first men of humanity did not think the same as modern men, but it also allows him to show that they did in fact *think*. The fact that their expressions are always poetic expressions is not the result of their naïveté or inexperience with language; such poetic expressions constitute a form of thought which contains its own version of class logic.

The imaginative universal, the fable, or poetic character is

[25]*New Science,* §§218–19.
[26]*New Science,* §§209, 225–35, 401–402, and 409.

more real than the individual, and the individual derives his reality from it. Vico says: "Poetic truth is metaphysical truth, and physical truth which is not in conformity with it should be considered false. Thence springs this important consideration in poetic theory: the true war chief, for example, is the Godfrey that Torquato Tasso imagines; and all the chiefs who do not conform throughout to Godfrey are not true chiefs of war."[27] The individual is what it is because its being is the being of the type. Since the figure of the fable or poetic character is not formed by abstraction from individuals or particulars already commanding their own empirical reality, the poetic character *is* the reality, and physical reality is to shape itself in terms of it. This connection between the metaphysical and physical orders, expressed in terms of poetic mentality in the *New Science,* had been expressed in general terms as early as Vico's defense of the *Ancient Wisdom* in the first *Risposta.*[28]

It is because poetic characters are themselves the conditions of reality for poetic mind, rather than abstractions or generalizations from an empirical order of individual things, that Vico can claim that fables have "univocal, not analogical, meanings for various particulars comprised under their poetic genera."[29] For the poetic mind poetic characters are not colorful or "rhetorical" embellishments of genera abstracted from empirical particulars; the particulars are not thought of *analogically,* as being *like* the ideal portraits of the generic individual of the fable. The individual cannot be thought of as having a reality apart from the generic character; he is what he is only through his identity with it.

The warrior does not conceive of his nature as apart from that of Godfrey, the true war chief. To the extent that he *is,* he and Godfrey have an identical reality. According to Vico's view, the distinctive characteristic of mythic or primordial poetic thought

[27]*New Science,* §205.
[28]*Risposta* (1711), sec. 2.
[29]*New Science,* §210.

is its power to assert *identities,* not *similarities.* The intelligible universal comes about through the development of the mind's ability to objectify experience through the discovery of similarities and differences in perceptual objects and the formulation of them in terms of common properties. The poetic mind structures experience through the formulation of immediate identities between elements.

Vico's conception of imaginative universals is not based on a nominalism in which a particular is raised to the level of a universal type and taken to stand for the nature of the class out of which it arises. Instead the reverse is true; the particulars are directly conceived as universals. The primordial poetic mind can formulate relationships and make assertions that are nonsense for the modern logical mind: "We cannot at all imagine and can understand only by great toil the poetic nature of these first men."[30] The poetic mind can univocally predicate a poetic genus of a collection of elements in a way that makes no sense to the mind that thinks in terms of intelligible class concepts. The way in which this univocal predication is accomplished in poetic thought involves the connection in Vico's thought between the fable and the allegory. Vico states: "Allegory is defined as *diversiloquium* insofar as, by identity not of proportion but (to speak scholastically) of predicability, allegories signify the diverse species or the diverse individuals comprised under these genera. So that they must have a univocal signification connoting a quality common to all their species and individuals (as Achilles connotes an idea of valor common to all strong men, or Ulysses an idea of prudence common to all wise men)."[31]

For the poetic mind, Ulysses is not a particular member of the class of wise men which is used to stand for the other members of the class, nor is Ulysses simply the substitution of a proper name for a class term, nor is Ulysses a kind of master type or composite individual that each member of the class of wise men

---

[30]*New Science,* §34.
[31]*New Science,* §403; cf. *Scienza nuova prima,* bk. 3, ch. 6.

could be said to resemble. The poetic mind can make assertions that are nonsense for the rational mind. It can assert meaningfully for or to itself that each member of the class of wise men is literally Ulysses, not that each individual is *a* Ulysses or is *like* Ulysses, but that each is identical with Ulysses. Each individual can be said to *be* Ulysses in the sense that Ulysses is their reality; each is to be identified as literally being Ulysses in a sense analogous to the assertion a rational mind would make in maintaining each to have the quality of being "prudent." In the first *New Science* Vico illustrates this point of the univocal meaning of the poetic character through the figure of Hercules.[32]

For the mind in possession of intelligible universals and abstract words, in possession of the fundamental distinction between thing and property upon which Aristotelian class logic rests, such forms of predication by the mythic mind appear as either nonsensical thought or unnecessary literary embellishments of what are in reality properties common to a class of objects. Primitives have often been seen as naïve or confused or as simply giving "metaphorical" accounts of ordinary empirical events, but this is not true in Vico's view.

I wish now to turn to the second point, that of the imaginative universal as a theory of metaphor. In my discussion of the first point, my aim was to show how the generic universal of class logic presupposes the imaginative universal. This approach is limited in that it treats the imaginative universal as a proto-concept rather than as the form of the image seen as having its own particular function in thought. In what sense is the *universale fantastico* not simply a principle necessary to one type of knowledge, poetic or mythic knowledge, but the principle of human knowledge itself? The answer to this question lies in the sense in which the metaphor is the basis of thought. It involves the metaphor or image as an embodiment of both the *verum-factum* and the *verum/certum* principles. If the *universale fantastico* were only a conception of a particular kind of knowing and not

---

[32]*Scienza nuova prima*, bk. 3, ch. 5.

of the basis of human knowledge itself, it would be an important epistemological idea but could not be called the master key of a new science.

Vico names metaphor as one of the four tropes that constitute the basis of the logic of poetic wisdom. Through the tropes and other rhetorical and poetic devices the imaginative universal is expanded into the language of mythological consciousness. Metaphor is the first of the tropes: "The most luminous and therefore the most necessary and frequent is metaphor."[33] The other three tropes are metonymy, synecdoche, and irony. Irony, Vico says, is not part of the poetic mind because its use requires the sophistication of the reflective mind that can distinguish between truth and falsehood and thus manipulate this distinction to achieve ironic statement.[34] Andrea Battistini has claimed in an essay, "Antonomasia e universale fantastico," that has as its background his longer study, *La degnità della retorica*,[35] that Vico's view of this fourfold taxonomy of the tropes derives from the view of Gerard Jan Voss.[36] The Vossian conception of antonomasia reverses the classical conception. In the classical view antonomasia is a device of *species pro individuo,* the substitution of an epithet or appellative for a proper name. In the Vossian view antonomasia becomes *individuum pro specie,* the use of a proper name to express a general idea or common noun.

The Vossian conception of antonomasia is the precursor in rhetorical theory of Vico's *universale fantastico.* In the scheme of the four tropes of Voss, antonomasia is a species of synecdoche, but even as a rhetorical device it does not always remain within this classification.[37] Vico transforms this rhetorical conception of antonomasia into the fundamental principle of mythic mental-

---

[33]*New Science,* §404.

[34]*New Science,* §408.

[35]Andrea Battistini, *La degnità della retorica: Studi su G. B. Vico* (Pisa: Pacini, 1975), esp. ch. 4.

[36]Andrea Battistini, "Antonomasia e universale fantastico," in *Retorica e critica letteraria,* ed. Lea Ritter Santini, Ezio Raimondi (Bologna: Società Editrice Il Mulino, 1978), pp. 105–21.

[37]Ibid., p. 119.

ity. In his conception of the four tropes as the basis of a logic of poetic wisdom, the *universale fantastico* becomes joined with metonymy and metaphor, as well as synecdoche and other devices of poetic thought such as metamorphoses, and the conception of monsters.

I wish to add to Battistini's discussion of the imaginative universal in rhetorical theory a conception of the imaginative universal as the basis of epistemological theory. Vico's transformation of this special rhetorical principle into a principle of mythic mentality has implications for the philosophical conception of metaphor as the basis of thought. In discussing this I wish to understand metaphor in a broader sense than it has in the fourfold scheme of the tropes, seeing it as the first principle of mind.

Cohen and Nagel, in discussing the logic of fictions, state: "Metaphors may thus be viewed as expressing the vague and confused but primal perception of identity, which subsequent processes of discrimination transform into a conscious and expressed analogy between different things, and which further reflection transforms into the clear assertion of an identity or common element (or relation) which the two different things possess."[38] With the exception of calling the perception of identity in metaphors "vague and confused" (which, from the point of view of analogical or conceptual forms of mentality, is in fact the case), Cohen and Nagel's threefold distinction is quite close to Vico's. This is especially true if one considers Vico's description of the Egyptians' imaginative identification of their inventions with Thrice-great Hermes (*Mercurius Trismegistus*) as based on their inability to form the genus "civil sage" and, moreover, their inability to conceive of civil wisdom.[39] Vico's discovery of the imaginative universal is the discovery of a principle of identity that is linked with the notion of metaphor as the fundamental epistemological element. The metaphor is that by which identity is originally achieved in perception. It is the form perception

---

[38]Morris R. Cohen and Ernest Nagel, *An Introduction to Logic and Scientific Method* (New York: Harcourt, Brace, 1934), p. 369.

[39]*New Science*, §209.

most immediately takes. Metaphor is the first of the tropes and the first of the operations of mind in the act of knowing.

Vico's conception of knowledge arises from a question fundamentally different from those asked by modern theory of knowledge. Modern philosophical theories of knowledge begin with something present to the mind. Descartes in the sixth *Meditation* wished to prove the existence of material things, to prove that the mind really had corporeal objects before it. Such proof, were it successful, would not explain how we know such things in particular ways. It could only supply us with a certain sign that we are not mistaken that there are things before the mind. In classical British empiricism the given is made up of ideas or impressions of sense. Vico's view might be thought to have a similarity with that of Kant in that Vico's *verum-factum* principle implies that the mind is active in the formation of its object. Kant's notion of this activity is founded on a passive moment in which the mind has a given in sensibility, in *Sinnlichkeit,* and is able through the synthesis of a manifold to achieve a certain content. We cannot discover from Kant, or for that matter from Hegel, how the mind actually gets something before it. There is a sense in which I think Kant is struggling with this question in the *Critique of Judgment* in his conception of the "reflective judgment." In this work Kant is attempting to understand how the mind can form the object without the use of the category.

Hegel's phenomenology of consciousness begins with the apprehension of the "here" and "now" from which the object is constructed in the development of consciousness, but we never learn how we come by a "here" or a "now" in the first place. Hegel's "here" and "now" are blanks, without the emotional directionality of the mythical consciousness. For Vico, the beginning point of mind like the primitive world, is filled with benign and malignant forces. In the theory of the *universale fantastico* Vico makes the question of the given the basis of his conception of knowledge. He asks a completely new epistemological question. He does not ask how the mind functions in relation to the object to produce knowledge, or the even less profitable question of whether the mind has objects actually before it, whether it has an external world.

Vico asks how the mind comes to have something before it at all. In this way he moves behind the given. By asking how there ever comes to be something, rather than nothing, before the mind, Vico is able to see knowledge as beginning directly with the image. In their drive from the perceptual given to the concept, non-Vichian views of knowledge regard the image only as that which readies the perception for the concept. The full-blown images of myth and art that do develop their own reality directly from perception appear to such epistemologies as a world outside the concept. They are regarded as images "of something," perhaps of the given, or as compressed analogies.

The power of the mind to have something before it rests on its power to rise beyond immediacy. Immediacy is the state of pure particularity in which each moment is new, in which there is no place, no *topos* for thought. Vico says: "We can now scarcely understand and cannot at all imagine how the first men thought who founded gentile humanity. For their minds were so limited to particulars that they regarded every change of facial expression as a new face."[40] This immersion in the particular in which one appearance or perception follows the other without the achievement of meaning is a nullity, a kind of nothingness. It describes a mentality that is on the border between that of animals and that of humans. Vico says further that "the minds of the first men of the gentile world took things one at a time, being in this respect little better than the minds of beasts, for which each new sensation cancels the last one."[41] This thought of the immediate is one that we who are in possession of conceptual thought can barely grasp. *Fantasia,* with its power to give imagistic form to experience, is always approached by us from the touchstone of the constancy of the abstract concept. But the

[40]*New Science,* §700.
[41]*New Science,* §703. Cf. Vico's remarks on animal mentality, *Vici vindiciae,* sec. 16.

minds of the first men achieve the stability of meaning within the immediate flux of sensations that cancel each other in succession by the power of *fantasia* alone. Through *fantasia* the particular is formed as a universal.

Time here is only the motion of this flux in which "each new sensation cancels the last one." Meaning can be achieved only if a sensation can become a particular that is not cancelled by the presence of the next sensation. The mind can have something before it through its power to produce an identity. A sensation is apprehended as the being of the other sensations in the motion of the flux. The time of the flux is cancelled by a locus within itself. A single sensation becomes a permanent reference point of the flux of sensations which now have their being in it. Through this fixed point of sensation, or particular, the meaning of the flux can be repeatedly grasped. This is very like the process that Cassirer describes by the term "finding again," "*Wiederfinden,*"[42] the difference being that Cassirer ultimately bases his conception on a cognitive model of thought. This "finding again" in a fixed sensation the meaning of the whole of the flux is achieved through the power of *fantasia*. It requires the formation of an image or metaphor. This interruption of the flux for Vico is initially done by the gesture, by the mute sign. The identity of the flux with itself is accomplished by bodily speech, by an action. Such actions precede for Vico the more abstract actions of ordinary human speech which can hold the flux at a greater distance.[43]

The fixing of sensation in the flux does not occur by analogy, by likening one sensation to another, by finding similarities in this flux. The fixation of the particular is not a process in which one sensation in the flux is grasped as *like* the rest. It is a process in which the *is* itself is made. Vico says that *mythos* is *vera narratio* or true speech: "The fables in their origin were true and severe narrations, whence *mythos*, fable, was defined as *vera narratio*."[44] Every fable is true speech and every metaphor is "a fable in

[42]Ernst Cassirer, *The Philosophy of Symbolic Forms*, III, 108 and 124.
[43]*New Science*, §446.
[44]*New Science*, §814.

brief."[45] Vico says that metaphors involving "likenesses [*simi-glianze*] taken from bodies to signify the operations of abstract minds must date from times when philosophies were taking shape."[46] In the fixing of sensation the meaning of the whole of the flux is found again in the single sensation. In this way a universality is achieved through the particular. An identity is made. The power of the *is*, the power of identity itself is realized.

No element of analogy is here possible because the flux of sensation is in no way *like* one of its sensations, the universal is not *similar* to the particular. These two elements are never the same, nor are they derived from similarity. They originate at once. The fable or metaphor is true speech because it makes this identity; it brings forth the *is* as the given of human mentality. This given is something made. The *verum-factum* principle is the inner working of the *universale fantastico* because, through the image, which is the metaphor understood on this level, the primary act of intelligibility takes place. The *verum/certum* principle applies here as an element within this process of making. The *verum* and *certum* are not convertible, but they are held in an original and indissoluble bond. What is made is a *certum*, but not a mere *certum*. What is made is not a simple fact. The particular that is made manifests a universal element that connects it to all other particulars within a total mentality which makes up its intelligibility, its dimension of *verum*. The metaphor is the power of true speech, the narration that makes the particular appear as an image within the movement of sensation.

Vico's primary example of the fixation of sensation in the image is Jove. Jove is the first *universale fantastico* of poetic mentality and "every gentile nation had its Jove."[47] The primordial sensation in the flux of sensations is thunder and the fear of thunder.[48] Thunder is the first thought. Joyce understood this when, under the influence of his reading of Vico, he placed his

[45]*New Science*, §§403–404.
[46]*New Science*, §404.
[47]*New Science*, §193.
[48]For Jove's relation to thunder see *New Science*, §§9, 192, 193, 195, 377, 379, 383, 385, 387, 389, 447–48, 491, 516, 689, and 1098.

hundred-lettered clap of thunder on the first page of *Finnegans Wake*: "bababadalgharaghtakamminarronnkonnbronntonner-ronntuonnthunntrovarrhounawnskawntoohoohoordenenthur-nuk!" Jove speaks.

The flux of sensation in which one sensation cancels the next is a total flux. The first thought, or name, is a total name, one that provides a fixed point for the total flux. It is that through which the whole can be "found again" in the negative time of flux, the original motion that lacks place. The divine is the first name. Vico regards the first men as beginning to think by becoming aware of the sky. They were giants, "all robust bodily strength, who expressed their very violent passions by shouting and grumbling, they pictured the sky to themselves as a great animated body, which in that aspect they called Jove, the first god of the so-called greater gentes, who meant to tell them something by the hiss of his bolts and the clap of his thunder."[49] This first thought is the thought of Jove as an active moving body that shouts back to their shouting with the original shout. Jove calls attention to himself as the largest of the *giganti* by his powers of light and sound. The divine arrives in noise. His body flashes and shakes and the bodies of the giants shake with sympathetic motion out of fear. Jove is not an alter ego, but a vast body to be feared.

This awareness of the sky as a body of a different order is, for Vico, the first distinction of thought. Through it a distinction of sky and earth can be made. Such a distinction allows the first men to live in a world. Jove is not the name for the whole in the sense of all that there is, everything. The thought of Jove allows not only the first men's eyes to turn toward the sky for the first time, but also allows them to discover that they are of the earth. The primordial distinction between sky and earth is the fundamental distinction within which the realities of the world can come about.

Once this distinction is made others can follow so that nature

[49]*New Science*, §377.

comes alive as an activity of bodies. The world of human institutions can develop later, when the orientation toward Jove is transferred to the fathers who found the original families. The sky was apprehended as Jove and the earth and sea were seen as Cybele and Neptune, "and similarly by means of the other divinities they signified the other kinds of things appertaining to each, denoting all flowers, for instance, by Flora, and all fruits by Pomona."[50] All of nature is composed of bodies who communicate to the first men by the signs of their natures, just as Jove speaks through his signs of thunder and lightning. Vico says: "They believed that Jove commanded by signs, that such signs were real words, and that nature was the language of Jove."[51]

The first men lived in a world of "real words," of the passionate action of the bodies of nature moving in relation to each other. This is not a harmonious situation because the first men, as Vico pictures them, did not immediately know how to understand this activity. Divination, the ability to read real words, was of great importance. Vico asks us to imagine a beginning point of human experience in which all was body and bodily motion, in which meaning was an action between bodies, and in which human thought was nothing more than the bodily act of sensation. There is no mere sensation for Vico. Sensation is the act that underlies or is the first moment in any act of knowing. It is a necessary act through which the mind initiates for itself what is to be known or thought. There is true speech only at the level of sense.

Sensation is not understood in traditional epistemology as itself a form of thought but as the material of thought. In Vico's view there is a thought of bodies. To think this thought of bodies would require that we revert to the life of a purely bodily state of existence, where all thought is just bodily sensation. Since we as modern men live on a different level, one involving abstract thought, we cannot truly get back to the level of the first men.

[50]*New Science*, §402.
[51]*New Science*, §379.

But since we possess to some extent the power of *fantasia,* even though reduced and monitored by our powers of intellectualization, we can move back in the direction of this thought of sense by becoming attentive to the myth.

Vico speaks of three different ways in which primordial thought is bodily thought: (1) Language was originally used to give form to inanimate things by means of metaphors derived from the body, such as eyes of potatoes, shoulders of hills, and teeth of rakes.[52] (2) The mind itself is immersed in the body and cannot be apprehended apart from it. Thus, "the human mind is naturally inclined by the senses to see itself externally in the body, and only with great difficulty does it come to understand itself by means of reflection."[53] And (3) the thought of the first men was literally a bodily act of sensing. Vico says that Jove was a "truth of the senses for them,"[54] and that human ideas began as divine ideas through the contemplation of the heavens with "bodily eyes."[55] Also the first acts of meaning are connected to mute acts of bodily gestures.[56]

The first of these forms of bodily thought is a process in which the world is embodied by the first men by apprehension of their own bodies; and they see the forms of nature and their bodily activities, their work and life, as alter bodies. Because the largest dimensions of nature are apprehended as bodies—sky, earth, and water as the divine bodies of Jove, Cybele, and Neptune—the more specific embodiment of the world by the same metaphorical process is possible. Thus the indentations on potatoes, the contours of hills, and the tines of a rake are not simply *like* eyes, shoulders, and teeth, they *are* such, just as the sky is the body of Jove and not merely similar to Jove. Potatoes, hills, and rakes are bodies of different shape than the human body. They are alter bodies of the human body.

[52]*New Science,* §405. These bodily metaphors vary between languages; e.g., Vico uses *occhi delle viti.* See Fisch's footnote to this passage.
[53]*New Science,* §236; see also §§331 and 1045.
[54]*New Science,* §508.
[55]*New Science,* §391.
[56]*New Science,* §401.

The first men make their world intelligible through the senses. The true is the made and all that is made is true because at this level there is no contrast between what is sensed and what is thought, or between what is sensed and what is signified. The world is all bodies in motion, and meaning is achieved through the action and reaction of bodies on each other. When the great body of Jove vibrates with his signs of lightning and thunder, the movements of other bodies have significance. The meaning of Jove's signs is initially nothing more than the trembling of the bodies of the *giganti* and the motion of their flight in fear into their caves. Divination of the more specific meaning of these signs is a development from this initial bodily gesture. Here there is also no grasp of mind or self as separate from body. To be all body or all sense is to be able to achieve meaning only through bodily action. To mean something is to do it. If fear is meant it takes the form of actual flight. It cannot be spoken about; speaking involves a more sophisticated form of symbolism.

Articulate speech and writing allow us to use other bodily motions, the special motions of our vocal chords or fingers to respond to what is there. With this deflected form of motion we can also respond to what is not there. The mute gesture is bodily thought because it requires the bodily presence of what is meant and it itself is a bodily act. The mute gesture is a bodily movement toward another body—the thing that is meant. A bodily motion is brought forth on the same plane of what is there to be meant. In this act distance is achieved between what is there as object meant and the motion wherein significance is achieved. Sensation does not cancel sensation but fixes it. What is fixed is something sensuous, a bodily action. This mute sign is a metaphor in the sense that it is a bodily form—the immediate representation in gesture—of what is there, of what *is*.

The third perspective from which I wish to consider the imaginative universal is as a theory of the existential conditions of thought. Thought for Vico arises from fear. Fright or fear, *spavento* or *timore,* is the condition for the experience of the divine and for the founding of a world of human institutions developed over and against the world of nature.[57] The basis of the metaphorical formation of the sky as Jove, the founding of an *is* or identity within the sensible flux, arises from fear. The *universale fantastico* does not arise as the answer to a problem thought sets for itself. It is given birth through the master passion of fear.

The *giganti*, whom Vico pictures as wandering in the vast forests of the earth after the biblical flood, are awakened to their essentially human condition by mortal terror of thunder. This thunder occurs just above their heads, Vico says, the sky for these first men was only as high as the mountain tops.[58] The body of Jove was like a cover. The fright of their own bodies causes them to apprehend the sky as the body of Jove. Religion originates in fear, in Vico's view, and is the first of his three "principles" or basic generative conditions of the human world. The fear that initiates religion leads to the second principle, marriage, since it is from fear that the first humans retreat to copulate out of sight of the sky in caves and then begin to live in constant relationship.[59] Fear is also part of the third principle, that of burial. Since places of the dead are associated with the divine, they too are feared.[60]

Why is thunder the primordial phenomenon of human experience? Vico certainly saw great lightning and heard thunder rolling across the bay of Naples and over Ischia and Capri. Yet Vico does not consider this question beyond reiterating the classical association of Jove with the hurling of thunderbolts. The Etruscans, an ancient people in whom Vico had some particular interest, had a system of divination based on thunder, which Pliny describes in his *Natural History*.[61] These ancient Tuscans

[57]On *spavento* and *timore* see, e.g., *New Science*, §§13, 14, 16 (*orridi*), 178, 183, 190–91, 338, 369, 371, 376, 377, 379, 382, 385, 387, 449, 502–504, 518, 529, 550, 554, 629, 916, 1098, and 1099.

[58]*New Science*, §712.

[59]*New Science*, §1098.

[60]*New Science*, §529.

[61]Pliny, *Natural History*, II, 137–48.

divided the sky into sixteen sections from which to observe and interpret thunderbolts and distinguished eleven different kinds of thunderbolts, of which Jove was entitled to throw three different kinds. The thunderstorms over Tuscany can be large and all-encompassing in their tremor. Vico thought the Etruscans to have a particular wisdom of the divine. This wisdom ultimately involved the connection of the study of thunder with hepatoscopy, divining the future from the livers of animals—connecting the external order with the internal order.

Had Vico attempted to explain why thunder is the primordial phenomenon, he might have pointed out that the association of thunder and Jove in religion and mythology cannot be regarded as accidental. The primordial mind makes primordial associations. Thunder is a special noise. Vico's conceptions of thunder and fear are not inductive. To understand the importance of thunder in human activity, we must consider the imaginative grasp of human consciousness which caused Joyce to create the longest word in the English language, the sound of Finnegan's fall.

I believe Vico would have liked the following words of the Tasaday, the "primordial" people of the Philippine rain forest discovered by the modern world in 1971, as reported by the journalist John Nance. The Tasaday were asked:

> "What is the worst thing in the forest?"
> "The big word is the worst thing. We are afraid of it. Our ancestors also were afraid."
> This was puzzling. Mai, who could readily convert metaphorical language into common terms, smiled and said, without asking them, that the "big word" was thunder—the worst thing in the forest was thunder.
> "What do you do when the big word comes?"
> "We stay in our places and some of us put our hands to our ears."
> "Where does this big word come from?"
> "We don't know . . . we don't know."[62]

[62]John Nance, *The Gentle Tasaday* (New York: Harcourt Brace Jovanovich, 1957), p. 58.

One is not surprised when several pages on in Nance's reportage the local interpreters and the Tasaday discuss the nature of the moon (about which there is some confusion) and the sun in terms of their having bodies.

In the *Kaṭhopaniṣad* of the Indian *Upanisads,* can be found the following: "The Prāṇa [Brahman as the master of creation] being present this whole universe comes out of Him and vibrates with Him. He is a great terror like the raised thunderbolt. Those who know this become immortal. For fear of Him the fire burns; for fear of Him shines the Sun; for fear of Him do Indra, Vāyu and Death, the fifth, proceed (with their respective functions)."[63]

Vico's conception of the origin of religion is not derived from the empirical study of myth, although thunder and sky mythology play a central role in much primitive and religious mentality. Vico's placement of the origin of religion in fear has a connection with the ancient tradition of Epicureanism, of which Naples was the center in Roman times, and specifically with Lucretius, who saw fear of the gods as the basis of religion. Vico's earliest surviving writing, his poem of 1692, "Affetti di un disperato" ("Feelings of One in Despair"), is Lucretian: "It could not," as Fisch remarks, "have been written by a devout Christian."[64] This Lucretian orientation is not carried past Vico's earliest work. Although the origin of religion in fear is preserved in the *New Science,* Vico draws very different implications from it than does Lucretius.[65] Fear is understood by Vico not as passive, but as an active, formative passion. It has the positive result of ordering the bodily activity of the first men and concentrating their powers of sensation so as to provide the necessary basis for human thought and society.

Vico says: "Thus it was fear which created gods in the world; not fear awakened in men by other men, but fear awakened in

[63]Swāmī S'Arvānanda, *Kaṭhopaniṣad,* 8th ed. (Mylapore, Madras: Sri Rama-krishna Math, 1956), pp. 101–2.
[64]Fisch, Introduction, *Autobiography,* p. 36.
[65]*New Science,* §191.

men by themselves."[66] This original fear is not ordinary fear. It is not the fear of the other self, nor is it fear of natural events, of the dangerous in nature in an ordinary sense. The source of this fear is an immediate beyond. The thunderous motion of the sky that covers the world like a ceiling sweeps over the heads of the *giganti* whose bodies involuntarily tremble in imitation of the celestial motion. The motion instilled in their bodies becomes the quasi-mental motion of the gesture, the half-voluntary movements that fix their sensations on a difference between the conditions of the earth and of the sky. The ability to fear and fear again in the same way produces a common point of focus, an object, and a common form of feeling among the giants. They feel the same thing in the same way. In this constancy of feeling induced by fear human society is born.

For Vico, society and human experience itself do not originate in any practical response to existence or material needs. The *giganti* are robust and strong and successful dwellers of the forest. Their humanity is not initiated by themselves except in their ability to respond to the movements of the sky as signs of Jove. Before men fear Jove they experience fear only in a momentary sense. The response of fear is repeated in relation to each thunderstorm over and over without it becoming a deliberate action, a meaning. Each instance of the fright is a *there*. The first men live in a "thrownness" of existence in which there is no freedom to form their world until they are able to grasp the special fear that makes the thunder become Jove. It is a fear like that heard in the human outcry at birth.

Unlike the fear of another's movements or of a natural event such as a fire or flood there is no practical response to thunder, for it is an event in the face of which there is nothing specific to do. Thunder signifies the termination of the lightning bolt; in practical terms escape is not necessary. Fear of thunder is logically unjustified; yet, like the speech of the *archai* which bursts

[66]*New Science*, §382.

91

forth suddenly and from which we can then think, thunder activates the human condition. Modern men awake to thunder in the night, their minds full of confusion and movement. When its noise is heard in the day, they move furtively with little conversation; the thunder's presence is the unspoken explanation of their actions.

Vico says that in their most original state the *giganti* were without fear of the gods. These giants grew to such proportions because they absorbed their own excrement as it lay upon the earth. It reentered their bodies through inhalation and by passing through their pores during their great exertions. Vico says that among the survivors after the biblical flood mothers must have abandoned their babies, who grew as giants: "And these children, who had to wallow in their own filth [*le loro fece*], whose nitrous salts richly fertilized the fields, and who had to exert themselves to penetrate the great forest, grown extremely dense from the flood, would flex and contract their muscles in these exertions, and thus absorb nitrous salts into their bodies in greater abundance."[67] These giants were huge in bodily size but childlike in mentality, themselves being the "children as it were of the growing human race."[68]

Vico maintains that fear of the gods is the cause of the reduction of the *giganti* to normal bodily size. The fear of the gods which begins with the formation of Jove as the great body of the sky enlarges the mental capacity of the giants while causing the diminution of bodily size. Vico says: "It was by becoming imbued with this cleanliness of body and this fear of gods and of fathers—in both cases a fear we shall find amounting to terror [*spaventosissimo*] in earliest times—that the giants diminished to our normal stature."[69] This fear of the gods resulted in the activity of divination and sacrifice which involved the custom of sacred ablutions. These first baths, these forms of sacred cleansing, changed the relations of the *giganti* to their own excrement

[67]*New Science*, §369.
[68]*New Science*, §4.
[69]*New Science*, §371.

which had made them grow so big. Vico claims further that the fear itself, first of the gods and then of the fathers who founded the first families, reshaped the bodies of the giants into normal size. For Vico the body is a metaphor of the mind. As the mental capacities of the first humans develop in their powers to form the world, their bodies take on a controlled shape. There can be no institutions or society of giants.

Vico's view of fear suggests something broader than just a theory of the first thought. It implies that fear is the condition, the impetus for any first thought. Any beginning in thought subsequent to the primordial thought of the first men reenacts this fear of the beginning. The intelligible universal of modern men is not connected with fear. It is thought confident of itself. In Cartesian fashion it moves from one concept to another, but it does not make its own beginnings. It does not wrest from the negativity of the flux an identity of sensation, a *topos* within which mental activity can concentrate itself and overcome the erosion of its energy in the cancellation of one sensation by the next.

The mentality of the intelligible universal pretends that the negativity of the flux does not exist. Sensation is an element of anxiety for it, but it can grasp none of the terror of formlessness which accompanies the attempt to make a new intelligibility, the attempt to perform an original conversion of the true and the made. Any genuine beginning in thought requires the power of *fantasia* to produce true speech. The reflective mind is not the support of itself, any more than reflective society is the support of itself, but develops from and always has beneath its activity the imaginative forms of early life.

Vico's view suggests that the ability to fear is what gives us an origin point in thought when thought grows old in one of its patterns. The solution to the fatigue of thought at any point is not rest, but fear, the reemergence of the chaos of sensation which places us in a demiurgic position. Fear reinstates us as makers and forces us to remember how to speak. This can be accomplished only when we become afraid as, for example,

93

when Stephen Dedalus in Joyce's *A Portrait of the Artist as a Young Man* speaks of his fear of the materiality of the host in the Christian trinity and his fear of other things, among them thunder. He is freed from the fatigue of religious devotion and from its intellectual embodiment in scholastic language. He speaks with a Vichian sense of origin and making as the work ends: "I go to encounter for the millionth time the reality of experience and to forge in the smithy of my soul the uncreated conscience of my race. *April 27*. Old father, old artificer, stand me now and ever in good stead."[70]

Fear allows us to become the artificer, to practice the divine making in ourselves. It is not fear of danger; no practical solution of flight to safety is possible. The fear is generated between the thereness of the concept and the thereness of sensation, the negative times of both—the infinity of distinctions within the concept and the material flux of sensation. If we cannot fear, cannot feel our way back to touch the primordial act of thought, we simply remain fatigued, devout, anxious, logical, and unable to experience the *verum-factum*. Fear allows us to grasp an identity and through it we see a new difference between the divine and nature and between nature and culture. Any metaphor that is an element of a beginning is not only a fable in brief, it is the world in brief. When it is developed in the allegorical language of the fable, when its true speech is extended out in various directions, its version of the divine, natural, and human begins to emerge. Devotion is replaced by human piety, the artifice of the knower. A thought born out of fright, and not confidence, is not a thought in an ordinary sense. It is always a new reality.

Fear itself is a shape the body takes which in turn allows the mind to take the shape of *fantasia*. In *fantasia* all oppositions are held together in the manner of the opposition of particular and universal in the *universali fantastici*. As in the myth, these oppositions are not mediated. They achieve intelligibility as forces in a

---

[70]James Joyce, *A Portrait of the Artist as a Young Man* (Harmondsworth, Middlesex: Penguin Books, 1960), pp. 243–53.

bond having no third term. The myth is not a third term. It is not something separable from them as a third element which they are within. In the narration of the myth benign and malignant forces are placed in touch with each other but they are not unified or mediated. The poetic wisdom of the myth is a drama of unresolved oppositions which must be read by auspices, by the regions of thunder and their connection, as the Etruscans thought, with the regions of the liver. It is a world, as Vico says, that we can barely reach, if at all.

CHAPTER 4

Memory

In two places in the *New Science* Vico calls attention to Memory as the mother of the Muses—Mnemosyne.[1] He makes the same point in his early work, *On the Ancient Wisdom of the Italians*.[2] Vico says in the *New Science*: "Memory thus has three different aspects: memory when it remembers things, imagination when it alters or imitates them, and invention when it gives them a new turn or puts them into proper arrangement and relationship. For these reasons the theological poets called Memory the mother of the Muses."[3] Memory (*memoria*) is memory (*memoria*), imagination (*fantasia*), and invention (*ingegno*). Vico makes a similar association between these three terms surrounding his point that Memory is the mother of the Muses in the *Ancient Wisdom*.[4]

Mnemosyne is the mother of the Muses. The daughters of Memory govern the arts of civilization. Vico says that "Urania must have been the first of the Muses," and that "she and the

---

[1]*New Science*, §§699 and 819. See Paolo Rossi, *Le sterminate antichità: Studi vichiani* (Pisa: Nistri-Lischi, 1969), p. 183. Rossi remarks that Hobbes uses the same expression.

[2]*De Italorum sapientia*, ch. 7, sec. 3.

[3]*New Science*, §819.

[4]See also *Autobiography*, pp. 123–25.

96

other Muses were held to be daughters of Jove."[5] In making this point Vico refers to the saying from Virgil's *Eclogues* that *A Iove principium musae*, "From Jove the muse began."[6] This is also the saying that Vico affixed as the motto for his first *New Science* (1725). Urania is the daughter of Jove and is associated with the sky.

Vico says, "The first muse must have been Urania, who contemplated the heavens to take the auguries. Later she came to stand for astronomy."[7] Vico repeats several times in the *New Science* that Urania was understood by Homer as the *"scienza del bene e del male,"* the "science of good and evil."[8] He makes his point of the association of Urania with the auspices in discussing the gods in the second book of the *Universal Law* (*De constantia iurisprudentis*).[9] In the *New Science* Vico says that wisdom (*sapienza*) begins in this science or knowledge of good and evil: "Wisdom among the gentiles began with the Muse, defined by Homer in a golden passage of the *Odyssey* as 'knowledge of good and evil,' and later called divination."[10]

To summarize, memory is a faculty that consists of: (1) itself, (2) imagination (*fantasia*), and (3) invention (*ingegno*). Its fundamental character can be seen by the fact that Memory or Mnemosyne is the mother of the Muses, who are associated with the arts of civilization. The Muses were daughters of Jove, who is the first poetic character or *universale fantastico*. The first of the Muses is Urania, who is defined by Homer and Vico as the science of good and evil or the science of divination. From divination, the reading of signs through analysis of thunder, observing the flights of birds, examination of the entrails of slain animals, comes the assessment of the good and evil forces in the world. Among the arts of civilization, divination is the first. This first art derives from Mnemosyne and Jove. Put in philosophical

---

[5]*New Science*, §508.
[6]*New Science*, §391.
[7]*New Science*, §391.
[8]*New Science*, §508; see also, e.g., §§365, 381, 391, and 533.
[9]*De constantia iurisprudentis, pars posterior*, ch. 23.
[10]*New Science*, §365.

terms, this first art of humanity derives from the association of memory, in the sense of Vico's "three memories" described above, and the imaginative universal, in its most primordial sense of the transformation of nature into thought.

Memory, imagination, and invention are the primary faculties of the mind. They are the powers out of which human experience is formed. Vico says: "All three appertain to the primary operation of the mind, whose regulating art is topics, just as the regulating art of the second operation of the mind is criticism; and as the latter is the art of judging, so the former is the art of inventing. And since naturally the discovery or invention of things comes before criticism of them, it was fitting that the infancy of the world should concern itself with the first operation of the human mind." Vico concludes this passage by saying, "With reason, then, did the theological poets call Memory the mother of the Muses; that is, of the arts of humanity."[11] The power of beginning to think, the power of origin, is memory in this threefold sense.

Vico's connection of memory with the art of topics in the *New Science* has its origin in his oration *On the Study Methods of Our Time* in which he first breaks with Cartesianism and states his own original position. Here he emphasizes the importance of the art of topics as the "art of finding the medium," or middle term, and introduces this idea by discussing the interrelationship of the memory and imagination.[12] In the *Study Methods*, as previously discussed, Vico presents the art of topics as important for philosophical criticism of concepts and argumentation. He regards topics as having a proper basis in the early training of memory and imagination which is ignored in modern education. In the *New Science* the conception of the art of topics is expanded from its relevance for conceptual analysis and argumentation to its relevance for a general theory of humanity.

[11]*New Science*, §699.
[12]*Study Methods*, pp. 13–15.

Topics is central to our understanding of primordial mind. The art of topics involves the creation of the medium of thought itself and is associated with the first art of civilization, the divinatory science of good and evil.

How is this complex notion of memory to be understood? What does it signify for the construction of the *New Science* as a whole? The *New Science* is a theater of memory in which humanity originates and confronts itself. The answer to this question, or at least a good part of it, lies in the realization that there are two senses of *fantasia* and two senses of the *universale fantastico* at work in the *New Science*. One of these Vico describes directly in his theory of poetic wisdom, *sapienza poetica*. It is the basis of his theory of primordial mind. This is the sense of *fantasia* and the *universale fantastico* I have described in the preceding chapter. I wish to claim here that there is a second sense in which the *universale fantastico* is the "master key" to the *New Science. Fantasia* is not only a subject matter of the *New Science*; it is the form of Vico's science itself. In other writings I have called this second sense "recollective *fantasia*."[13]

In coining the term "recollective *fantasia*" I mean to designate the type of memory through which Vico's *New Science* is accomplished and also the type of thought from which it must ultimately be understood. This power of memory which Vico's work employs, but does not as such discuss, can be understood by seeing how the imaginative universal is the structure of memory for the first men. Recollective *fantasia* contains in itself elements that reflect in a one-to-one fashion the elements in the memory structure of original or mythic *fantasia*. It is the result of basing reflective thought on the image, rather than beginning with

[13]Donald Phillip Verene, "Vico's Philosophy of Imagination," in *Vico and Contemporary Thought*, ed. Giorgio Tagliacozzo, Michael Mooney, and Donald Phillip Verene (Atlantic Highlands, N.J.: Humanities Press, 1979), pt. 1, pp. 20–36. See also "Vico's Humanity," *Humanitas*, 15 (1979), 227–40; and "Vico's Philosophical Originality," in *Vico: Past and Present*, ed. Giorgio Tagliacozzo (Atlantic Highlands, N.J.: Humanities Press, 1981), pt. 1, pp. 127–43.

some notion of the concept and then working toward its concreteness. I wish to use "recollective *fantasia*" as a general term for the Vichian manner of thinking.

At several points in the *New Science* Vico says how difficult it is to grasp the mentality and life of the first humans; he gives this observation a special emphasis in the section on method. Here he states that his discovery of the mode of thought of the first humans, the imaginative universal, has cost him the work of a good twenty years and then goes on to say that he had "to descend from these human and refined natures of ours to those quite wild and savage natures, which we cannot at all imagine and can comprehend only with great effort."[14] Vico repeats the phrase about scarcely being able to imagine (*immaginare*) or to comprehend (*intendere*) the natures of the first humans elsewhere, using the same or nearly the same words.[15]

These statements may appear to oppose the thesis I have just suggested, particularly if they are considered only in English translation. In English both *fantasia* and *immaginazione* are rendered as "imagination." The term *universale fantastico*, based on the term *fantasia*, is "imaginative universal" in English. It is important for my view of recollective *fantasia*, as the form of thought whereby Vico reaches a knowledge of the first humans, to note that in such passages as those mentioned above Vico uses the verbs *immaginare* and *intendere*. To describe the thought of the first humans Vico most often uses *fantasia*, a term strongly associated with the arts and creative making, with varicolored thoughts.[16]

In passages where Vico says we can barely imagine and comprehend the thought of the first men I take him to be saying something quite simple, namely, that we as persons whose minds

[14]*New Science*, §338.

[15]*New Science*, §§378 and 700.

[16]*New Science*, e.g., §§1, 3, 6, 34, 159, 185, 211, 375, 376, 378, 699, 705, 708, 787, 816, 819, 825, 829, 916, and 933. Vico also uses the verb *immaginare*, e.g., §§9, 375, 401, 710, 739, 956, 1035, and 1098; and on occasion he uses *fantasticare*, e.g., §§7, 9, 392, 540, 714, and 734.

are formed by rational thought, by *generi intelligibili,* can barely grasp what a mentality governed entirely by *fantasia* is like. We cannot comprehend a world full of gods. We have lost touch with the powers of creative imagination which are present in the primordial sense of the *generi* or *universali fantastici.* For us to imagine (*immaginare*) or to comprehend (*intendere*) is to approach the object from the outside, as something external to ourselves. *Fantasia* is the power to know from the inside, to grasp the object in its inner nature. In such passages Vico is reminding us as moderns how difficult it is to grasp the life of the first men in any but the most external way. In his own thought Vico accomplished significant penetration into the thought of the first men. If Vico is not claiming this in the *New Science,* then he is claiming very little when he speaks of the twenty years required to discover the principle of the poetic character, the *universale fantastico.*

For the *verum-factum* principle to function in the *New Science* we must be able to make our way back in some way to the origin of human thought and activity and we must be able to do this in such a way as to remake the human world as something true for us. We must do this rather than merely formulate conceptual truths about the human world. If the human world is grasped in this conceptual fashion, we will know no more about it than we do of an object in physical science. Since physics does not create the object it knows, that object can never become fully intelligible to us. We cannot actually rethink the thought of the first men, not even fully grasp the form of their thoughts, but in Vico's view this world of our own origin is not closed to us. We must be capable in some way of seeing the origin of humanity as *our* origin. To identify with this origin is not something that can be achieved through empirical-scientific analysis of the thought patterns of primitives.

Each term of Vico's "three memories"—*memoria, fantasia,* and *ingegno*—is inseparable from the others. They are a totality. In speaking of *fantasia* as the form of Vico's science itself, I wish to use "recollection" for this composite sense of memory done on this self-conscious level or, more precisely—recollective *fantasia.*

I am suggesting that in Vico's philosophy the notion of recollection is made the basis of philosophical thought instead of reflection and speculation. Recollection and creative imagination are terms associated with the image. Reflection and logical implication are terms associated with the concept.

Hobbes expresses in large part how we have come in ordinary thought to regard memory and imagination. In the *Leviathan* Hobbes says: "For after the object is removed, or the eye shut, we still retain an image of the thing seen, though more obscure than when we see it. And this is it, the Latins call *imagination*, from the image made in seeing; and apply the same, though improperly, to all the other senses. But the Greeks call it *fancy*; which signifies *appearance*, and it is as proper to one sense, as to another. IMAGINATION therefore is nothing but *decaying sense*; and is found in men, and many other living creatures, as well sleeping, as waking."[17] Hobbes then connects memory with imagination: "This *decaying sense*, when we would express the thing itself, I mean *fancy* itself, we call *imagination*, as I said before: but when we would express the decay, and signify that the sense is fading, old, and past, it is called *memory*. So that imagination and memory are but one thing, which for divers considerations hath divers names."[18]

Hobbes's view is very close to that of common sense. Attachment to the concept as the true basis of thought makes us comfortable with placing imagination and memory near the level of sense, functions of the mind that prove their value as the means whereby sense is transported to the level of cognitive thought. Fancy, fantasy, and imagination are often associated in ordinary speech. Such powers, if allowed to follow their own route from their basis in sense, are thought to produce appearance, not reality. In this commonsense view the calling up of something in memory is not a form of knowledge but remains a psychological process unless connected with some fact or cognition. In

[17]Thomas Hobbes, *Leviathan*, vol. 3 of *The English Works of Thomas Hobbes*, ed. William Molesworth (London: John Bohn, 1839), pt. 1, ch. 2.
[18]Ibid.

ordinary discourse, terms such as myth and fable, which are structures of imagination and memory, function as opposites for truth, as synonyms for error. A myth is something that is not true, rather than itself being, as it is for Vico, the way in which an original truth is made.

There is much in Hobbes's view with which Vico could agree, in particular Hobbes's emphasis on the closeness to sense of imagination and memory. The difference is that Vico shifts such terms into a new key. Vico sees sense as itself a form of thought. Sense is not passive apprehension which then decays to the point of imagination as it is absorbed away from its object into a mental image, which then continues to the stage of a memory. Imagination in Hobbes's sense may be found in animals, but in Vico's sense it is what separates animal and human mentality. Animals cannot laugh, Vico says, because they are bound within the immediacy of sense.[19] In Vico's view memory is more than decaying sense because it has the power to take the knower back toward the level of sensation, to place the mind back in touch with the original formative powers of sensation. Memory is corrective of the mind in its thrust toward conceptual abstraction. Behind the Vichian orientation of these terms is the principle of the *verum-factum*, the principle that intelligibility is something made and that this making involves fundamentally what I am calling Vico's "three memories." Modern epistemology, whether Hobbesian or Kantian, has lost touch with this more ancient sense of memory and its connection with place and image—a connection to which Frances Yates has directed attention in *The Art of Memory*.[20]

The first of the three memories is memory. This is not a paradox if *memoria* is understood in two different senses. *Memoria,* understood not as the collective term for the three memories

---

[19]*Vici vindiciae,* sec. 16; English trans. of this section, "A Factual Digression on Human Genius, Sharp, Witty Remarks, and Laughter," trans. A. Illiano, J. D. Tedder, and P. Treves, *Forum Italicum,* 2 (1968), 310–14.

[20]Frances A. Yates, *The Art of Memory* (Chicago: The University of Chicago Press, 1966).

but as a term alongside the other two, is simply the power to remember, *rimembrare*. As Vico says in the passage quoted at the beginning of this chapter, it is "memory when it remembers things." *Memoria* in this sense is the power to bring to mind what is not before the mind, to find in the *here* the *not-here* and in the *now* the *not-now*. In terms of what was discussed in the preceding chapter, *memoria*, as part of the structure of the imaginative universal, occurs at the point where a moment is fixed within the self-cancelling flux of sensation. Once they can repeatedly grasp thunder and fear as Jove, the first men have made sensation into a kind of thought. What would have been mere moments in a flux can now be felt, remembered in the gesture, the mute images of Jove. The process of "finding again," which is accomplished through the imaginative universal's power of identity, provides the first men not only with the power of metaphorical thinking but also with the power of memory. The flux of sensation can be remembered through a part of itself.

Fantasia is memory when it "alters or imitates things" (*l'altera e contrafà*). *Fantasia* as a kind of memory is the power to reorder what has been recalled and to shape it after the general form of the subject. It is a power to give the object distinctively human form. Through *fantasia* the mind makes the object familiar; objects are not simply apprehended in themselves but are shaped as human objects. *Fantasia* places the shape of the subject on the object. *Contraffare* here is not to be taken in the sense of making something false or in the sense of a passive imitation of something more real. *Alterare* and *contraffare* are active as the way in which the subject "finds again."

The immediate presented through simple *memoria* is actively moved by *fantasia* into the medium of the subject. The sense of "imitation" is not that of pictorial realism. Jove as the fear felt by the first men is imitated by them; they shake their bodies like the sky-body of Jove himself. Jove is found again in the medium of their own bodies. Jove is "re-presented" in their own bodies. This primordial power of re-feeling Jove is slowly transformed into the world of human symbols, into the medium of language and cultural institutions in which all sensation is modified and given shape as humanity develops into the ideal eternal history.

Vico claims that memory as *ingegno* gives things "a new turn or puts them into proper arrangement and relationship." *Ingegno*, like the Latin *ingenium*, is a difficult word to translate or interpret. Fisch remarks that this term can take two directions: "Perception, invention, the faculty of discerning the relations between things, which issues on the one hand in analogy, simile, metaphor, and on the other in scientific hypotheses."[21] I wish to regard *ingegno* here as a primordial activity underlying the former of these two possibilities. What is recalled in the shape of the subject, in its medium, must also be understood as having a relationship to all other acts of recall. The world of human meaning is a totality in which any act of meaning leads to and is part of a total system of meaning. *Ingegno* is the power of the subject to move from one act of formation of sense to others, to create further acts of formation and to have past acts combine and influence present ones. *Ingegno* arises from the fact that in any act of forming sensation there is present all that is necessary to transform all of sensation into a world of meaning.

In terms of Jove *ingegno* arises from the fact that Jove is a *name*. Once this power of the name is realized in one instance, the name is spread over the whole of experience. All nature is full of gods. Jove, Cybele, and Neptune become names for the sky, earth, and sea.[22] *Ingegno* is memory in the sense that the process of *memoria* and *fantasia* which has made the thunder intelligible as Jove must be held in mind and moved across the field of sensation to create nature as gods, to transform all sense experience into a world of names. It is also a process of memory in that all such names are held in a total, each having bearing in all directions on all others. This process of *ingegno* is not mechanical in the sense of building up mind from part connected to

21*Autobiography*, p. 216, note 141.
22*New Science*, §402.

part. All three memories come about at once. All three are inseparable elements of the *universale fantastico*. *Ingegno* is that element which specifically makes the *universale fantastico* a total form of thought.

I have called the *New Science* a theater of memory because all of human history moves within it. It is a place within which the universal structures of the human world are brought together with its particulars by the bonding of philosophical and philological thought into a single form of mentality. These two kinds of truth are held together in a way such that one cannot be grasped without the other. The first experience of opening Vico's *New Science* is demonstration of this. The reader confronts an order of contents wherein the logic of what is to be discussed is not evident. Instead there is a collage of topics such as wisdom, giants, sacrifices, poetic logic, monsters, metamorphoses, money, rhythm, song, children, poetic economy, Roman assemblies, the true Homer, heroic aristocracies, natural law, duels, Jean Bodin, legal metaphysics, barbaric history. One encounters the scenery of the human world.

As the reader of the *New Science* studies the work it becomes clear that there is a general order and progress of thought, but Vico's account moves in terms of jumps and associations. Content is put on top of content; identifications between subjects are made unexpectedly. Many esoteric subjects are discussed, such as the origin of the wedding ring,[23] dragons,[24] and the history of roasting of meat.[25] Vico reverses Occam's sense of the economy of thought. We find not Occam's razor, but Vico's magnet. Principles are multiplied and as many as possible are drawn into the presentation of a given point. I do not mean that in its contents, its collage-like character, Vico's work is unlike any other. It is perhaps most like some ancient and Renaissance texts. Vico's account has its own sense of economy given the enormity of

[23]*New Science*, §514.
[24]*New Science*, §540.
[25]*New Science*, §801.

what it wishes to explain, an economy like that found in the myth or fable. What gives Vico access to the total human world? What is the *topos* of the *New Science,* that from which it draws forth the meaning of the human?

Human thought originates through the master imaginative universal of Jove. As thought develops its powers of formation, human qualities emerge as imaginative universals in the figures of heroes in the age of heroes. In one of the passages quoted above Vico claims that memory, imagination, and invention "all pertain to the primary operation of the mind whose regulating art is topics." This art of topics is a primary act of mind and is presupposed by the art of criticism or judging. The act of critical judgment presupposes invention. Vico's notion of the three memories shows how the human world was invented through the imaginative universal. When we assume the perspective of the third age of humanity we enter a world dominated by the mentality of criticism and reflective judgment. The third age, the age of men, is characterized by the thought of intelligible universals, *generi intelligibili.* Here we find logical or purely philosophical sentences. These presuppose the poetic sentences of the first two ages. Conceptual thought presupposes the *sensus communis* of the human world formed by the imagination from which it abstracts its order of logical genera. In the same fashion the institutions of the third age have behind them the primordial life forms of the first families and the heroic cities, their senses of customs and laws.

Any new form of understanding which is not simply the extension of implications from some form of thought already present, in short, that is more than intellectual analysis, requires a *topos.* The *topos* is what gives us access to what can be understood. The *topos* is the work of *fantasia. Fantasia* is required for the invention of the *New Science* itself. On the level of the *New Science,* the level of the work itself, *fantasia* is not "collective" but "recollective." At the level of the origin of thought, that which is described in the work, Vico's three memories function "collectively" to form sensation into the *universale fantastico.* In this way

107

thought is itself begun. The *New Science* has the problem not of beginning thought itself, but of re-beginning it. It must revive the activity of *fantasia* within an age, the third age of men, in which thought is dominated not by invention, but by criticism and logical judgment. It is an age in which memory has grown weak. Memory has become only the power to hold in mind a sequence of deduction, such as that required by Cartesian thought. Through the *New Science* Vico must establish memory as "recollection." This task demands a grasp of the origin of the human world. Vico's most important principle: "Doctrines must take their beginning from that of the matters of which they treat,"[26] requires that memory be the basis of science.

If Vico's three memories are considered as producing recollection, the form of this activity, as on the collective primordial level, is the imaginative universal or, more precisely, a "recollective imaginative universal." The recollective imaginative universal of the *New Science* is the *storia ideale eterna*. It is the *topos* through which all of the *New Science* is invented. As Jove is the master universal of mythico-poetic *fantasia*, so "ideal eternal history," I am claiming, is the master universal of recollective *fantasia*. The ideal eternal history is not one of the axioms of Vico's *New Science*. It appears within his list of axioms only as an aspect of their explication and emerges at the end of the work as his theory of the *corsi e ricorsi*.[27] The *storia ideale eterna* is Vico's master image of history and even more his master image of the human world itself. It is the perception that the human world as a whole and in every one of its parts moves through a beginning, a middle, and an end. It is an absolutely simple idea—that anything human can be understood in terms of an origin-end principle. It is obvious in the same sense that the *verum-factum* principle is obvious. What does this very simple principle entail?

Understood on this recollective level, Vico's three memories have functions parallel to their activity on the collective level.

[26]*New Science*, §314.
[27]*New Science*, e.g., §§145, 245, 294, 349, 393, and 1096.

Memoria on the recollective level is the power to fix the particulars of the human world as "certains." It is a philological sensibility to the particulars of the activity of past ages. Human activity is not simply apprehended as chaos or as a simple collection of moments of past activity. *Memoria* as philological sensibility allows us to fix certain points around which past cultures can be understood. From all the activity of a past nation, certain aspects, words, events, happenings are singled out and understood as such. This is ordinary historical memory—the finding in artifacts and documents that exist in the present what is not present, what is not here and not now. *Fantasia* shapes such particular understandings into living wholes. Ages and cultures are portrayed and felt as past forms of life. The specific philological understandings are given a total shape.

Memoria and *fantasia* underlie any great work of history. Historical consciousness requires both the empirical understanding of the past events and an imaginative reconstruction of them, a palingenesis such that we feel an identity between ourselves and the past. *Ingegno* as an element of recollective memory is the specific philosophical sense of history as involving principles of explanation. It is the notion that history as a whole can illustrate truths and patterns. Ordinary philosophy of history arises from the sense that there are truths of the historical world.

The middle term of these three moments of recollective understanding, *fantasia,* is what holds the philological and philosophical moments together; it is a sense of remembering particulars so that they have a total shape. Vico's philosophical-philological method depends upon the power of *fantasia* to think particulars in universal form. This act requires a master image of the human world in terms of which we can have access both to it as a whole and to any one of its concrete particulars. The *storia ideale eterna,* ideal eternal history, is the first name of recollective consciousness. It is the name of providence. It appears to consciousness as the sudden realization of a total sense of order to the human event. It is a sense that order in the human world

109

cannot be understood as something built up step by step, but that it can be perceived, grasped in *fantasia*.

If there is something in the formation of this recollective imaginative universal that corresponds to the element of fear in the creation of the imaginative universal of Jove, it is perhaps to be found in the night of the intellect. The metaphysics of the concept, rather than the image, yields the split between the *caso* (chance) of Epicurus and the *necessità*, or *sorda necessità* (the deaf or inexorable necessity), of Descartes, of which Vico speaks in his previously mentioned letter to Abbé Esperti following the publication of the first *New Science*.[28] Thought is left with only the power to express a preference for chance or necessity. Thought is deserted of providence and can strike only conceptual poses.

The *storia ideale eterna* is not a hypothesis for investigation and proof, but an immediate formation of the meaning of the whole of human activity. It comes from a stance of mind completely different from that interested in choices between the "chance" of Epicurus and the "deaf necessity" of Descartes. Vico summarizes his conception of the ideal eternal history in a sentence: "Men first feel necessity, then look for utility, next attend to comfort, still later amuse themselves with pleasure, thence grow dissolute in luxury, and finally go mad and waste their substance."[29] To understand this requires the sudden grasp that an origin in the human world comes out of necessity and that its end is always madness. Vico's much overworked and too frequently mentioned conception of *corsi e ricorsi* takes on a special meaning when seen from this perspective. A *corso* or cycle is a presentation in actual events of necessity developing into madness. Origin-end is necessity-madness. As Vico specifically says: men first *sentono il necessario* and *finalmente impazzano*.[30]

A common way to view any conception of human history

[28]"All'Abate Esperti in Roma" (1726), *Autobiografia*, ed. Fubini, p. 110.
[29]*New Science*, §241 (axiom 66).
[30]Ibid.

which is based on cycles is to regard the cycles as involving progress from one to another. Vico's view is frequently regarded in this way. We are so accustomed to Enlightenment ways of thinking that it seems natural to us that history must contain some progress or that it can be understood in terms of its moments of great achievement, as Voltaire was so interested to show. Vico himself at times speaks in a progressive fashion about his three ages, but there is nothing in Vico like Comte's "law of three stages"—the law which depicts human thought as emerging from poetic theological thought into the sunlight of positivistic rationality. The genius of Vico's view of the human world lies not in the fact that each *ricorso* differs from the previous *corso*. It lies in Vico's awareness that any real origin in human affairs meets with a real end.

The great Florentine historian, Francesco Guicciardini, understood this sense of history. He says: "It was no disgrace to great cities if after many centuries they at last fell into servitude, because it was inevitable that everything in the world should be subject to decay; but the memory of their greatness and noble past should engender in the minds of their conquerors compassion rather than harsh and bitter feelings—especially as all should consider that some day they might, indeed must, endure the same fate which is destined to overtake all empires and cities."[31] The noble, powerful, and heroic moments in the life of a people must be understood, even by the people themselves, if they are wise, in terms of the necessary motion of history that will prove to be their decline.

In Vico's view an origin is never really mastered. History is tragic. So is every human event. To emphasize that every end is a new beginning is to act as if there is more reality in the origin than in the end. It comes from our inclination to smuggle "progress" into the understanding of any human event. It is a natural

[31]Francesco Guicciardini, *History of Italy and History of Florence*, trans. Cecil Grayson and ed. John R. Hale (New York: Washington Square Press, 1964), pp. 196–97.

desire of the mentality of the third age of men and part of the barbaric arrogance of conceptual thought. The genius of Vico's recollective imaginative universal of ideal eternal history is its perception of the reality of ends. History is not tragic simply because it contains nothing but rise and fall. It is tragic because the movement of origins to ends opens the possibility of heroism within a cycle.

History is the body of providence. Development in history, in Vico's view, involves the birth of positive elements through their opposites. Vico says:

> Men mean to gratify their bestial lust and abandon their offspring, and they inaugurate the chastity of marriage from which the families arise. The fathers mean to exercise without restraint their paternal power over their clients, and they subject them to the civil powers from which the cities arise. The reigning orders of nobles mean to abuse their lordly freedom over the plebeians, and they are obliged to submit to the laws which establish popular liberty. The free peoples mean to shake off the yoke of their laws, and they become subject to monarchs. The monarchs mean to strengthen their own positions by debasing their subjects with all the vices of dissoluteness, and they dispose them to endure slavery at the hands of stronger nations. The nations mean to dissolve themselves, and their remnants flee for safety to the wilderness, whence, like the phoenix, they rise again. That which did all this was mind, for men did it with intelligence; it was not fate, for they did it by choice; not chance, for the results of their always so acting are perpetually the same.[32]

Truth is born through illusion. Human action in one direction gives birth to its opposite and the reality of providence is asserted once again. Specifically we can know one thing: all action on the part of "progress" in our current age of men will not result in "progress."

Vittorio Mathieu, in one of the few treatments of this question, "Truth as the Mother of History," has suggested that divine truth in Vico's view is revealed on the human level "in an upside-

---

[32]*New Science*, §1108.

down form."[33] Truth enters history upside down. The divine will is made manifest by the human will going in the opposite direction, as Vico describes in the passage quoted above. What is fundamentally made manifest is not a progression toward divine truth in history. Divine truth is affirmed by the lack of progress toward it in history. The periodicity of history is a manifestation of the inadequate participation of history in truth. History is an activity of the production of illusion, but the production of this opposite of truth is itself a truth. This is the truth that there is providence in history. The ideal eternal history once grasped in *fantasia* places us in a position to understand the specific nature of this process. The heroism of thought as I have mentioned it above is to grasp this connection of oppositions in history and to see them in terms of the permanence of the divine pattern. Heroic thought is a thought of unresolved opposites.

Vico's movements of opposites is not that of the traditional understanding of Hegelian *Aufhebung*. There is no higher synthetic moment in Vico's conception. As Vico schematically indicates in the above quotation, desire, first as sexual desire and then as desire for power, produces social form. From the pursuit of lust families arise; from an attempt to increase the power of families cities arise; from the attempt by lords to dominate the populace popular liberty is born; from the attempt of monarchs to increase their rule the over-extension of their power results in weakness; from an attempt to return to the state of desire social order is born again. This is not a movement to higher and higher kinds of unity. Desire creates grander and grander forms of illusion until there is collapse. Heroic thought is the recollection of this providential pattern.

The tragic sense of history contained in the recollective imaginative universal of ideal eternal history is not simply a theory of history. It is a perception, a fundamental image of human

---

[33]Vittorio Mathieu, "Truth as the Mother of History," in *Giambattista Vico's Science of Humanity*, ed. Giorgio Tagliacozzo and Donald Phillip Verene (Baltimore: The Johns Hopkins University Press, 1976), p. 119.

events. The primary context for the comprehension of any human event is the principle of origin-end. The event must be seen through this connection. An event can be comprehended as a memory structure. There is no tragedy in the logical comprehension of an event, because it has no plot. Logic is comic. The logical concept never faces the aspect of events that makes them tragic because it never participates in memory. Descartes' fourfold method of understanding in the *Discourse on Method* is comic rather than tragic. It begins with something already true, divides difficulties into parts, moves in due order from simple to complex, and ends in a review and enumeration to assure the clarity achieved.[34] There is no sense of beginning and no sense of end that can be connected with the human event as lived.

If Descartes' method is successfully enacted, the understanding reached is a perfect happiness or comedy of reason. In Vico's view such an analytic model of thinking removes from the very beginning any element of memory or plot that is distinctive of the human. We cannot, for example, achieve our own autobiography by such a method of thought. The elements of Descartes' autobiography in the *Discourse on Method* are simply segments of an existence inserted to give the theory a setting. Vico's *Autobiography* is the story of a beginning and an end. Vico deliberately places his method in the *Autobiography* in opposition to Descartes' presentation of himself in his work.[35]

The fact that human events have beginnings and ends does not in itself make them tragic. They are tragic because ends, as Vico shows, are real declines. The hope born of necessity in the moment of origin finally dissipates into barbaric conditions, into the madness and waste of the end. Vico sees such ends as the conditions for new beginnings. From the wilderness of the end arises the phoenix. The death of the course is the birth of the recourse. I do not think that this tie between births and deaths is

[34]*The Philosophical Works of Descartes*, 2 vols., trans. Elizabeth S. Haldane and G. R. T. Ross (Cambridge: Cambridge University Press, 1931), p. 92.
[35]*Autobiography*, p. 113.

the true greatness of Vico's view. I do not think, in fact, that Vico was much interested in this shift between termination and arisal. He has no particular theory or discussion of such transition. He has a theory of the first thought (poetic wisdom) and the last thought (the barbarism of reflection).[36]

Tragedy and heroism are connected. Heroism can occur within the cycle of the given human event, within the confines of origin-end. The fact that a given cycle, after its decline, will result in a new beginning can have little actual meaning for action within the cycle. Life goes on within the cycle, the given *corso*, and it presents the problem of how to act within it. Heroism is the ultimate form of meaningful human action within the tragedy of the *corso*. There is no heroism of pragmatic activity, of solutions to problems and goals achieved. A philosophy of the human based on pragmatic action, growth, or progress does not fit with the notion of heroism or with the concept of tragedy. It does not fit with the notion of the *corso*. The heroic occurs in the state of the dissolution of events. Heroism creates a point of meaning but does not actually solve the problem of dissolution.

This can be seen, for example, in the process of the most famous tragedy of Western consciousness—*Oedipus Rex*. Oedipus finds himself in the midst of events, the plague and troubles of Thebes. His actions require ultimately that he seek a knowledge of his own origin. The revelation of the origin places Oedipus in effective relationship to the dissolution of events around him. The flaws of the origin of Oedipus have caused him to kill his father, Laïus, and wed his mother, Jocasta. He has done this in ignorance, living as a man without memory. His position as king of Thebes leads him finally to a situation that only memory will resolve.

There is no pragmatic solution to Oedipus' situation. There is no logical concept of it or method. He has been living without knowledge of his origin. Once the power of memory has been introduced in a final manner by Tiresias, Oedipus can act. His

[36]*New Science,* §1106.

self-induced blindness and exile is the heroic response to the understanding of an end, the understanding of which required the grasp of an origin. That Thebes will enter another phase of its ideal eternal history is part of the meaning of the heroic act of Oedipus, when seen in Vichian terms. Each origin has a day side and a night side. Oedipus encounters, finally, the night side. The drama gives these opposites form.

Ideal eternal history understood as a master image of thought is a mode of vision for human events. It sees them as memory structures, plots capable only of dissolution or heroic resolution, or as dramas in which both these elements are set against each other at the moment of collapse. In Vico's ideal eternal history, seen in its broadest sense as his three historical ages, the heroic age is the middle age. It is often said that Vico takes a special interest in this age. It is the medium of the other two ages. It is a response to the dissolution of the first age—the receding of the world of gods and the reality of the cities over the families. And it is a reaction to the dissolution that brings on the third age—the receding of the imaginative particular and the appearance of the autonomy of law and popular liberty.

The two major moments of dissolution in the *New Science* involve heroism. The first moment is the dissolution of the *universale fantastico* that structures the first two ages and its replacement by the *generi intelligibili* of the third age. The second moment is the struggle by recollective *fantasia* to produce the *New Science* in the memory-deficient world of the third age. This struggle is not the true heroism of combined thinking and acting of the second age, but the heroism of thought that Vico speaks of in *De mente heroica*.

The hero is heroic in that he surmounts the immediate conditions of existence. Vico usually emphasizes this aspect of the hero. But the hero never surmounts the ultimate condition of existence—the ideal eternal history. The hero never overcomes his own end. When connected with the conception of ideal eternal history as the theory of the human event itself, the heroic is tragic. The hero struggles with, but cannot surmount the ideal

116

eternal history. The heroic age dissolves into that of reflective life. The hero himself cannot surmount the plot of beginning, middle, and end which is within any human event.

Oedipus' fear is mastered by memory, the recollection of his origin in both its day and night sides which moves him back toward the heroic middle of his *corso*. He can act finally only through his heroic self-blindness and self-exile. The perception of the end against the origin gives us access to ourselves as humans. The notion of ideal eternal history as something felt has a ground in the individual's ability to grasp his existence as a structure of birth and death, in which both the birth and the death are real points bridged by memory, by the human's power to grasp himself recollectively as a particular universal. *Fantasia* is the basis of self-knowledge. It gives us access to ourselves as makers of the true.

The kind of intelligibility Oedipus himself requires in order to act and that which we also require to understand his actions cannot be had from the standpoint of a problem-solving or pragmatic logic. Oedipus requires autobiographical memory that is tied to the real order of the human world itself embodied in the city of Thebes. I do not mean that the figure of Oedipus fits Vico's notion of the hero in all its points. It illustrates Vico's sense of memory and the tragic necessity of ideal eternal history understood as the form of a human event. In "On the Heroic Mind" Vico says: "'Hero' is defined by philosophers as one who seeks ever the sublime. . . . the hero generates for himself an immortal name."[37]

In the passages quoted at the beginning of this chapter, Vico says that the first of the Muses was Urania who, as Homer says, was the "science of good and evil" or divination. The appearance of the primordial universal of Jove results in the need to read the movements of the sky and other natural phenomena as signs. In this way the first men achieved orientation in the world

---

[37]*De mente heroica, Opere* 7: 3–20; English trans. "On the Heroic Mind," trans. Elizabeth Sewell and Anthony C. Sirignano, in *Vico and Contemporary Thought,* pt. 2, p. 230.

and developed social institutions. The altar which appears in the center of the frontispiece of the *New Science*, Vico says, signifies that the first human institutions took their origin from the auspices.[38] From divination of the actions of the gods in nature the fathers of the first families derived their wisdom and power. Is divination also a part of the recollective imagination as it is part of the mythic-poetic imagination? Is there something that corresponds to divination associated with the recollective imaginative universal of ideal eternal history?

The *storia ideale eterna* is the principle of providence in history. It is the image of history as eternal pattern in which divine truth is at any moment being revealed through its opposite. What appears as progress at any moment is actually movement toward dissolution. God enters history upside down and remains so. The divine never becomes right side up in history. History is a topsy-turvy of the divine, but it is not a nightmare. An end is a beginning. Social order is born through chaos, law through violence, religion through fear. The order of social institutions for Vico is not achieved through contract between primitive men or a deliberate will to reason. Fear is transformed as religion and remains the basis of religion. Desire for the extension of power by those in control produces the demand for rights by those who are ruled, which in turn creates new possibilities for the desire for power.

God as providence dominates these metamorphoses of opposites. In axiom seven Vico says: "Out of ferocity, avarice, and ambition, the three vices which run throughout the human race, it [legislation] creates the military, merchant, and governing classes, and thus the strength, riches, and wisdom of commonwealths. Out of these three great vices, which could certainly destroy all mankind on the face of the earth, it makes civil happiness. This axiom proves that there is divine providence and further that it is a divine legislative mind."[39] Legislation is the

---

[38]*New Science*, §9.
[39]*New Science*, §§132–33.

power to turn natural vices into bases of social order and to produce civil happiness. Jurisprudence as the embodiment of this process of opposites is a reflection on the social level of the process of opposites whereby providence legislates history.

On the level of individual activity prudence is the element corresponding to providence in history. In the *Pratica*, remarks prepared in 1731 on the practice of the *New Science* but excluded from the third edition of 1744, Vico advocates teaching the young the wisdom of living in accordance with providence.[40] In discussing the meaning of the *Pratica* and its relationship to the notion of prudence and providence, Alain Pons remarks: "History no longer gives counsels of prudence; it is prudence realized, since it is divine providence which is its principle."[41]

The *storia ideale eterna* makes prudence possible. Prudence is a form of recollective divination. It is the ability to read the signs of history, to understand the *ius gentium,* or universal law of the gentes, that lies at the basis of all societies. To be prudent the individual must master the fundamental metamorphoses of the human world as portrayed in the three ages of the ideal eternal history. By understanding the process of opposites which is involved in the generation of these ages, the individual acquires the power of insight to grasp any event placed before him in terms of its opposite, to see through it to its opposite outcome.

Prudence is this art of metamorphological thought. It requires the mentality of the image, of thought that is double-minded. This art cannot be achieved by the single-minded mentality of logical and conceptual thought, the thought that flattens an event into a single meaning. History cannot be read in logical terms and categories because human action does not originally

---

[40]*Scienza nuova seconda,* §1407. English translation of the *Pratica*: "Practic of the New Science," trans. Thomas G. Bergin and Max H. Fisch, in *Giambattista Vico's Science of Humanity,* pp. 451–54. For the relationship of the *Pratica* to the *New Science* see Max H. Fisch, "Vico's *Pratica,*" ibid., pp. 423–30.

[41]Alain Pons, "Prudence and Providence: The *Pratica della Scienza Nuova* and the Problem of Theory and Practice in Vico," in *Giambattista Vico's Science of Humanity,* p. 443.

have logic as its guide. The human event must be grasped in the image, as having a plot that moves from a point of origin to a dissolution of the impetus of this origin. But prudence as based in metamorphological understanding has nothing to do with a teleological understanding of events. Prudence does not see events in terms of a goal or possible perfection.

Imprudence is to be lost in the event, to be without memory. Memory produces contact with an origin through which the signs of an end can be read. Social science, understood as the application of logic and conceptual form to comprehend human affairs, is an example of imprudence. Social science acts as if conceptual analysis and the application of conceptual structures to human experience will enable us to know something about the reality of human events. This is imprudent because such thought is cut off from the plot that is the inner reality of the event. To seek intelligibility of the human without the ability to contact the human world through the *verum-factum* principle is to miss the sense of prudence, wisdom, and perception upon which the human depends. Social science, like physical science, is outside its object. In contrast, Vico's science begins from a grasp of the inside of human reality.

Vico says that "poetic morality began with piety, which was ordained by providence to found the nations, for among them all piety is proverbially the mother of all the moral, economic, and civil virtues. Religion alone has the power to make us practice virtue, as philosophy is fit rather for discussing it. And piety sprang from religion, which properly is fear of divinity."[42] In the last sentence of the *New Science* Vico says: "This Science carries inseparably with it the study of piety."[43] The morality of poetic or mythic mentality is the observation of the signs of Jove understood through the auspices. The mentality of the age of men is characterized by a loss of piety. The emphasis on the conceptual thought of the non-poetic age strips the mind of memory.

[42]*New Science*, §503.
[43]*New Science*, §1112.

120

Morality becomes a matter of discussion. Divination depends upon the memory structure of the imaginative universal whereby experience is given the shape of the divine.

Whereas conceptual thought shapes experience wholly in human terms and cannot serve as a basis for piety, the exercise of recollective *fantasia* makes piety possible once again. Piety and prudence, rather than deduction and prediction, become guides to human action. History is seen not as made by men but as enacted by them through the eternal pattern of providence. Recollective thought is pious because the understanding of any human event requires a sense of divination of its place within an eternal pattern. The heroic response to the tragedy of any *corso* is based on piety toward the eternality of its structure. But the heroic is at the same time a manifestation of the power of the human will in the face of tragedy.

I have approached Vico's view of the *storia ideale eterna* in a manner quite different from other interpreters,[44] deliberately expanding Vico's meaning beyond what is explicitly said in the *New Science*. What I have said differs from other more standard views in two fundamental ways. First, I have approached the notion of ideal eternal history as a way of understanding any human event, rather than as a concept limited to a theory of history. In my view it is a theory of history, but only because it is even more fundamentally a theory of how anything human can be understood. Second, I have taken Vico's notion of end as seriously as his notion of origin. Thus I have understood a *corso* within the total providential structure of ideal eternal history as a tragic unit. The positive moment in such a unit is the heroic act that can produce specific meaning by uniting its origin and end within a single action.

I have not, as others very often have, regarded Vico's cycles of *corsi* and *ricorsi* as exhibiting a kind of progress wherein a later cycle is understood as an advance beyond an earlier one. This

[44]E.g., Leon Pompa, *Vico: A Study of the 'New Science'* (Cambridge: Cambridge University Press, 1975), chs. 9–10.

progressive view places the positive moment outside the cycle, in that its demise will be a new beginning. But this positive factor can have no specific meaning for the cycle itself, except that it can give itself the stoic assurance that "history will go on." Any cycle develops differently than another. The content and specific forms of a cycle are not repeated in a subsequent one. The beginning of any *ricorso* is the ruin of the *corso* that preceded it. The conditions of the end of a specific course make a difference in the character of the recourse, but this involves no general progress toward a state of *absolute Geist,* to use Hegel's term, nor movement toward some perfected state of affairs as in Enlightenment thought.

For Vico the *storia ideale eterna* is the condition of the Fall of Man. Through his making man can exercise his divine nature in imitation of the divine who makes by knowing, but in his making man cannot work his way up to a state of the divine. Human making done at its very limits produces heroism. The hero is the living presence of memory, the recollection of the origin pitted against the end. Vico joins the principle of pagan mythology, the Hero, with that of Christian mythology, the Fall.

How do we acquire the *fantasia* of recollection? How can we enter back into the world of the first men? How do we know what we say of this first world to be true? We do not know the nature of this first form of humanity through an analogy made from our own remembrance of ourselves, our perception of ourselves as moving from childhood, to adolescence, to maturity, to old age. The kind of memory involved in such a recollection of ourselves would already presuppose the standpoint of mind required for the recollection of the development of the world of nations. Croce is right in his observation: "Vico's *Autobiography* is, in a word, the application of the *Scienza Nuova* to the life of its author, the course of his own individual history."[45]

On the first page of the *Autobiography* Vico describes the first

[45]Benedetto Croce, *The Philosophy of Giambattista Vico,* trans. R. G. Collingwood (New York: Russell and Russell, 1964), p. 266.

memorable incident of his life as a fall from the top of a ladder in which his cranium was fractured and which produced a long, life-threatening period of unconsciousness. Vico sees this incident as having shaped his temperament, making him melancholy and irritable. It produced in him, as in other men of such temperament, he says, ingenuity (*ingegno*) and depth. The former made him, like such men, quick as lightning in perception (*che per l'ingegno balenino in acutezze*), and the latter made him capable of an orientation toward truth and away from any pleasure in mere verbal cleverness or falsehood. Vico's powers of *fantasia* begin in a thunderous fall that produced in him a capacity of mental lightning. This thinker of primordial experience began the experience of his own mental life in this primordial way. This incident, although a real event in Vico's life, is full of symbolism for Vico's thought, a symbolism that was not lost on Joyce when he associated Finnegan's fall and the sound of thunder on the first page of *Finnegans Wake*.

Is the power of recollective *fantasia*, the power of imaginative memory, possible only for certain persons, perhaps those of melancholy and irritable temperament? Is some special element or experience required in the human person to be able to think through the power of the imagination? Is there a temperament of the logical concept and a temperament of the image? Vico's discussion of the nature of the first men would convince no contemporary anthropologist,[46] although Vico's principles of religion and burial have some status for the identification of human societies in the archeological investigation of early man. Vico's description of the giants and how they grew to their great size by reabsorption of their own excrement would convince no

---

[46]Edmund Leach, "Vico and the Future of Anthropology," in *Vico and Contemporary Thought*, pt. 2, pp. 149–59. Cf. Leach's remarks on the contemporary significance of Vico's conception of myth: Edmund Leach, "Vico and Lévi-Strauss on the Origins of Humanity," in *Giambattista Vico: An International Symposium*, ed. Giorgio Tagliacozzo and Hayden V. White (Baltimore: The Johns Hopkins University Press, 1969), esp. p. 315.

physiologist; nor does Vico's description of the environment of the first men fit with natural history.

In speaking as he does about early life, in his sometimes unique etymologies and fanciful descriptions of human customs, Vico is not simply reflecting the state of empirical knowledge of his time that has now become obsolete. As Croce and others have noted, Vico often passes over known details and describes things as he wishes. Croce observes that Vico's attitude seems to be that if the theory is in itself true, it does not matter if there are errors.[47] What is important is to sustain the enthusiasm of the theory. Vico is at times like a novelist whose aim at a given point is to get the reader to see something about the reality he is presenting, and to do so he arranges events in a way that they never could be outside the form of the novel.

Something that Vico says of the *universale fantastico*, of the nature of the fable, is also true of the thought of recollective *fantasia*: "These fables are ideal truths suited to the merit of those of whom the vulgar tell them; and such falseness to fact as they contain consists simply in failure to give their subjects their due. So that, if we consider the matter well, poetic truth is metaphysical truth, and physical truth which is not in conformity with it should be considered false."[48] Vico completes this point with the view, discussed in chapter three above, that the true war chief is that which the poet Tasso imagines. It is an ideal truth which expresses the reality of the empirical individuals, but it is not made by an inductive examination of them. Metaphysical truths are like poetic truths.

De Sanctis suggested that Vico's work is like Dante's *Divina commedia*, a total poetic embodiment of human reality. There are great similarities between Vico's and Dante's work. Both are gigantic structures of memory. Vico regarded Dante's *Divina commedia* as a special kind of poem. As Homer is the mind of the early Greek people, so Dante is the historian of the *ricorso* of

[47]Croce, *The Philosophy of Giambattista Vico*, pp. 151–53.
[48]*New Science*, §205.

Italian barbarism.[49] But Vico's work is not a poem or a history of the consciousness of a particular nation. His philosophical-philological method makes it a different kind of thought—philosophic *fantasia*. The *New Science* is a metaphysical fable. It creates a *vera narratio* of the recollective imagination. The *storia ideale eterna* is an ideal truth, but not an a priori or fictional one. As the master image of the recollective mind it precisely contains all of the human event. Metaphysical truth, achieved through the exercise of *fantasia,* gives access to physical truth, but it is not generated from it. Such truth is generated out of the mind itself, but not transcendentally as synthetic a priori categories. It is generated as images that actually contain the providential structure of reality. This is a power of original speech that lies behind any power of speech to form thought reflectively as categories.

Can all persons think this way? As Vico suggests, some do by temperament. In Vico this temperament was fixed in his fall but most of his life was required for him to be led by melancholy to the discovery of the poetic character and ideal eternal history. Vico's own tragic sense of life, which I find present in his tragic sense of history, led him to say that "misfortune would pursue him even after his death."[50] Certainly all persons can in a sense think this way, can think by means of *fantasia,* because it is the first form of thought itself. Isaiah Berlin, in *Vico and Herder,* a work that treats *fantasia* in a manner with which the present study is much in sympathy, speaks of "reconstructive *fantasia*" as a "faculty with which some men (Lucretius, Tacitus, Bacon) were more generously endowed than others; and of which, evidently, no mortals have enough."[51]

[49]"Discoverta del vero Dante, ovvero nuovi principi di critica dantesca," *Opere* 7:79–82; English trans. "Discovery of the True Dante," trans. Irma Brandeis, in *Discussions of the Divine Comedy,* ed. Irma Brandeis (Boston: Heath, 1961), pp. 11–12.

[50]*Autobiography,* p. 204.

[51]Isaiah Berlin, *Vico and Herder: Two Studies in the History of Ideas* (New York: The Viking Press, 1976), p. 112.

My term "recollective *fantasia*" was coined independently of Berlin's *Vico and Herder* but it has a similarity to terms Berlin occasionally uses in his work, "recon-

But modern men are barbarous. They are like nations in their barbarous state. Vico says: "Nations in their barbarous state are impenetrable; they must be either broken into from the outside by war or voluntarily opened to strangers for the advantages of trade."[52] The barbarism of modern men is the mentality of the concept, the *generi intelligibili*. This must be broken into from the outside or voluntarily become open to strangers. One or the other of these possibilities must take place. If the latter does not occur, then the former will. We can be led to *fantasia* by the concept's failure before the human event.

---

structive imagination" and "reconstructive *fantasia*" (see, e.g., pp. xix, 108, 136). See also Donald Phillip Verene, "Vico's Philosophy of Imagination"; Sir Isaiah Berlin, "Comment on Professor Verene's Paper"; Verene, "Response by the Author," in *Vico and Contemporary Thought*, pt. 1, pp. 39–43.

[52]*New Science*, §303.

CHAPTER 5

Science

Vico intended his major work to be a science and to be a new science. He intended the key words of his title, *scienza nuova*, to be taken in a literal not a figurative or approximate sense, the title in full being *Principj di scienza nuova di Giambattista Vico d'intorno alla comune natura delle nazioni* (Principles of New Science of Giambattista Vico concerning the Common Nature of the Nations). At the end of the fifth book Vico says this science contains not only the particular history of the Romans or Greeks, but "the ideal history of the eternal laws which are instanced by the deeds of all nations in their rise, progress, maturity, decadence, and dissolution [and which would be so instanced] even if (as is certainly not the case) there were infinite worlds being born from time to time throughout eternity. Hence we could not refrain from giving this work the invidious title of a *New Science*, for it was too much to defraud it unjustly of the rightful claim it had over an argument so universal as that concerning the common nature of nations, in virtue of that property which belongs to every science that is perfect in its idea."[1]

Vico concludes this statement with a quotation from Seneca's *Natural Questions*: "and which Seneca has set forth for us in his

[1]*New Science*, §1096.

vast expression: *Pusilla res hic mundus est, nisi id, quod quaerit, omnis mundus habeat*—'This world is a paltry thing unless all the world may find [therein] what it seeks.'" By changing the wording of this quotation from Seneca's *nisi in illo quod quaerat* to *nisi id, quod quaerit* Vico emphasizes that future researches into the histories of nations will not affect the basis of his science.[2] The "ideal history of the eternal laws" is true of all actual and possible nations. The "ideal eternal history" makes possible a science that is "perfect in its idea."

What kind of science is this that is perfect in its idea, that expresses the common nature of all known nations and even of those possible in an infinity of worlds? How is it like the science that we associate with natural science and theoretical thought, the science involving process of hypothesis, deduction, prediction, and models? What kind of a science is it whose *chiave maestra,* whose master key, is *fantasia*? Are science and imagination opposites, or is there a science of the imagination, a science that *is* imagination? These are the questions I wish to treat. To begin I wish to consider how Vico presents the basis of his science in Book I of the *New Science,* entitled "Establishment of Principles."

Book I begins with a Chronological Table and annotations concerning the ancient civilizations of the Hebrews, Chaldeans, Scythians, Phoenicians, Egyptians, Greeks, and Romans. This is followed by a section of Elements containing 114 axioms which are to give form to the materials of the Chronological Table. Two short sections follow: one on Principles in which Vico claims there are three fundamental customs common to the world of nations—religion, marriage, and burial; and one on Method in which Vico states in a very condensed form the manner of thought upon which his science depends.

The first four axioms constitute the basis of Vico's elements and "give us the basis for refuting all opinions hitherto held about the principles of humanity."[3] These four axioms express a

---

[2]Fisch, Introduction, *New Science,* pars. I·11–12.
[3]*New Science,* §163.

theory of ignorance which we require in order to acquire a doctrine of truth concerning the nature of humanity. They have a similarity to Bacon's idola. Croce noticed this similarity, but he specifically compares only Vico's first axiom to Bacon's first idol, as does Nicolini in his commentary on the *New Science*.[4] Vico's first axiom also has some similarity to Hobbes's statement in his chapter in the *Leviathan* on imagination: "For men measure, not only other men, but all other things, by themselves."[5] Hobbes's specific example is the propensity of men to project their own need for rest after motion into their understanding of motion in other bodies and in general.

(1) Vico's first axiom is: "Because of the indefinite nature of the human mind, wherever it is lost in ignorance man makes himself the measure of all things."[6] When in ignorance (*nell'ig-noranza*), man makes himself the measure (*la regola*) of all things (*dell'universo*). Vico says that this tendency arises from the construction of the mind; it can apprehend things indefinitely and thus can experience ignorance. To relieve this ignorance, to rest from this motion, it makes things after its own *regola*, its own measure or order.

Bacon's idols of the tribe arise when the human senses are taken to be the true standard of things.[7] This is a difficulty common to the tribe (race) of men itself because we as humans can experience the objects of the world only through our senses. Our senses are like "uneven mirrors" that distort and refract the

[4]Benedetto Croce, *The Philosophy of Giambattista Vico*, trans. R. G. Collingwood (New York: Russell and Russell, 1964), pp. 155–57. Croce makes no comment on axiom two and imprecisely draws two points out of axiom four. Fausto Nicolini, *Commento storico alla seconda Scienza nuova*, 2 vols. (Rome: Edizioni di Storia e Letteratura, 1949–50), I, par. 120. Nicolini states: "Già Bacone, *De dignitate et augmentis scientiarum*, V, 5: 'Homo fiat quasi norma et speculum naturae.'" Nicolini's citation is in error. The sentence from Bacon occurs in V, 4 (bk. 5, ch. 4). Bacon discusses the idols briefly in *De dignitate et augmentis scientiarum*, bk. 5, ch. 4, and more fully in *Novum Organum*, bk. 1.
[5]Thomas Hobbes, *Leviathan*, vol. 3 of *The English Works of Thomas Hobbes*, ed. William Molesworth (London: John Bohn, 1839), pt. 1, ch. 2.
[6]*New Science*, §120.
[7]Bacon, *Novum Organum*, bk. 1, 41 and 52.

properties of objects. In principle our senses contain a kind of ignorance because they show us the object only in human terms. We apprehend the world with more measure, in a more standardized fashion than it actually exhibits.[8]

(2) Vico's second axiom is: "It is another property of the human mind that whenever men can form no idea of distant and unknown things, they judge them by what is familiar and at hand."[9] This axiom expresses in general fashion how the mind relieves its ignorance and makes things after its own order. Men relieve their ignorance of unknown things by valuing or considering them in terms of things with which they have experience and that are present (*le stimano dalle cose loro conosciute e presenti*). The unknown is made known by the standard of the familiar.

Bacon's idols of the den are those blindnesses of vision common to all men because each is an individual with an orientation peculiar to himself.[10] This orientation is shaped by such factors as the individual's disposition generally, his education and reading, his intercourse with others, the authorities he admires, and the state of his mind at any given moment. These conditions vary from person to person and cause each to see the world in the context of his own understanding.

Bacon's idols of the den are very like Vico's second axiom because it too is a principle of the familiar. The mind distorts what comes to it from a distance in terms of what it has already made familiar or in fact assimilated to itself. Vico's first two axioms are parallel to Bacon's first two idols in that they express aspects of the individual mind that are held in common by the race. Vico divides his second axiom into two versions, two "conceits" or *borie*. These are literally "arrogances" of the familiar, ways in which the mind arrogantly takes what it does not know and claims knowledge of it. Through this process of familiarity, the mind moves from a kind of ignorance that is natural to it to a

[8]*Novum Organum*, bk. 1, 45.
[9]*New Science*, §122.
[10]*Novum Organum*, bk. 1, 42 and 53–58.

covering over of this ignorance with a more elaborate ignorance which it then claims as knowledge. Bacon does not develop his second two idols, those of the market and the theater, as parts of the idols of the den, but they are connected to it in that they represent social and intellectual frameworks in which the individual's den is shaped. Vico's two conceits have several points of similarity with Bacon's second two idols.

(3) Vico's third axiom is the "conceit of nations" (*boria delle nazioni*), a nation's belief "that it before all other nations invented the comforts of human life and that its remembered history goes back to the very beginning of the world."[11] Vico's immediate explanation of this is in terms of the falsity of the claims of various ancient civilizations to be the founders of humanity.[12] But if we reflect on it more broadly as an axiom of the *New Science* as a whole, it is a general principle of culture and history. All cultures are arrogant because they do not see themselves as subject to the ideal eternal history. The ideal eternal history shows that: (a) there are many cultural origin points of humanity, just as there are many Joves and many Herculeses; and (b) each of these is subject to the three-stage structure of providence, each nation moves between its own origin and its own approaching end. No nation is the first nation of history, and none can claim that it dominates the historical process because it is only one cycle within the total set of *corsi* and *ricorsi* that make up providential reality. All gentile nations arrogantly maintain that they are special children of providence and thus erroneously believe that they live beyond the effects of the *storia ideale eterna*.

Bacon's idols of the market arise from the intercourse between persons in society.[13] The basis of this commerce is language. The meanings that words acquire in this process of social exchange and thought lead the understanding to approach experience in certain ways. These meanings become traps because

[11]*New Science*, §125.
[12]*New Science*, §126.
[13]*Novum Organum*, bk. 1, 43 and 59–60.

131

language builds its own world of meanings apart from the objects to which such meanings refer. Bacon's idols of the market and Vico's conceit of nations are similar in that both are fallacies that arise in the social definition of reality. Human beings acting socially develop total versions of reality through which all is familiarized and which deny reality to all that lies outside the familiar terms of their interpretation. Vico's focus is on the historical principle of providence as reality "outside" any nation. Bacon's focus is on an empirical reality of objects outside the world of linguistic meanings, meanings that are often just drawn out of the power of words themselves.

(4) Vico's fourth axiom is the "conceit of scholars" (*boria de' dotti*), "who will have it that what they know is as old as the world."[14] Vico says that this arrogance of the scholarly mind is responsible for reading mystic meanings into Egyptian hieroglyphs and treating Greek fables as if they were allegorical statements of philosophical truths. This conceit has prevented us from understanding the true form of ancient poetic or mythic mentality by regarding oracular texts as if they were esoteric ways of stating theoretical truths.[15] This conceit prevents us from having a theory of the origin of human mentality. It shores up its own narrow version of thought by claiming that what it knows is what all learning has always been about.

Bacon's idols of the theater are scholarly dogmas that have crept into men's minds from various systems of philosophy.[16] Like large fictions of the nature of the world or like stage plays of ideas not grounded in any empirical understanding, these idols transfix the understanding and prevent the consideration of experience as it actually is. This idol of Bacon, like Vico's fourth axiom, describes a falsity of the scholarly mind. In Bacon's conception of scholarly error we are cut off from the reality of empirical experience, in Vico's conception we are cut off from the reality of the past.

[14]*New Science*, §127.
[15]*New Science*, §128.
[16]*Novum Organum*, bk. 1, 44 and 61–67.

132

Vico's first four axioms are an answer to a most important question: What prevents man from making the nature of his own humanity intelligible to himself? What hinders him from turning his own nature into true knowledge? Vico's answer is that through ignorance man makes himself the measure of all things; he measures things by what is familiar and present; he makes things familiar by means of the popular notions every nation has of its own self-achievement, its customs and belief in its special place in history, and by means of the notion every scholar has of the reality and timelessness of conceptual knowledge, that is, that all knowledge from the earliest times has been of a philosophical sort.

Bacon asks: What prevents the mind from making proper inductions from its experience of nature? He answers that it is the same as what confutes judgment in ordinary logic—the false use of images or idols that he says are the deepest fallacies of the human mind.[17] In saying this I am interpreting Bacon to mean that idols are a species of illusion and not a type of divinity to which the mind bows down. These idols confute not only judgment but also the interpretation of nature. They sever us from empirical experience.

There are many differences between Bacon's *idola* and Vico's first axioms and *borie*. Bacon was one of Vico's "four authors," one of the four sources of his original thought referred to in the *Autobiography*.[18] The title of the *New Science* was inspired in part by that of Bacon's *Novum Organum*.[19] Bacon understands his idols as impediments to induction.[20] Vico is not seeking a science that is inductive, but a science of nations that is "perfect in its idea." Vico's science is man's true production of a knowledge of his own nature. This knowledge can be reached only by overcoming the mind's tendency to substitute awareness for what should be the generation in the mind of the true causes of the

[17]*De dignitate et augmentis scientiarum*, bk. 5, ch. 4; *Novum Organum*, bk. 1, 40.
[18]*Autobiography*, pp. 139 and 154.
[19]Fisch, Introduction, *Autobiography*, p. 20.
[20]*Novum Organum*, bk. 1, 40.

human world. Vico's first four axioms are not a portrait of simple ignorance, but a portrait of how ignorance is turned into arrogance. He depicts a process of a total falsity of mind wherein nations preposterously believe themselves to be greater in their reality than history itself and wherein thinkers believe their own form of thought to have always been the form of human thought.

I think Vico, like Bacon, thought that there is no certain means by which the mind can overcome its tendencies to illusion. It can only strive to avoid illusion through the proper presentation of knowledge. Vico says in the first axiom that rumor (*fama*) is deflated by the presence of the thing itself.[21] The two conceits are deep tendencies, propensities of the mind in its understanding of the human world. Vico says that, until his correction of it in the *New Science*, philology, the study of human language, customs, and institutions, had been only a reflection of the conceit of nations. Philosophy had been only a reflection of the conceit of scholars.[22]

In order to overcome this state of affairs Vico advances a doctrine of ignorance. Vico's view of ignorance and *boria* is reminiscent in a sense of the thought of Nicholas of Cusa, the first modern philosopher, who, in *De docta ignorantia* (1440), advanced the doctrine of "learned ignorance." Vico says: "So, for purposes of this inquiry, we must reckon as if there were no books in the world."[23] Nicholas says: "Nothing could be more beneficial for even the most zealous searcher for knowledge than his being in fact most learned in that very ignorance which is peculiarly his own."[24] Ancient philosophy and modern philosophy both take their beginnings from doctrines of ignorance, from the method of Socratic ignorance and from Nicholas' doctrine of learned ignorance.

[21]*Novum Organum*, bk. 1, 68; *New Science*, §121.

[22]*New Science*, §330.

[23]*New Science*, §330.

[24]Nicholas of Cusa, *Of Learned Ignorance*, trans. Fr. Germain Heron (London: Routledge and Kegan Paul, 1954), pp. 8–9.

I see Vico's statement that we must reckon "as if there were no books in the world" as a statement of the importance of genuine ignorance for the creation of true science. This is a sense of ignorance that can help prevent the mind from turning ignorance (defined as uncertainty and indefinition of mind) into *boria,* or arrogance and false science. I see this same attitude in Vico's previously mentioned insistence that "we cannot at all imagine and can comprehend only with great effort" the natures of the first men.[25] The illusory thought of the *borie* of nations and scholars and the philology and philosophy that reflect this arrogance lead to the claim that we can comprehend exactly the natures of the first men. Such conceits uphold the view that the first men were like us and that their world was essentially that empirical collection of objects which is so familiar to us.

Vico's reckoning "as if there were no books in the world" is a doctrine of the importance of learned ignorance as a principle of inquiry, and his conceit of scholars is a doctrine of the mind's propensity toward an ignorance of learning. His statement concerning a world with no books is followed directly by perhaps the most famous and frequently quoted passage in the *New Science*: "But in the night of thick darkness enveloping the earliest antiquity, so remote from ourselves, there shines the eternal and never failing light of a truth beyond all question: that the world of civil society has certainly been made by men, and that its principles are therefore to be found within the modifications of our own human mind."[26] To understand how this development from the "night of thick darkness" has come about we must reinterpret philology and philosophy, understanding each in a new way and combining them into a single mode of thought. This will demonstrate how the *verum-factum* principle can give the human mind a knowledge of itself, of its own modifications seen in their connection with human actions in civil society.

Vico's axioms are divided into general (1-22) and particular

[25]*New Science,* §§338, 378, and 700.
[26]*New Science,* §331.

135

(23-114). Within the general, as mentioned above, the first four "give us the basis for refuting all opinions hitherto held about the principles of humanity"; those that follow (5-15) "give us the foundations of the true," that is, proper philosophical understanding; the others (16-22) "give us the foundations of the certain," that is, proper philological understanding.[27] The mass of particular propositions (23-114) that follow are associated with each other in various ways, such as those relating to the beginnings of divine poetry (28-38), beginnings of historical mythology (42-46), divisions of poetic theory (47-62), ideal eternal history (66-96), and natural law as instituted by providence (109-114). There are subgroupings within these groups of particular propositions but there is no overall classification as there is with the three groups of general propositions. In general, the first half of the particular propositions can be characterized as treating topics relating to poetic wisdom, while the second half deal mostly with ideal eternal history. Some of the propositions in this second half are very specific, for example, those treating questions of Roman history, law, and custom.

In the general axioms that give the foundation of the true, Vico states his distinction between science and awareness or consciousness, between *scienza* and *coscienza*: "Men who do not know what is true of things take care to hold fast to what is certain, so that, if they cannot satisfy their intellects by knowledge (*scienza*), their wills at least may rest on consciousness (*coscienza*)."[28] This distinction recalls Vico's presentation of the *verum-factum* principle in *On the Ancient Wisdom of the Italians* (1710). He distinguishes between *scientia*, which involves knowing in the sense of possessing the genus or form by which a thing is made, and *conscientia*, which is a consciousness of things without the power to demonstrate the genus or form involved.[29]

Seen in light of Vico's conception of false knowledge, of ignorance made into grand illusion by the *borie* of nations and of

[27]*New Science*, §163.
[28]*New Science*, §137.
[29]*De Italorum sapientia*, ch. 1, sec. 3.

scholars, this distinction between science and consciousness takes on special meaning. "Men who do not know what is true" hold on to what is certain (*il certo*). Not knowing how to make the unknown according to its genus or form, that is, being without the power to demonstrate its nature, they familiarize it to themselves. They make a knowledge of acquaintance. They develop elaborate structures of their awareness of it. These structures appear to be *scienza,* but in fact they are only grand schemes of *coscienza.* This is because the *verum-factum* principle whereby they could make the object truly intelligible is not part of their apprehension of the object. The conceit of nations acts as if there is no need to make the customs of the past known in terms of their own form or genus, because the past is just in essence an incomplete version of the present. The conceit of scholars acts as if it is unnecessary to make mythicopoetic te˙ 's intelligible in terms of the form of their own thought, the thought of the texts themselves. This conceit sees these texts as just signs of its own wisdom, its own form of understanding, which it claims to be truth itself. The conceits of nations and scholars are the arrogances of the certain thrown in the face of the true.

This substitution of awareness or consciousness (*coscienza*) for true knowledge (*scienza*) rests on a failure to be able to connect *verum* with *certum* through the activity of reciprocal making expressed in the *verum-factum* principle. Vico wishes to achieve true science (*scienza*) by uniting philological understanding, which studies the certain, with philosophical understanding, which studies the true. He wishes to associate them in the sense that the certain when regarded in the proper way will show its aspect of the true; the particular will reveal its universality. The true, regarded not in itself, but as it embodies itself in a particular of the human world, will appear as something actual and concrete. The mentality required to think *verum* against *certum* against *factum* is special. It is philosophical philology, a new critical art. It is not only *scienza* but *scienza nuova.* Fisch points out that no thinkers prior to Vico remotely approached what Vico has done, and concludes: "In the end, therefore, if we concede

137

that what he has done is science, we must also concede that it is a new science."[30] I agree with this and would add that if Vico had no true predecessors, he also has had no true successors.

Vico's 114 axioms or elements, like Euclid's *Elements,* contain axioms, definitions, and postulates and, like Euclid's work, they suggest that the *New Science* contains a total system of thought. Vico's system of thought is not achieved by the use of a geometric method. There are no proofs and demonstrations laid out in Euclidean fashion. Vico does claim that some propositions are proved by others and some are said to have corollaries, but there is no deductive order to Vico's elements. As mentioned above, the overall arrangement is classificatory and not deductive. This classificatory structure, especially in relation to the mass of particular axioms, is quite loosely done.

Vico's axiomatic list is characterized by apparent jumps from one subject to another and from one level of generality to another. It is difficult to say why some axioms that appear as particular (23-114) should not with equal ease appear as general (1-22). Some of the particular propositions seem to have such specific meaning as not to be axioms at all. One of Vico's most dramatic acts of placement is that by which his most fundamental axiom, the axiom that he makes the basis of his section on Method, becomes axiom 106: "Doctrines must take their beginning from that of the matters of which they treat." He explains this arrangement by saying that the axiom's import for understanding the natural law of the gentes can better be seen by placing it in relationship to this subject matter.[31] Such possibilities of arrangement make clear that we cannot interpret Vico's elements as a deductive system of propositions. How are we to regard elements of this sort?

A constant feature of Vico's axioms is that each proposition, whether general or particular in its classification, is given immediate philological embodiment in terms of some reference to

[30]Fisch, Introduction, *New Science,* par. G4.
[31]*New Science,* §§314–15.

custom, etymology, law, or mythology. Vico's elements are each miniatures of the philosophical-philological bond upon which the *New Science* as a whole is based. They are each demonstrations of this bond. In their microcosmic embodiment of both this philosophical-philological bond and the interconnection between *verum, certum,* and *factum* that lies within it, Vico's elements are different from Spinoza's geometrics. Each element reflects the whole of the *New Science* and their internal order is one of internal mutual reflection and not geometric deductive order.

Vico introduces his axioms in the *New Science* with this metaphor: "And just as the blood does in animate bodies, so will these elements course through our Science and animate it in all its reasonings about the common nature of nations."[32] This notion of the motion of the blood goes back to *On the Study Methods of Our Time* (1708/1709) in which Vico says that the aim of the learning process should be truth. This aim "should circulate, like a blood-stream, through the entire body of the learning process. Consequently, just as the blood's pulsation may best be studied at the spot where the arterial beat is most perceptible, so the aim of our study methods shall be treated at the point where it assumes the greatest prominence."[33]

Vico was interested in the metaphysical significance of the motion of the blood stream. In his dedication to Paolo Mattia Doria at the beginning of the *Ancient Wisdom,* Vico claims that all things live and die in terms of a sort of systole and diastole and he specifically pursues this idea in his discussion of mind and soul, "*De animo et anima.*"[34] Vico followed this with a short treatise, *De aequilibrio corporis animantis* (On the Equilibrium of the Living Body), which is now lost.[35] For Vico the notion of life as pulsation-like movement is related to the Egyptian medicine of "slack

[32]*New Science,* §119.
[33]*Study Methods,* p. 6.
[34]*De Italorum sapientia,* dedication and ch. 5, sec. 1.
[35]See Fisch's remark on the history of this work in *Autobiography,* p. 219, note 168.

139

and tight," and he discusses this question at some length in the first part of the *Autobiography* (1725). He says: "Accordingly the soul, that is the air insinuated into the blood, would be the principle of life in man, and the ether insinuated into the nerves would be the principle of sensation." And at one point he concludes: "The operating principle of all things in nature would be corpuscles of pyramidal shape."[36]

In his metaphor introducing the list of axioms, Vico is claiming that just as blood functions as the life of animate bodies, so the following elements (*i seguenti assiomi o degnità*) will course through his *Scienza* and give it life. Contrary to Hobbes's view, Vico believes that when the relationship is between their bodies and the human world, men can measure other things by themselves, even in terms of their pattern of motion and rest, if this pattern is understood as systole and diastole. This can certainly be done if the pitfalls of Vico's conceits are avoided. The body of the human world as we come to it prior to the *New Science* is inanimate, dead from the conceits of nations and scholars. Vico's axioms can be moved about singly and in clusters to animate the material of history, to make truth emerge in the pattern of history's pulsations. There is no set order in which the axioms are to be employed. They can be moved in an indefinite number of ways in their animation of the material of the human world so that its ideal eternal history can be grasped.

This varied use of axioms is in fact how Vico proceeds in the four books of the *New Science* once he has established its principles. Vico does not make systematic application of the axioms or lay out proofs or demonstrations from them. He speaks of them only from time to time; yet they are his guides as he animates the materials of the nations. The meaning of the philosophical-philological bond is achieved by means of the expansion and contraction of its dimensions—expansion of a philological certain into a philosophical truth, and contraction of a philosophical truth into a particular custom, word, or legal form. These

[36]*Autobiography*, pp. 148–51.

expansions and contractions are the motion of the *New Science* of which the axioms, each being a philosophical-philological bond, are the primary exemplars. Vico's elements are the air, or *mens,* that can be "insinuated into the blood," the circulating pattern of human history. History is systole and diastole. History expands into a *corso* and contracts to form the beginning of a *ricorso.* The ages within a *corso* have this same movement, as do the pulsations of opposites within them. Any given corpuscular bond of philosophy and philology has within it the pyramidal shape of *verum, certum,* and *factum.*

Vico is the discoverer of the nature of the motion of human events in the way that Nicolas Oresme, in his treatise *On Intensities,* is the discoverer of the graphic representation of physical motion from which the modern understanding of motion springs.[37] Vico attempts to picture the pulse of the *corso* and *ricorso* in history and in any human event. There is a parallel between Newton's interest, in the preface of the *Principia,* in bringing together that which is "perfectly accurate," the geometrical, with that which is "less so," the mechanical, and Vico's concern to unite methodologically the true and the certain— what we can assert with philosophical precision and what we can assert philologically.[38] Vico greatly admired Newton and sent him a copy of the *New Science* but Vico's science is not that of Newton. It does not attempt to apply mathematical structure to the motion of human events, as Newton does to the motion of bodies in nature. It is not a science of the "rational mechanics" of the human.

History is the body of providence and the purpose of the axioms of the *New Science* is to allow us at any given point to bring out providential structure that is there, to make it intelligible as a point wherein the eternal pattern can be seen. Vico begins the section on Principles by inviting the reader to test what has been said against the materials of the Chronological

[37]Siegfried Giedion, *Mechanization Takes Command: A Contribution to Anonymous History* (Oxford: Oxford University Press, 1948), pp. 16–17.
[38]See Newton's *Principia,* preface to the first edition.

Table. If any of these materials can be found to be inconsistent with the propositions expressed in the elements, Vico says, the entire science is faulty: "For inconsistency with one of them would amount to inconsistency with all, since each accords with all."[39] At any given point whatsoever in history, when we look for its truth, these axioms must allow it to be seen. It must emerge as a pressure point wherein providence, the *mens* of history, is present making intelligible the motion of the systole and diastole of its great body.

There is no rule whereby a truth of human motion can be produced. In the *Ancient Wisdom* Vico says that the ability to produce knowledge with certainty requires prudence. Prudence, he says, does not operate by rules; it is not prudence if it does. Vico claims, quoting Terence's *Eunuchus*, that any man who would try to conduct his life by geometrical method would be striving only for rational madness.[40] The making of a truth of history in thought is like the making of a certainty in a prudent action. The axioms cannot be worked as a geometry of the human world.

How does Vico's short section on Principles relate to the axioms of the elements? Vico says that the principles of human society are religion, marriage, and burial. Fisch points out that the term "principles" here can be understood as "the necessary and sufficient generative conditions of the *gens,* the minimal society that can outlive its members and thus make possible an evolution of culture."[41] Religion, marriage, and burial are the conditions out of which social life can arise. I suggest that they are also the conditions necessary to the creation of *sensus communis,* that is, the topical structure upon which any human sensation or thought depends. Religion, marriage, and burial designate conditions that must be present before axioms can be employed to understand the providential pattern of truth in society. If these conditions are not present, life does not exhibit

[39]*New Science,* §330.
[40]*De Italorum sapientia,* ch. 7, sec. 5.
[41]Fisch, Introduction, *New Science,* par. I·2.

providential structure and cannot be so understood. We are presented with animal life, perhaps, but not with human life. Our ability to sense the presence of these principles in evidences of early man, for example, makes it possible for us to think of what we see as human and providential.

The brief section on Method is Vico's most complete statement of the sense in which the *New Science* is a science. In originally defining science (*scientia*) in the *Ancient Wisdom* as that which we arrive at through the *verum-factum* principle, Vico has stolen the club of Hercules. He has taken the term "science" from the hands of the scientists themselves. What we understand above all to be science—physical science—Vico has described as a kind of simulated form of real science achieved by making objects intelligible in experiment. This is not the only occasion of such a theft. Hegel, after Vico, took the term *Wissenschaft* from the hands of the scientists. Just at the moment when nineteenth-century science was beginning its dominance, Hegel identified the reasoning of scientists as *Verstand*, understanding, rather than true reason, *Vernunft*. Vico made his distinction between *scientia* and *conscientia* against the zenith of seventeenth-century scientific genius. Vico is a thinker writing in the eighteenth century but he is a thinker in the spirit of the founding of new sciences coming out of the seventeenth century. Vico also had a strong sense of science as empirical investigation. He participated in the Academy of the *Investiganti* which was for a long period a center of natural scientific investigation in Naples. Fisch concludes his study of the history of this Academy with this sentence concerning Vico: "It is not too much to say that he lived under the shadow of the Investigators."[42] It seems reasonable to think that Vico took his metaphors of the motions of bodies and the circulation of the blood and, more generally, his sense of inquiry from the activity of the Academy. Perhaps he took more.

---

[42]Max H. Fisch, "The Academy of the Investigators," in *Science, Medicine, and History: Essays on the Evolution of Scientific Thought and Medical Practice Written in Honour of Charles Singer*, ed. E. Ashworth Underwood, 2 vols. (London: Oxford University Press, 1953), I, 552.

Vico's notion of science as it appears in the *New Science* is a very special one, one not familiar to us. In *Ulysses* Joyce writes: "It had better be stated here and now at the outset that the perverted transcendentalism to which Mr S. Dedalus' (Div. Sep.) contentions would appear to prove him pretty badly addicted runs directly counter to accepted scientific methods. Science, it cannot be too often repeated, deals with tangible phenomena. The man of science like the man in the street has to face hard-headed facts that cannot be blinked and explain them as best he can. There may be, it is true, some questions which science cannot answer—at present—such as the first problem submitted by Mr L. Bloom (Pubb. Canv.) regarding the future determination of sex."[43] None of the questions of Vico's science can be answered in terms of the thought of "hardheaded facts," nor by science in any sense in which we usually understand it. It requires us to reconsider what can be meant by science.

In the section on Method Vico claims that there are three principal aspects of his science: (1) it is a "rational civil theology of divine providence"; (2) it is a "history of human ideas"; and (3) it is a "philosophy of authority."[44] This science is at once a particular kind of theology, history, and philosophy. These are aspects (*aspetti*) of this science; they are not parts or divisions of it, but ways in which it can be viewed.

Seen as a civil theology, Vico says, "Our new Science must therefore be a demonstration, so to speak, of what providence has wrought in history."[45] Vico invites the reader to consider history and see if he "can conceive more or fewer or different causes than those from which issue the effects of this civil world."[46] He intends the reader to regard the variety of human customs, diversity of conditions, and variations in the development of institutions and see if all this activity does not fit

---

[43]James Joyce, *Ulysses* (London: The Bodley Head, 1960), p. 547.
[44]*New Science*, §§342, 347, and 350.
[45]*New Science*, §342.
[46]*New Science*, §345.

together with "naturalness," "order," and "end."[47] Although men undertake courses of action consonant with their own interest and self-love, their actions work to promote society and to serve the preservation of the human race.

The "divine" proofs of Vico's rational civil theology have a certain similarity to the classical teleological argument as applied to history rather than to nature. The teleological argument commonly asks the thinker to reason from the design of causes and effects, orders and ends, which can be found in nature, to the existence of God as creator. Vico asks us to examine history in all its diversity, its individual aims, its oppositions and chaotic moments and to see if there is not present an elegance, an economy of structures, of causes and effects which all act toward the preservation of the human race. The presence of such elements of design will allow us to see divine providence in history. At the basis of our perception of the economy of causes (*cagioni*) and effects (*effetti*) should be the awareness that the whole civil world, the immense number of civil effects, comes from four causes. These causes are stated by Vico in his presentation of poetic wisdom (*sapienza poetica*) in Book II of the *New Science* as a variation on the three principles he has presented in Book I, that is, religion, marriage, and burial. Burial is omitted and two other features of poetic society are added; thus there "are four elements, as it were, of the civil universe, namely religion, marriage, asylum, and the first agrarian law."[48]

Despite these similarities, there is an important difference between Vico's argument from design and the teleological argument for God. The teleological argument regards the elements of design in nature as evidence of the existence of God as creator. Vico's proof is not an argument from evidence of design in history to the existence of providence as the creating force of history. His proof does not function as a means to obtain the

[47]*New Science*, §344.
[48]*New Science*, §630.

145

existence of an infinite being from the finite. Vico's proof is an act of combining the divine with history. The reader has before him both providence and the material of history. He is asked to see that what is before him is in fact providential. The pattern is not evidence of providence. It is not a proof of providence since both providence and history are givens. Providence is given not as a rational inference but as an act of imagination, of recollective *fantasia*. We obtain it when we grasp directly and suddenly the sense of ideal eternal history. In an expanded list of the aspects of his new science in Book II, Vico lists ideal eternal history.[49]

Vico's proof asks the reader to meditate one given against another, that is, the notion and reality of providence given in *fantasia* against the materials of history given in ordinary historical investigation. This method might be described as transcendental in that providence is the answer to how history is possible, but providence is not derived as a synthetic a priori basis of history in the way Kant derives the categories of the first *Critique*. Providence is not produced for the mind through a procedure of rationally developed presuppositions of historical experience. The mind comes to the notion of providence in an immediate fashion through its powers of *fantasia*, and it directs its vision toward apprehending the universality present in the particulars of history. As transcendental thinking, Vico's procedure has more in common with the type of subjective universality involved in Kant's conception of the reflective judgment (*reflektierende Urteilskraft*) of the third *Critique* than with the determinant judgment (*bestimmende Urteilskraft*) which determines the particular through a cognitive rule or law of thought that Kant explores in the first *Critique*. Neither Kant's nor Vico's understanding of science would convince a man of "hardheaded facts."

Vico associates the third principal aspect of his science, that of a philosophy of authority, with the type of proofs involved in it

---

[49]*New Science*, §393.

as a rational civil theology. I wish to consider this third aspect before turning to the second. By a philosophy of authority (*autorità*) Vico means that his science offers an understanding of the bases on which human prudential and legal judgments are made. It is an understanding of the grounds that have guided human actions, the grounds of human choice in its direction of society. Vico's new science is a history of common sense, of the shifts in the *sensus communis* which have marked the development of the human race as it has moved from divine authority, to an authority of human nature, to that of the authority of natural law.[50] Human choice, the decisions by which the human world is given order, is not based on rational inference from rules or laws but is accomplished by acting from a common perception of things, a *sensus communis*.

Human choice makes things certain in the midst of uncertainty. The results of these free acts of human choice are the certains that philology investigates and turns into particular pieces of knowledge. In the section on Method Vico gives a list of seven philological proofs that are to be joined with the philosophical proofs of the three principal aspects of the science. In Book II he also indicates that the philosophy of authority has a special relationship to philology. He says that it "reduces philology to the form of a science."[51] In its aspect as a philosophy of authority, the new science specifically demonstrates the truth of what is philologically certain.

The new science as philosophy of authority shows the ideal eternal history of human choice. Its proofs are in form like those of the broad consideration of history that is the task of the new science considered as rational civil theology. The proofs of the philosophy of authority are made by combining two givens—the ideal eternal history and the specifics of human choice or authority. The philosophy of authority must see how any act of human choice is based on a specific kind of authority which is a

[50]*New Science,* §§387–89.
[51]*New Science,* §390.

reflection of some specific form of common sense. A specific form of common sense is always connected with some sense of property, which is connected in its original meaning with authority.[52] Our understanding of authority is made scientific by showing how each act of prudential choice whereby human consciousness makes something certain is in fact providential. It is providential in that each specific act follows the same principles and source from which the jurisprudence of the human spirit derives. Each act of human choice has its own beginning, middle, and end, its own ideal eternal history that reflects the structure of history as a whole.

The most important passages for an understanding of Vico's proof of the *New Science* are those that concern the second aspect of his science. In introducing this aspect Vico says that the "natural theological proofs will be confirmed for us by the following sorts of logical proofs."[53] These logical proofs are achieved on the basis of a method of understanding human mentality itself, a method which above all requires an ability to begin our understanding of the human where the human itself begins. The first principle of the method of this science is that "it must begin where its subject matter began."[54] Vico's science thus depends upon a theory of origin. This science must be able to grasp the nature of human mentality in its original moment and unfold the human world from this moment. In this unfolding the human world must be explained in terms of its causes and effects or this would not be truly a science. Science requires more than the narration of events. Science requires an explanation of (1) particulars and (2) their causes. Vico says of the features of the human world: "We explain the particular ways in which they come into being; that is to say, their nature, the explanation of which is the distinguishing mark of science."[55]

Vico makes it clear that in his view human thoughts arise from

[52]*New Science*, §386.
[53]*New Science*, §346.
[54]*New Science*, §338.
[55]*New Science*, §346.

the "human necessities or utilities of social life."[56] His science in the sense of a history of ideas is not an idealism. It is not an account of the idea developing itself in terms of itself. At the same time Vico's view is not compatible with a conception of the strict economic determination of history. Vico believes that types of mentality also shape social life. Forms of society and forms of thought act reciprocally on each other. In Vico's view all features of human existence are codeterminative. History's course is determined by divine providence. There is no independent material basis that determines human action. The tragedy that arises from the fact that any *corso* has a real end prevents history from having a future. Providence repeatedly teaches its lesson of the three ages. In Vico's view there is no ideal state of human existence toward which history moves or can be made to move as a goal.

Vico's notion of his science as a history of human ideas (*una storia dell'umane idee*) is not a notion of the history of ideas as a special field of knowledge such as that which is associated with the work of A. O. Lovejoy. Vico's science aims instead at a complete and true account of human mentality itself. Its aim is essentially metaphysical in the sense of being a true science of human reality. It seeks to encompass more than the special task of understanding and tracing the interconnections between various moral, intellectual, and aesthetic outlooks. Vico's science can be viewed in this regard as the history of the human mind itself, a history that makes possible the history of ideas in its more ordinary sense.

Vico's science is a "metaphysics of the human mind," a "new art of criticism," a "metaphysical art of criticism." Vico uses the terms *nuova arte critica; Nuova Scienza, o sia la metafisica; arte critica, pur metafisica; critica metafisica* and variations on these.[57] These terms of the *New Science* reflect back in Vico's thought to the first *New Science* (1725), in which Vico employs as a chapter

[56] *New Science*, §347.
[57] *New Science*, e.g., §§7, 31, 143, 348, 350, and 905.

149

title, *Idea d'una nuova arte critica*,[58] and in the *Autobiography*, where Vico uses the same terms to describe his achievement of the first *New Science*.[59] Vico's work of twenty years, which resulted in the discovery of the *universale fantastico* as the master key of the *New Science*, was made possible by his creation of this new art of criticism. All of the truth of Vico's *New Science* is reached through this art. What is this new art that is simultaneously a new science?

The answer to this question can be approached through Vico's notion that chronology and geography (*cronologia* and *geografia*) are "the two eyes of history" (*i due occhi della storia*). Vico uses this phrase in the *New Science*[60] and in the first *New Science*.[61] He also uses it in the *Autobiography*.[62] History requires two modes of vision—time and place, chronology and geography. A nation is a time and a place. Vico's *New Science* is a science of the common nature of nations (*nazioni*). In paragraph 348 of the section on Method Vico makes three statements that are of great importance for understanding the basis of his science.

The first statement of paragraph 348 is: "To determine the times and places for such a history—that is, when and where these human thoughts were born—and thus to give it certainty by means of its own (so to speak) metaphysical chronology and geography, our Science applies a likewise metaphysical art of criticism with regard to the founders of these same nations, in which it took well over a thousand years to produce those writers with whom philological criticism has hitherto been occupied."

Previous study of human history has been based on philological criticism. Although such criticism may offer an explanation of the particular, it does not offer an explanation of causes; it does not construct a knowledge of things from their origins. The new art of criticism involves a metaphysical understanding of time and place, a metaphysical chronology and geography. This new

---

[58]*Scienza nuova prima*, bk. 2, ch. 9. See also, e.g., bk. 2, ch. 57.

[59]*Autobiografia*, ed. Fubini, p. 56; *Autobiography*, p. 167.

[60]*New Science*, §§17, 348, and 741.

[61]*Scienza nuova prima*, bk. 2, ch. 57.

[62]*Autobiografia*, ed. Fubini, p. 57; *Autobiography*, p. 167.

art requires a type of understanding that can show that all nations order themselves temporally and spatially according to the same principles. The new art of criticism must be a means whereby we can reach back to discover this process by which nations originate themselves.

If we connect a number of Vico's statements, using what he says in the above statement concerning metaphysical chronology and geography as a key, we can see that there is a precise analogy between divination as the first art of humanity and metaphysical criticism as the first art of the understanding of humanity. This analogy offers a confirmation of my thesis of the parallelism of mythicopoetic *fantasia* and recollective *fantasia*. The former produces the first human knowledge, divination; and the latter produces the first scientific knowledge that humanity has of itself.

In Book II of the *New Science* Vico describes the structure of the thought of *fantasia,* of poetic wisdom or *sapienza poetica,* in terms of a tree, one of the two main branches of which contains the poetic sciences.[63] Among these sciences is poetic astronomy, which has two daughters—poetic chronology and poetic geography.[64] These two daughters are said to be the eyes of poetic history.[65] Poetic history here may be understood as the total activity of *sapienza poetica,* including the other poetic sciences of physics and cosmography and the activities of the other main branch, poetic logic, morals, economics, and politics, as well as poetic metaphysics, which is the trunk of the tree of poetic wisdom. In poetic mentality astronomy is identified with Urania.[66] As discussed in the preceding chapter, Urania is the first Muse. She is called the "science of good and evil" or the science of divination.[67] Urania is the Muse of the first art of humanity.

This first art of humanity, divination, is the art of reading the

---

[63]*New Science,* §367.
[64]*New Science,* §367.
[65]*New Science,* §741.
[66]*New Science,* e.g., 391 and 739.
[67]*New Science,* §§365, 391, and 508.

signs of Jove. When Jove is formed as a *universale fantastico*, the meaning of his existence for the first men is elaborated through the art of divination. From the power of mind to form the sky as Jove's body develops the power to shape all of nature as a system of gods whose signs can be read by divination. Chronology and geography are the daughters of astronomy because through attention to the sky the power to order experience as gods is derived. Chronology appears through the phenomenon of theogonies of the gods; geography appears through the identification of certain gods with certain places.[68]

Divination is the way in which *fantasia* is extended into a total mode of the formation of experience. As the science of good and evil it is the science of understanding opposites. Through it the first men learn how to read good in relation to evil. From this art grows our knowledge of those elements in experience that are truly divine and eternal. Wisdom itself, Vico says, is this understanding of the eternal that has its origins in poetic divination: "a science which, among the Tuscans, considered as knowledge of the true good and true evil, perhaps owed to that fact the first name they gave it, 'science in divinity.'"[69]

Scienza in divinità, when practiced not on the movements of the sky, but on the movements of history, gives us an understanding of providence. The science of providence is a science of true good and true evil. This science depends upon our access to history through the recollective imaginative universal of the ideal eternal history, through a special combination of memory and imagination. Vico's science, following the wisdom of the Tuscans, is *scienza in divinità* made possible by *scienza in fantasia*.

The *nuova arte critica* or *critica metafisica* is a *scienza in fantasia* in which things are understood through their opposites. The providential order of history is accomplished by a kind of reverse movement, as was discussed in the preceding chapter. God as the true good appears upside down in history. Man's self-love,

---

[68]*New Science*, §§732–40 and 741–78.
[69]*New Science*, §365.

his pursuit of power, and the passions of fear, violence, and greed yield religion, cities, and governments. History is not dissolved in its chaotic and negative moments, but emerges from them with new patterns of social order. In the pulsation of *corso* and *ricorso* the human race is preserved. Vico's science requires the critical art of reading oppositions in terms of pattern. When opposites are read in this way human events can be arranged in a causal account.

Vico notes that Clio is the second Muse and is the narrator of poetic history.[70] Urania as the first Muse is the narrator of the science of good and evil, of the metaphysical knowledge upon which poetic history is based. Philological criticism that has preceded Vico's new art of metaphysical criticism is like the narration of Clio, not Urania. Vico is seeking the art of the first Muse, the true narration of history in which the reality of the human world is made fully articulate. As divination develops the first knowledge of the world from Jove, so the new art of criticism develops the first true metaphysical knowledge of history from ideal eternal history.

The second statement of paragraph 348 is: "And the criterion our criticism employs is that taught by divine providence and common to all nations, namely the common sense of the human race, determined by the necessary harmony of human institutions, in which all the beauty of the civil world consists."

This statement concerns the eye of metaphysical geography in that the common sense, the *sensus communis*, of the human race is the basis upon which any nation develops the *topoi* from which its thought can develop. Jove is the first *topos* common to the beginnings of all nations. Jove is a "sensory topic" in that as imaginative universal Jove is a fixed point in the self-cancelling flux of sensation. Jove is not consciously invented as a place for memory to fix the flux of sensation. He is only *felt* as a point to which thought can return and reexperience the meaning of the sky and thunder. From the experience of this mental fixation of

[70]*New Science*, §533.

153

a first place in sensation, thought learns to shape all of nature. This gives the first men a sense of physical and mental location. As Vico pictures it in the frontispiece of the *New Science*, the altar upon which to perform sacrifices and take auspices is a locus in the center of the clearing in the great forests. This altar is a first location of physical place made possible by the apprehension of Jove as a mental place. Through the guidance of divination controlled by the ancient fathers, society evolves and cities develop.

The third statement of paragraph 348 is: "The decisive sort of proof in our Science is therefore this: that, since these institutions have been established by divine providence, the course of the institutions of the nations had to be, must now be, and will have to be such as our Science demonstrates, even if infinite worlds were born from time to time through eternity, which is certainly not the case."

This science must be made as an absolute chronology, the second eye of the metaphysics. History must be seen as a process that had, has, and will have to be, *dovette, deve, dovrà.*[71] This metaphysical sense of chronology requires the *fantasia* of the ideal eternal history to be joined to that *fantasia* employed in the original construction of the *sensus communis.* Any nation can then be seen as a unity of place and time and this unity is achieved and understood in the same way for each. Any nation is a microcosm of the total human world.

At every point *fantasia* is the means of our access to this science. The kind of knowledge it involves is not as such self-reflective. Self-reflection is a kind of cognition that the agent has of himself. This kind of knowledge is present in Vico's science. But Vico's science shows that self-reflective knowledge depends upon the activity of *fantasia.* This process of seeking an origin is not one of simple chronological tracing, nor is it one of metaphysical reasoning to the principle of a ground. It is a process in which the origin is approached as if it were something present to the senses. Recollection aims at having its object as something

---

[71]*New Science,* §349.

quasi-perceptual, as a phenomenon. To grasp this origin the mind must actually attempt to enter into the original exercise of its powers.

To recollect is to order things in terms of their origin, to obtain a totalization of all the fragments of the activity of the human spirit through a progressive ordering of things between the origin point, once found, and the form of the present mentality from which the ordering takes place. This process cannot be fully typified by the notion of *reflection*. Reflection is essentially a logical term. Even if it is taken in a transcendental sense as the mind's self-conscious reflection upon itself, reflection falls short because it does not necessarily involve the notion of a time that moves from a primordial point of origin to the present. What must be sought is a sense of self-identity that extends through time from the origin to the present. We must reperceive with our memory what this first world is like before it can become an object of reflection. Any sense in which we might call Vico's mode of thought in the *New Science* reflection presupposes that we are able first to form through *fantasia* what we are to reflect upon.[72]

---

[72]Leon Pompa employs the term *reflection* to characterize the type of knowledge in the *New Science*: "The concept of *reflection* is therefore the crux of Vico's later theory of knowledge. Vico is claiming that by self-conscious reflection upon our own ways of seeing our world and our own attitudes to it, we can come to understand what are the natural propensities which cause these" (*Vico: A Study of the 'New Science'* [New York: Cambridge University Press, 1975], p. 166). When Pompa's meaning of reflection is developed fully in the final two chapters of his study it comes, I believe, quite close in the principles of its definition to what I mean by the term *recollection*. The central difference, and I believe it to be a very important one, is that his view is not grounded in Vico's notion of *fantasia*. Pompa does not explore the sense of *fantasia* present in the origin of human mentality, upon which the *New Science* rests; nor does he explore the sense in which *fantasia* raised to a different level is involved in the "reflective" activity of the *New Science* itself. Pompa has discussed the imagination in Vico in a paper at the Vico/Venezia Conference, Venice, August 1978. See *Vico: Past and Present*, ed. Giorgio Tagliacozzo (Atlantic Highlands, N.J.: Humanities Press, 1981), pt. 1. The difference remains that Pompa's view approaches Vico's thought through cognition and the philosophical argument and the present study comes to Vico through the basis of his thought in rhetoric and the image.

Vico's science is performative. The proof of the science is found through the reader making it for himself. Vico's science is a true or necessary narration wherein the reader correctly orders events. Vico says, "And history cannot be more certain than when he who creates the things also narrates them."[73] Since the human is the maker of the world in which he exists, he can be the certain knower of this world. His account of the human world will be *vera narratio,* or true speech; it will be like the natural speech through which the mind originally gives form to the world.[74] Vico's science is a science of the divine and a divine science. It is a science of the divine because it reveals what providence has wrought in history. It is a divine science because we are god-like in our making of its knowledge. God makes by knowing. Vico says, "O reader . . . these proofs are of a kind divine and should give thee a divine pleasure, since in God knowledge and creation are one and the same thing."[75] God does not create through an abstract knowledge of forms. *Fantasia* is the knowledge of concrete forms.

How do we find an origin and enter the mind of these first men? How do we know what we have constructed as ideal eternal history is true and not just a grand illusion?[76]

The answer to these questions lies in the theory of ignorance with which the new science begins. Our attempt to find the origin of the human world and to discern the necessary structure in the events of its development depends upon our understanding of ignorance. The mental lightning of which Vico speaks on the first page of the *Autobiography* depends upon an acute sense of ignorance. We must learn first the ignorance appropriate to our science. Vico has explained the keys to this in his first four axioms—the anxiety of the uncertain, the propensity to familiarize, and the two conceits.

[73]*New Science,* §349.

[74]*New Science,* §401.

[75]*New Science,* §349.

[76]Isaiah Berlin, "Comment on Professor Verene's Paper," in *Vico and Contemporary Thought,* ed. Giorgio Tagliacozzo, Michael Mooney, and Donald Phillip Verene (Atlantic Highlands, N.J.: Humanities Press, 1979), pt. 1, pp. 336–39.

If we ask what is the connection between Vico's natural scientific activity in the Academy of the Investigators and the science of the *New Science*, the answer lies in the sense of inquiry present in these first axioms. The methodological similarity between the natural sciences and Vico's science is not a transference of specific methods of empirical description and hypothetical reasoning, but the sense of the need for the mind to correct its directions of thought against what is clearly brought before it. This is the way the book of nature can be read, and this is the way the book of humanity can be read. We must "think [and] see" (*cogitare videre*) in relation to the philologically empirical in order to read the book of humanity as science.[77]

Vico's science offers no guarantee against the discovery of false origins or the creation of explanatory illusions. In this Vico is like Bacon, who knows no way we can assure ourselves of avoiding the idols in inductive science and natural investigation. Although Vico's science is not inductive, the notion of the propensity of the mind toward the certain and the familiar rather than the true is as basic to it as are the idols to the empirical understanding of nature. *Fantasia* must apprehend its own nature in relation to ignorance as its opposite. In this case ignorance is the willingness of the mind to reduce its uncertainty by the use of the concept, to see all thought as the same as modern thought and all life as the same as modern life. This makes a flatland of history. Wherever mind looks it finds the monotones of cognition. *Fantasia* must act counter to this ignorant and arrogant state of affairs.

I do not think there is any answer to the question of the proof of Vico's new science apart from the *New Science* itself. The problem the *New Science* poses for us is to imagine and at the same time to control imagination. As early as the *Study Methods* Vico insists that the imagination must be trained. We must come to the question of metaphysical chronology and geography, of time and place, and see if *fantasia* can offer the answer. Vico's

---

[77]*New Science*, §§359 and 163. See Fisch's note to §359. Vico's reference is to Bacon's *Cogitata et visa*.

work is a training in *fantasia,* as are the works of Joyce. We know very little about *fantasia* because we live in a Cartesian world. The grasp of a meaning through *fantasia,* upon which metaphysical criticism depends, occurs suddenly, like original speech itself. The image opens the world.

Once we have imaginative access to the human world, once we possess it as an imaginative universal, then Vico's questions about the human world make sense. There is no general mode of investigating these questions that can function apart from Vico's philosophy. There is not some criterion that exists independently of Vico's *fantasia* that guides *fantasia* toward truth. All that guides *fantasia* is the sense of ignorance, an unwillingness to reduce the mind's uncertainty by embracing what is familiar to the mind. This sense of ignorance leads us to reach out past our inclination to make experience familiar through the power of the concept and to engage the power of the image. We must reconstruct the human world not through concepts and criteria but as something we can practically see.

CHAPTER 6

Rhetoric

Vico's conception of a science of the human world combines elements from the two spheres of his activity—his involvement in the natural scientific researches of the Academy of the *Investiganti* in Naples and his profession as a teacher of rhetoric, including his study of jurisprudence. At the end of his discussion of poetic logic in the *New Science* Vico says: "Providence gave good guidance to human affairs when it aroused human minds first to topics rather than to criticism, for acquaintance with things must come before judgment of them. Topics has the function of making minds inventive, as criticism has that of making them exact. And in those first times all things necessary to human life had to be invented, and invention is the property of genius."[1] The distinction between criticism and topics dates back to Vico's oration *On the Study Methods of Our Time* (1708/1709), in which he connects this distinction to the quarrel between the moderns and the ancients, between the conceptual criticism of modern scientific thought and the topical and inventive powers of language employed by the ancients to give form to the thought and activity of the human world.

In the *Study Methods*, Vico's aim is to balance the merits of the

[1]*New Science*, §498.

moderns and the ancients.[2] These two forces in the thought of Vico's own historical period are incorporated as forces within the personality of his own thought—in his understanding of the practice of the new sciences of nature and in his grasp of the importance of language and eloquence for acts of human will and decision, especially in law. The *New Science* does not balance the merits of these two modes of thought against each other as does the earlier *Study Methods*, but combines them as factors in a single mode. I wish to understand the role of rhetoric in the *New Science*, and in so doing to focus on what is traditionally only a part of rhetoric—topics.

In its specific subject matter and approach my account differs from Andrea Battistini's *La degnità della retorica: Studi su G. B. Vico*[3] and Hayden White's discussion of "tropics."[4] But it agrees in general spirit with these approaches, sharing their view that Vico's conception of rhetoric is new and causes us to rethink our traditional view of rhetoric. Both of these approaches, in quite different ways, emphasize Vico's theory of tropes—metaphor, metonymy, synecdoche, and irony—with White making special use of "tropics," the older English word for tropes. My interest is in moving from topics to tropes. I wish to go back in philosophical terms to a sense of topics, or "places," as the basis for ordering and initiating human speech, and to understand tropes, figures of speech, as the logic for the narration of topics.

The Academy of the Investigators, as I have mentioned in the preceding chapter, and as Fisch has shown in his essay on this subject,[5] was part of a tradition of thought in which members

[2]*Study Methods*, p. 5.

[3]Andrea Battistini, *La degnità della retorica: Studi su G. B. Vico* (Pisa: Pacini Editore, 1975), esp. ch. 4.

[4]Hayden White, "The Tropics of History: The Deep Structure of the *New Science*," in *Giambattista Vico's Science of Humanity*, ed. Giorgio Tagliacozzo and Donald Phillip Verene (Baltimore: The Johns Hopkins University Press, 1976), pp. 65–85. See also Hayden White, *Tropics of Discourse* (Baltimore: The Johns Hopkins University Press, 1978).

[5]Max H. Fisch, "The Academy of the Investigators," in *Science, Medicine, and History: Essays on the Evolution of Scientific Thought and Medical Practice Written in Honour of Charles Singer*, ed. E. Ashworth Underwood, 2 vols. (London: Oxford University Press, 1953), I, 521–63.

prepared papers on natural scientific and historical subjects and conducted some experiments and empirical observations. None of the work of the successive versions of the Academy during the almost ninety years of its life (1649–1737) had any important effect, except whatever effect it may have had on Vico's *New Science*.[6] One of Vico's specific contributions to the Academy was his paper in 1699, "Delle cene suntuose de' Romani" (On the Sumptuous Dinners of the Romans),[7] written in the same year as Vico's first Inaugural Oration at the University of Naples. Vico's friend, Lucantonio Porzio, was a researcher in natural scientific subjects and had been a member of several academies, including that established in Rome by Queen Christina of Sweden. Porzio was a member of the *Investiganti* and taught at Naples during the period of Vico's conception of the *New Science*. He was a critic for Vico's scientific treatise, now lost, *De aequilibrio corporis animantis* (On the Equilibrium of the Living Body).[8]

Perhaps Vico took specific ideas or absorbed particular methodological elements from his participation in the activity of the *Investiganti* and his friendship with thinkers such as Porzio but, above all, he took from this activity a spirit proper to scientific inquiry. Vico comes closest to the attitude of inquiry characteristic of natural scientific thought in his emphasis on considering the specifics of the human world and considering them in their own terms. Vico wishes to see the universal aspects of the particulars of the human world, but he wishes to find these universals in what is actually there. He thinks in terms of finding the inner form of things rather than in terms of making a prior metaphysical decision about the nature of human society and then proceeding to extract the meaning of the particular from the metaphysics of the universal. The reader is invited to ascertain the correctness of the views of the *New Science* by an examination of the details of human history. Vico's conceits (*borie*) of nations and of scholars are foundations of his science in that

[6]Ibid., p. 552.
[7]Ibid., p. 547.
[8]Ibid., p. 552.

they present the pitfalls the mind can encounter in its attempt to comprehend its own nature. This spirit of investigation is in tune with the spirit of the Academy's device of a setting dog and their motto, adapted from Lucretius, of *Vestigia lustrat.*[9] The members of the Academy aimed to seek out the truth for themselves and not to profess to have found it already by a priori arguments.

This spirit of inquiry, of seeking the light of truth without dogmatic claim to possess it already, is an important part of Vico's science, but it is not enough for a science of the human world. To have a science of things human we must be able to do more than look carefully and inductively at the materials of history. We must be able to grasp the inner form of the philological particulars, to comprehend how they function to make up the whole of the human world. For this Vico employs his original understanding of law and rhetoric. As he points out in the *Study Methods,* the study of jurisprudence and rhetoric, as well as poetic, is tied to the art of topics.[10] As was indicated previously, the first sketch of the idea of the *New Science* arises within his study of the basis of law. In the second part of *Universal Law, De constantia iurisprudentis* (On the Constancy of the Jurisprudent), Vico not only advances an outline of the new science[11] but also discusses heroic language in terms of ingenuity (*ingegno*), which

---

[9]Adopted by the *Investiganti* in 1663. Ibid., p. 526. In Lucretius:

I could mention many things,
Pile up a heap of argument-building proof,
But why? You have some sense, and these few hints
Ought to suffice. You can find out for yourself.
As mountain-ranging hounds smell out a lair,
An animal's covert, hidden under brush,
Once they are certain of its track, so you,
All by yourself, in matters such as these,
Can see one thing from another, find your way
To the dark burrows and bring truth to light.

(Lucretius, *The Way Things Are: The De Rerum Natura of Titus Lucretius Carus,* trans. Rolfe Humphries [Bloomington: Indiana University Press, 1968], p. 32.)

[10]*Study Methods,* sec. 3.

[11]*De constantia iurisprudentis, pars posterior,* ch. 1.

162

is connected with the origin of poetic speech and the tropes that characterize its form.[12] Vico's understanding of rhetoric goes back to his Inaugural Orations (1699–1707) and *Study Methods* (1708/1709) and to his *Institutiones oratoriae* (1711), all of which show that Vico always believed rhetoric, philosophy, and law to have primary connections with each other.[13]

Vico's conception of rhetoric is the key to his construction of the inner form of the human world. His concern with rhetoric and its relation to truth reaches from the earliest work of his original philosophy to his last, his 1737 address to the Academy of Oziosi on the connection between philosophy and eloquence.[14] Latin eloquence, or rhetoric, was the subject in which Vico was completely learned. To approach the *New Science* without attention to Vico's conception of rhetoric is to miss one of the bases on which it is founded. What is Vico's concept of rhetoric? How does it provide him with a basis for a science of the inner form of the human world?

Traditionally rhetoric is seen as separate from the concerns of philosophy. Logic is understood as the concern for truth in its proper form and rhetoric as the concern for the means of persuasion. In this common view rhetoric is regarded as a type of thought that plays on the emotions, an instrument to be used for good and for ill. This view holds that if we have come to a truth through proper reasoning, we may then avail ourselves of rhetoric as a means to persuade and communicate its value to others. If we possess no such truth to communicate, but possess the means of rhetoric to play on the emotions and sensibilities, we may persuade listeners of what we will, of whatever our talent and their reason will allow. In this view rhetoric, if not directed by truth founded on logical grounds, becomes an instrument of power over listeners. In this sense rhetoric is seen as

[12]Ibid., ch. 12.

[13]On the significance of the *Institutiones oratoriae* see Alessandro Giuliani, "Vico's Rhetorical Philosophy and the New Rhetoric," in *Giambattista Vico's Science of Humanity,* pp. 31–46.

[14]"Le accademie e i rapporti tra la filosofia e l'eloquenza," *Opere* 7: 33–37.

the guise of thought, a way of seeming to think without any standards of correct thinking.

This notion of rhetoric as the speech of the emotions and as the instrument for the swaying of opinion is grounded in the Cartesian conception of knowledge and constitutes the modern side of the quarrel between the moderns and the ancients. This quarrel had developed in Italy from the sixteenth century up to the time of Vico. As Vico treats this quarrel in the *Study Methods,* the educational concepts of the moderns are based on a view of thought as essentially propositional, deductive, and evidential. The activity of memory and imagination, which the ancients connected with poetic, rhetoric, and jurisprudence, is seen as superfluous to the production of knowledge.

In the *Discourse on Method* Descartes bases the conception of knowledge as centered in the scientific concept on the notion that there is a single method for all knowledge. Only that which can be understood through a single method of thought is regarded as knowledge, all else is not a true and profitable way of thinking. The unity of knowledge which can be visualized from Descartes' four-step method of understanding is attained at the expense of dismissing the powers of memory and imagination and the variability of thought forms that they generate. Cartesian mentality is singlemindedness. All oppositions between elements of thought are eliminated in the success of the method. All connections between concepts and all supporting evidence brought from the senses are articulated through the method.

Poetic, rhetoric, and jurisprudence cannot be pursued in terms of a unified method because they comprehend oppositions in diverse ways. They make them intelligible without the articulation of a category that reduces the opposition to a single plane. Poetic, rhetoric, and jurisprudence are narrations of the oppositions of human experience. At their root is the *mythos* or true narration,[15] which gives immediate form to the benign and malignant forces that characterize the experience of the first

[15]*New Science,* §401.

164

men. In the language of poetic, rhetoric, and jurisprudence oppositions are moved in tandem. The oppositions of human experience are seen but there is not a resolution of these oppositions through a single method.

The production of a poem, a speech, or a legal interpretation allows us to hold in mind a fundamental opposition between universal and particular. The opposition is held within their form. It is not possible to turn such a form into a determinate rule or to arrive at such a form through an analytic method. The forms generated by our powers of memory and imagination orient us toward oppositions and make possible human choice. Oppositions are dealt with in a determinate fashion only in such acts of choice. Out of these acts human society is made in accordance with the conception of authority discussed in the preceding chapter.

Vico's science is a science of narration. It is a science that presents in language the inner form of the life of humanity. This is a literary science, the proof of which is in its meditation in the language of narration. There are no experiments to be performed or evidences to be gathered to confirm its truth that are independent of its act of meditation. The *New Science* is a representation by the mind to the mind of the way in which humanity has all elements in common with itself. This must be done in such a fashion that the bond between the particular and the universal is expressed and all the elements of the human world are understood through causes. This requires that rhetoric be understood as a science of narration which can comprehend the particulars of the human world in terms of necessity. Narration must tell us the story of the human world as the necessary sequence of the ideal eternal history. Narration and necessity are joined.

Understood in this sense rhetoric is an activity in which the mind constructs a knowledge of itself. As this master form of thought, narration is always as much about the subject to which its attention is directed as it is about its own nature. In narration a particular *subject* is constituted for thought, and at the same time what *narration* is is constituted for thought anew. There can be no method of narration in the sense of method advanced by Descartes in the *Discourse on Method*. Not only is narration self-reflexive, but, even more important, in narration the universal element never brings the particular element under a determinant principle of unity. Narration is the language of oppositions of which there is no dialectical or categorical resolution. Oppositions are embraced in the form of narration but not resolved.

In the "Author's Letter" to the *Principles of Philosophy* Descartes speaks of philosophy as a tree in which morals is the highest branch and the "last degree of wisdom," but he produces no such science.[16] Although Descartes has views on morals, conduct, and society which he expresses in various places, in particular in his letters to Princess Elizabeth, the relationship of knowledge to action and society remains largely that of the provisional maxims of conduct set down in the third section of the *Discourse*.[17] Once the possibility of narration as a form of knowledge is excluded, no philosophy of society or authority is possible.

Thought does not begin its life among the first men as an activity of problem solving and analysis, nor does it maintain itself as a living spirit in the course of the ideal eternal history in terms of such a method. What Vico calls criticism (that which the moderns made the basis of knowledge and education) exists always within the larger life of human culture, which itself depends upon our powers of poetic, rhetorical, and jurisprudential formation. To confine thought to a single method, to truth as clarity, as Vico says in *On the Ancient Wisdom of the Italians*, is to see as if by a lamp at night.[18] We see only what the lamp will show us. Conceptual criticism presupposes the powers of thought to

---

[16]*The Philosophical Works of Descartes*, trans. Elizabeth Haldane and G. R. T. Ross, 2 vols. (Cambridge: Cambridge University Press, 1931), I, 211.

[17]See the letters to Princess Elizabeth in *Oeuvres de Descartes*, ed. C. Adam and P. Tannery, 13 vols. (Paris, 1897–1913), IV.

[18]*De Italorum sapientia*, ch. 4, sec. 2.

originate forms. The theory of topics, or *topoi*, in rhetoric provides the key for understanding how thought brings forth form. What is a *topos*? What is Vico's special understanding of it?

I wish to consider these questions from three standpoints: (1) the relation of *topos* to Vico's "three memories," principally the third of these, ingenuity (*ingegno*); (2) the relation of *topos* and metaphor; and (3) the relation of *topos* to the common sense of humanity, *sensus communis*.

(1) In the passage quoted at the beginning of this chapter Vico says that "topics has the function of making minds inventive" and that the power of invention, or *ingegno*, was crucial in the times of the first men when out of necessity everything had to be invented. In his composite notion of memory consisting of *memoria, fantasia,* and *ingegno*, Vico says that *ingegno* occurs within memory when in relation to things "it gives them a new turn or puts them into proper arrangement and relationship."[19] *Ingegno* does not function alone, but is always connected with the other two powers of memory. It is part of the originating power of mind, of the mind's ability to make an object appear within the flux of sensation in which every sensation cancels the one before it. Specifically, *ingegno* is the power to extend what is made to appear from sensation beyond the unit of its appearance and to have it enter into connection with all else that is made by the mind from sensation.

In the *Study Methods* Vico discusses the notion of topics in relation to reasoning and conceptual judgment. Arguments must be invented before they can be criticized according to the principles of logic. Such invention requires *ars topica*, or the art of finding the middle term.[20] In his discussion of the art of judgment in *De dignitate et de augmentis scientiarum* (Of the Dignity and Advancement of Learning), a work that Vico cites in the first line of the *Study Methods*, Bacon says: "So then this art of judg-

[19]*New Science*, §819.
[20]*Study Methods*, p. 15.

ment by syllogism is but the reduction of propositions to principles in a middle term."[21] The middle term of a syllogism, that is,
the term common to the two premises of a syllogism and that
which makes possible the connection between the subject and
predicate of the conclusion, is the traditional basis of any line of
reasoning.

The invention of an argument requires the invention of the
middle term of the syllogism. The creation of the middle term
and the needed premises are aspects of a common process; they
come into being at the same time. One of the editors of Bacon's
works in the last century, Joseph Devey, remarks on this passage:
"Thus, to develop his thought, when a certain attribute does not
appear to belong to a proposed subject, the logician must present another subject, in which the contested quality is admitted
by his hearers to enter, and having shown that this new subject—
the middle term—may be affirmed of the original subject with
which he set out, he concludes that its inseparable attribute must
also belong to it. If these two primary propositions, viz. those
which affirm the attribute of the middle term, and connect this
term with the original subject, need proof, he is obliged to seek
other middle terms, and employ them in the same manner, until
he establish his disputed premises on the basis of experience or
consentaneous principles. If such fundaments, common to the
minds of the disputants, do not exist, the argument is nugatory,
and rational conviction impossible."[22]

This invention of an argument depends upon seeking out
something that will be generally accepted by a community of
hearers. This element of general acceptance gives the argument
a locus or place from which to work, without which no argument
is meaningful. We may apply the principles of evaluating syllo-
gistic reasoning as much as we like, but we are then engaged
only in the abstract process of criticizing the argument's form. If

[21]*The Works of Francis Bacon*, ed. J. Spedding, R. L. Ellis, and D. D. Heath, 14
vols. (London: Longman et al., 1857–74), IV, 429.

[22]*The Physical and Metaphysical Works of Lord Bacon*, ed. Joseph Devey (London:
George Bell, 1894), pp. 204–5, note.

the syllogism's subject is not based on the mentality of the hearers, nothing is being illuminated.

In the preceding chapter of *De dignitate*, Bacon discusses topics and says that "the invention of arguments is not properly an invention."[23] This, Bacon says, is because arguments must exist between persons who have a command of a subject matter. Thus what is invented is more a matter of recalling what is already known than real invention. Bacon concludes: "Nevertheless, as the name has come into use, let it be called invention; for the hunting of any wild animal may be called a finding of it, as well in an enclosed park as in a forest at large."[24] Ingenuity in this sense is more an art for the ready use of thought than for the enlargement of thought itself.

In the *Study Methods* Vico discusses *ingenium* in terms of the invention of arguments; he ties the faculty of ingenuity to imagination and memory and says that the young must be educated in common sense, or *sensus communis*.[25] Only if the young are given this orientation can they reason successfully when they attain maturity and command full powers of reasoning and metaphysical thought. In both the *Study Methods* and the *Ancient Wisdom*, Vico suggests but does not develop a deeper sense of topics and invention.[26] In the *New Science* Vico deepens his view of topics and invention by connecting them to his conception of the origin of mind and the imaginative universal. The sense of invention that Bacon compares to real hunting as opposed to hunting in a park, wherein the mind brings into being the middle terms of experience itself rather than just the middle terms of specific arguments within the frameworks of existing subject matters, is developed in the *New Science*. In so doing Vico develops a view much wider than Bacon's notion of invention. In Vico's account the human world is itself invented through the art of topics.

[23]*Works*, IV, 421.
[24]Ibid., 422.
[25]*Study Methods*, pp. 12–13.
[26]*De Italorum sapientia*, ch. 7, sec. 5.

Vico's concern in the *New Science* is not how *ingegno* functions to discover the middle term between premises within a known subject matter, but how *ingegno* functions in a primordial way to produce any connection in experience at all. In terms of the art of logical judgment this is not the question of the connection between premises done by the middle term, but the question of how a first premise is generated at all. Vico carries Bacon's notion of real hunting far beyond Bacon. Vico says in the *New Science*: "The first founders of humanity applied themselves to a sensory topics, by which they brought together those properties or qualities or relations of individuals and species which were, so to speak, concrete, and from these created their poetic genera."[27]

Vico's notion of a "sensory topics," a *topica sensibile,* is tied to his conception of sensibility as a way of thinking—the notion that when sense takes the form of the imaginative universal in the *fantasia* of the first men, it is a kind of thought. A sensory *topos*, as Fisch points out in a remark on this passage, is related to Aristotle's conception of topics, or places, that could be kept in mind and serve for the inventing of probable arguments.[28] The fundamental difference is that the sensory *topos* is achieved through feeling and not achieved as an element within discursive thought.

In the first sentence of the *Topics* Aristotle says that the purpose of his study is to find a way whereby we can reason from generally accepted opinions about any topic presented to us. Topics is not a process of rational demonstration because such reasoning proceeds from premises that are primary and true. Topics is the basis of what Aristotle calls "dialectical" reasoning, lines of reasoning which proceed from what is generally accepted opinion rather than what is primary and true. In Aristotle's view what is generally accepted is what is generally held in a discursive sense. It is what is believed by everyone, by most people, or by those particularly learned. Vico's view asks the

---

[27]*New Science*, §495.
[28]Fisch, Introduction, *New Science*, par. K5, note.

fundamental question of how we come to have such commonalities of mind at all. On what do these discursive topics depend? His answer is his notion of the sensory *topos*.

In Vico's view we come to what is generally accepted on the basis of felt unities, felt places or *loci*. Our ability to feel in common through our senses brings into being commonplaces of the human world. The sensory *topos* of Jove is the first commonality. Jove is the first name and the first place from which human thought brings itself forth. Through *ingegno* this power of the first name is extended throughout experience. As a name the first men are able to find the universal meaning of the thunder as Jove in each repetition of thunder. Through their powers of *ingegno* they are able to name all of nature in terms of gods, once one feature of nature is named. All nature is put "into proper arrangement and relationship." The sensory *topos* is not a primary truth for demonstrative reasoning but a kind of probability in terms of which the mind can become alive and against which it can develop its life. Its meaning is "tested out" in the subsequent development of mind.

In the *Rhetoric* Aristotle presents the notion of topics as a theory of speaking on a subject. A *topos* is literally a "place" or region, a commonplace. It is something the speaker may in advance of his speaking commit to memory as a place to be retained in the background of his mind. While speaking he can return to this original association and bring it forth as a means to develop a point he needs at the moment. Lane Cooper, in commenting on the *Rhetoric*, remarks that a topic is something from which we literally draw forth something. "But the sound rhetorician does draw one thing *from* another. Thus we come to the preposition *ek* (or *ex*), which is characteristic of Aristotle's thought, but often is hard or impossible to translate directly. The speaker is supposed to have resources, *from which* he draws his arguments and illustrations."[29] Vico says: "Topics is the art of finding in any-

---

[29]*The Rhetoric of Aristotle,* ed. and trans. Lane Cooper (New York: Appleton-Century-Crofts, 1960), p. xxiii.

thing all that is in it."[30] To prove (*apodeiknynai*) is to show something on the basis of something else. But to speak in accordance with a *topos* is to draw forth something from something. The topic involves an active sense of drawing from a place. The rhetorician must reach into the background of his mind and draw out what is needed in his speech. In the second book of the *Rhetoric* Aristotle lists twenty-eight *topoi* from which to draw enthymemes. These are topics understood as ways in which lines of argument can be found.

The sensory *topos* of Vico differs from Aristotle's conception in that it is a theory of how the background of the mind itself is created. It is the basis of human speech itself rather than the notion of even general topics from which particular speeches can be developed. The sensory *topos* is presupposed as the notion of fundamental places or images that give the human mind its character and on which it must draw in order for human speech to achieve meaning. Jove as the first name is drawn forth from the flux of sensation. The mind then has a place from which it can find again a basis for meaning in the placeless movement of sensation. *Ingegno* as the ultimate moment of Vico's threefold sense of memory is the *drawing from* Jove, as the original imaginative universal, the power to move human speech across nature and turn other sensations of it into gods. Through this inventive process nature is turned into culture.

(2) A sensory *topos* is an imaginative universal, a *universale fantastico*. As discussed in the third chapter, the imaginative universal is a theory of the metaphor that sees metaphor as based in identity rather than likeness or similarity. The traditional notion of the metaphor as the likening of one thing to another arises from Aristotle's definition in the *Poetics*: "Metaphor consists in giving the thing a name that belongs to something else."[31] This transference can be done in various ways, from genus to species, species to genus, etc. Metaphor in its root meaning is to bear or

---

[30]*Autobiography*, p. 124.

[31]Aristotle, *On the Art of Poetry*, ed. and trans. Ingram Bywater (Oxford: Clarendon Press, 1909), p. 63.

to carry. Metaphorical speech is that which transfers signification (*metapherein*). A name or descriptive term is borne or carried
to an object different from but analogous to that to which the
term is properly applicable. The bonding between things
achieved by metaphor is traditionally understood as the power
to perceive the similarity between things. Aristotle says: "But the
greatest thing by far is to be a master of metaphor. It is the one
thing that cannot be learnt from others; and it is also a sign of
genius, since a good metaphor implies an intuitive perception of
the similarity in dissimilars."[32]

The sense of metaphor present in Vico's notion of the imaginative universal requires us to take a step back in consciousness and consider the notion of transference in the metaphor as
linked more to identity than to the notion of similarity. The
universale fantastico is a conception of how the mind has anything
before it at all, how it has something before it from which to
draw forth meaning rather than nothing at all. It is a theory of
the first thought. The mind's first act is a transference or bearing of meaning from sensation as placeless, momentary flux to
the fixation of sensation as a god. First and foremost the *universale fantastico* is a conception of the *is*. The carrying of particular
sensation to a fixed place or universal of sense, an imaginative
universal of Jove, is the appearance of *is* in experience. The *is*, or
identity, appears from the first moment with a double meaning—as *being* and as *copula*, as permanence and as relation. In
the imaginative universal something *is* for the mind, whereas
otherwise there exists only the nothing of sensation in flux, and
something *is* "in relation."

Jove and thunder are identical. The thunder is Jove. What
is first felt as an imaginative universal can later be formulated
as elements of a logical judgment, once consciousness has
developed to the level of conceptual criticism in the ideal eternal history. Originally what the mind can think resides in the
imaginative universal's power to transfer thunder as sense into

[32]Ibid., p. 71.

Jove as sensed. Jove is sensed as fear, but not merely as fear. Fear is a place, a sensory *topos*, a fixation of the body wherein the experience of Jove's great shaking body of the sky is found and found again. The identity between the elements of this first thought is that presupposed in the logical judgment. The law of identity that A is A does not describe the relation of subject and predicate in the traditional logical proposition since the predicate is always a B and not another A. This has been well known since Antisthenes the Cynic in the fourth century B.C. It is a scandal of logical thought that it cannot make clear the very basis upon which judgment itself is possible. Vico's theory of imaginative universals provides us with such a basis.

The conception of metaphor involved in the *universale fantastico* is an understanding of how the *is* itself comes into consciousness. The *is* is not given in nature. It requires a sense of language that is beyond the powers of logical language. The key to such language is found in rhetorical language, in topics, which treats of how bases for speech can be brought forth in the mind. Vico's *universale fantastico* as a conception of both topic and metaphor is a conception of how the mind brings forth its own being. Before we can speak of metaphor as the transference of signification between objects, we must be able to speak of transference itself as present in consciousness. This is the sense of transference from particular to universal meaning which occurs within *fantasia* as structured by Vico's threefold form of memory, the harmonious working of *memoria, fantasia,* and *ingegno*.

The genius or *ingegno* required for finding what is common between things is possible only because of the primordial power of transference between particular and universal which is accomplished within *fantasia*, within the unit of the *universale fantastico*. Metaphor can be understood as likeness or similarity only if we ignore its role in relation to the *is*. To regard the constructive power of metaphor as based on its analogical capacity is also to presuppose its primordial power to construct the *is*. In a metaphor not deliberately formed as a logical proportionality, the two objects involved are no more *like* each other than is the subject *like* the predicate in the logical judgment. When we view a living metaphor as an object of analytic examination or employ it as a theoretical tool, it can be turned into an analogy. But the notion of analogy or similarity does not describe the nature of its being.

Vico's conception of metaphor as based on identity and not on likeness between things reverses the understanding of metaphor which has developed since Aristotle. Metaphor conceived as the imaginative universal is also the touchstone between topics and tropes. The metaphor is that through which a *topos* is originally formed. It is a fundamental image from which the mind can begin to speak. The speech of the first men as brought forth from such *topoi* is not developed through the elements of logical form. It is developed through the figures of speech, or tropes, that make up the form of poetic or rhetorical speech. Metaphor, as Vico says, is the most fundamental of the tropes; it is "the most luminous and therefore the most necessary."[33] Metaphor is the primary figure of speech, the trope through which mythical speech is elaborated once it is begun by metaphor in its role as *topos*.

(3) A *topos* in Vico's sense is brought about by a metaphor conceived as an imaginative universal. Sensory topics are the primordial places, or *loci,* of the human mind. They make up its common sense, its *sensus communis*. In the *Study Methods* Vico says that the young must be educated in memory and imagination so that they can acquire common sense. Without common sense there is no basis for the mind to bring forth the basis of arguments. Vico's notion of *sensus communis*, like that of Shaftesbury,[34] is not a body of empirical knowledge to be understood as quasi-scientific in nature. Common sense understood as *sensus communis* is not a loose form of scientific or theoretical thought. *Sensus communis* consists of those modes of speech, feel-

---

[33]*New Science*, §404. Cf. *Institutiones oratoriae* (1711), *Opere* 8, No. 38, p. 190.

[34]Shaftesbury, "*Sensus Communis*: An Essay on the Freedom of Wit and Humor," Treatise II of *Characteristics of Men, Manners, Opinions, Times*, ed. John M. Robertson (Indianapolis: Bobbs-Merrill, 1964).

ing, and outlook which are the communal ground of the life of a nation.

This *sensus communis* is formed through the sensory topics which Vico calls the primary operation of the mind. The primary operation of the mind involves the three faculties of memory, imagination, and ingenuity "whose regulating art is topics."[35] Vico says: "So that we may truly say that the first age of the world occupied itself with the primary operation of the human mind. And first it began to hew out topics, which is an art of regulating well the primary operation of our mind by noting the commonplaces that must all be run over in order to know all there is in a thing that one desires to know well; that is, completely."[36] The commonplaces that must be run over to know humanity, to know the common nature of nations, are the *universali fantastici* that stand behind all nations. These make up what Vico calls the common mental dictionary.[37]

This notion of the mental dictionary, of the *vocabolario* or *dizionario mentale*, is one of the three passages from the first *New Science* (1725) that Vico says should be retained in relation to the definitive version of the *New Science* (1730/1744).[38] In the second *New Science* Vico mentions the concept of a mental dictionary in various places.[39] He connects it with the notion of a common sense of the human race in the general philosophical axioms of Book I. In axiom twelve Vico states: "Common sense is judgment without reflection, shared by an entire class, an entire people, an entire nation, or the entire human race." He continues: "This axiom, with the following definition, will provide a new art of criticism concerning the founders of nations."[40] The definition to which Vico refers is stated in axiom thirteen as:

---

[35]*New Science*, §699.

[36]*New Science*, §§496–97.

[37]*New Science*, §§35 and 145.

[38]*Autobiography*, p. 192. See also *Scienza nuova prima*, bk. 3, ch. 43. *New Science*, §445.

[39]E.g., *New Science*, §§35, 141–45, 161–62, 445, 482, 527, and 542.

[40]*New Science*, §§142–43.

"Uniform ideas originating among entire peoples unknown to each other must have a common ground of truth."[41]

Common sense, *il senso comune*, is "judgment without reflection" shared by a human social group, including a group as large as the "entire human race." A sensory *topos* is a judgment without reflection. It proceeds directly from sensation as formed by the imagination or *fantasia*. Such a *topos* is made by feeling the world in concert with other humans. There is a *senso comune*, or *sensus communis*, for the entire human race that underlies all human activity and does not vary from nation to nation or people to people. This is the basis of the "new art of criticism," the *nuova arte critica*, upon which all of Vico's *scienza nuova* depends. This new art, which was the subject of the preceding chapter, allows us to achieve a science of mythology by joining philology and philosophy.

Vico says that "the first science to be learned should be mythology or the interpretation of fables."[42] We learn from this that thought as it exists at the origin of any *nazione* begins in the same way. It has the same form regardless of the time (chronology) or place (geography) of its origin. The thought of the origin is uniform from nation to nation. Judgment without reflection takes the same form at any origin although the particular content of mythology can differ from people to people. The gods have different names but they become gods by a common act of thought. Because all thought begins in *fantasia* and because *fantasia* is a genuine kind of thought, there is a common sense of the human race. Vico says: "Thence issues the mental dictionary for assigning origins to all the diverse articulated languages. It is by means of this dictionary that the ideal eternal history is conceived, which gives us the histories in time of all nations."[43]

The solution to the Tower of Babel is that behind all articulated languages there is a linguistic function that is identified

[41]*New Science*, §144.
[42]*New Science*, §51.
[43]*New Science*, §145.

with *fantasia*. This mental language, this *lingua mentale comune*, is what is made articulate in language as it appears in symbols.[44] Whenever we use an actual language to communicate, our ability to achieve meaning is based on the common mental language that contains the commonplaces of human mentality itself and that is a product of our *fantasia*. Fundamental human communication depends upon us making touch with this common mental language in a direct fashion. Something of this process can be grasped from the later works of Joyce, *Ulysses* and *Finnegans Wake,* in which Joyce uses a kind of language behind language. In reading these works we sense that below the articulations of our specific language there lies a language of all languages. Words and meanings are conjoined in a kind of first language of imagination, of imaginative universals. It is as if in *Finnegans Wake* Joyce tried to speak the unspeakable language of the *lingua mentale comune*.

The first language was mute, Vico says. In it the common mental language is directly expressed in the gesture, in the physical object and the act. The *sensus communis* is employed as a means of direct communication in Vico's recounting of the "five real words" that Idanthyrsus, king of the Scythians, sent to Darius the Great, who had declared war on him. "These five were a frog, a mouse, a bird, a ploughshare, and a bow. The frog signified that he, Idanthyrsus, was born of the earth of Scythia as frogs are born of the earth in summer rains, so that he was a son of that land. The mouse signified that he, like a mouse, had made his home where he was born; that is, that he had established his nation there. The bird signified that there the auspices were his; that is, that he was subject to none but God. The ploughshare signified that he had reduced those lands to cultivation, and thus tamed and made them his own by force. And finally the bow signified that as supreme commander of the arms of Scythia he had the duty and the might to defend her."[45]

These objects can be understood as *topoi* sent by Idanthyrsus

[44]*New Science,* §161.
[45]*New Science,* §435.

to Darius. They are memory places, things to remind him of certain things he already knows from the fact that he is the ruler of a nation. What he is reminded of is in fact what a nation is. His memory is called back to the *sensus communis* of the origin of any nation. These objects are *topoi*, not unlike what an orator might arbitrarily use to remind himself of points in a speech, things which he would think of to move from point to point. Here the *topoi* are not employed as artificial aids to memory but as direct means to achievement of communication. Idanthyrsus in effect sent to Darius the Great some pieces of the common mental vocabulary. One is reminded of Vico's use of the various objects in the frontispiece to instruct the reader of the fundamental points of the *New Science*. He uses the ploughshare in the same sense as this example, to signify the reduction of lands to cultivation.

Human choice as well as human thought is based on common sense. Law, which gives basis to human choice, is not based in Vico's view on conceptual criticism. Law grows from the common sense of a people. Human choice exercised in the furthering of social order is based on the recollection of this common sense. The interpretation of law, in Vico's view, is not done solely through conceptual criticism but involves the connecting of the law with the common sense out of which the law itself has developed. Vico points out in the *Study Methods* that jurisprudence is based on the art of topics, of invention rather than criticism. *Ingegno* is required for the making of a legal interpretation as well as the making of a poem or a speech. *Ingegno* allows us to call forth what we need from the *sensus communis* of humanity or a particular people.

Vico considered his interpretation of the Roman Law of the Twelve Tables to be a major discovery. His passages on this subject in *Universal Law* are one of the few portions of his early work that he wishes remembered in connection with the *New Science*.[46] Vico maintains on the basis of his new science that the

---

[46]*Autobiography*, p. 193; *New Science*, §§26 and 29. See also *De constantia iurisprudentis, pars posterior*, chs. 36–37.

traditional notion that the Twelve Tables, the basis of Roman law, were brought to Rome from Greece is false. Vico holds that the Tables were without authorship; they were simply the expression of the common sense or consciousness of the Roman people themselves.[47]

Fisch points out in his essay, "Vico on Roman Law," that Vico's treatment of this great discovery parallels his other great discovery, that of the "true Homer."[48] The third book of the *New Science* concerns the discovery of the true Homer as a demonstration of the truth of the theory of poetic wisdom presented in Book II. Vico's purpose is to show that there is no authorship to Homer's works in the ordinary sense and that the mind of the Greek people is their author. This view derives from Vico's discussion of the origin of poetry in *Universal Law*.[49]

For Vico the Twelve Tables and the true Homer are instances of the *sensus communis*. Not only are they embodiments of the unconscious wisdom of humanity, but once in existence they function as keys to common sense such that we can call forth from them commonplaces for subsequent decisions and choices. The Law of the Twelve Tables and the true Homer are not pieces of esoteric philosophical wisdom. They are pieces of common wisdom.

Behind the senses in which topics is related in Vico's thought to *ingegno*, metaphor, and common sense is a wider understanding of topics and of the relation of philosophy to rhetoric. Vico's new art of criticism that is the basis of the *New Science* is not an art of criticism in the sense of the criticism of concepts that requires the art of topics for its middle terms. Vico's *nuova arte critica* is not an art of the concept. It is an art whereby we grasp philosophical meanings through narrative speech and not through argumentative process. Vico does not base what he is

---

[47]*New Science*, §§284f.

[48]Max H. Fisch, "Vico on Roman Law," in *Essays in Political Theory, Presented to George H. Sabine*, ed. Milton R. Konvitz and Arthur E. Murphy (Ithaca, N.Y.: Cornell University Press, 1948), p. 69.

[49]Ibid. See also *De constantia iurisprudentis, pars posterior*, ch. 12, sec. 21; *Dissertationes, Opere* 2, ch. 4; and *New Science*, §873.

fundamentally saying on arguments, but attempts to present the nature of things directly in his speech. Vico's aim is philosophical wisdom or *sapienza*, not conceptual justifications in the sense of philosophical arguments. To explain this I wish to relate my views to Ernesto Grassi's conception of rhetoric and to move from this to the sense in which Vico's work is a theater of memory with similarity to the work of the Venetian Renaissance thinker Giulio Camillo.

Grassi's view of rhetoric is based on a rereading of classical sources and a revival of the philosophical importance of the views of rhetoric and imagination advanced by the Renaissance Humanists, including such figures as Salutati, Landino, Poliziano, and Gianfrancesco Pico. He sees Vico as part of this Humanist tradition.[50] Grassi has connected rhetoric with the art of first speech rather than with the art of persuasion. To prove something in the sense of a rational process of thought requires that something is shown on the basis of something else. The speech of the rational proof requires a starting point which is not shown within the proof. It can only show something on the basis of something else if its beginning point is itself shown.

The speech of an origin point, of a beginning point of thought, is nondeducible. It is indicative. It shows something directly. Such speech is archaic in the sense of a speech of first principles or *archai*. In his essay, "Rhetoric and Philosophy," Grassi says: "Such speech is immediately a 'showing'—and for this reason 'figurative' or 'imaginative', and thus in the original sense 'theoretical' (*theorein*—i.e., to see). It is metaphorical, i.e., it shows something which has a sense, and this means that to the figure, to that which is shown, the speech transfers (*metapherein*) a signification; in this way the speech which realizes this showing 'leads before the eyes' (*phainesthai*) a significance. This speech is and must be in its structure an imaginative language."[51]

---

[50]E.g., Ernesto Grassi, *Macht des Bildes: Ohnmacht der rationalen Sprache, Zur Rettung des Rhetorischen* (Cologne: M. DuMont Schauberg, 1970), esp. pt. 3.

[51]Ernesto Grassi, "Rhetoric and Philosophy," *Philosophy and Rhetoric*, 9 (1976), 202. See also Ernesto Grassi, *Rhetoric as Philosophy: The Humanist Tradition* (University Park: The Pennsylvania State University Press, 1980).

Rhetoric in its fundamental function is identified with this speech of the *archai*, with the transference through metaphor of the common mental language, to use Vico's terms, into articulate speech. This primary speech, as Grassi holds, reveals itself suddenly. It does not lie in historical time but bursts forth into historical time. To put this in Vico's terms, any archaic speech bursts forth into consciousness with the suddenness of the original burst of Jove which, as the first speech, is the original place or *topos* of consciousness. Such primary speech is providential and prophetic. This speech is not the starting point of rational thought in the sense of employing a proposition that may be derived as a conclusion from another process of reasoning or system of propositions. It is the notion of a beginning point in thought that allows us to reason at all about a subject. Such a beginning point requires that we call forth a *topos* from the *sensus communis*. It requires a fundamental metaphor of reality that allows us to think, to initiate the art of criticism which, Vico says, presupposes the art of invention.

In Grassi's view we can distinguish between three kinds of speech: (1) *"external, 'rhetorical speech'"* that involves images in the sense that it employs them to affect the passions. This is rhetorical speech in the sense of persuasion. It is rhetoric in the common and pejorative sense. (2) A second type of speech is that *"which arises exclusively from a rational proceeding."* Such speech does not have rhetorical effect as its intention. Its aim is to avoid affecting the passions. It is theoretical speech in the standard sense of logical speech. (3) The third type is *"true rhetorical speech.* This springs from the *archai*, non-deducible, moving, and indicative, due to its original images. The original speech is that of the wise man, of the *sophos* who is not only *epistatai* but the man who with insight leads, guides, and attracts."[52]

My contention is that Vico's science is this third type of speech. The speech of recollective *fantasia* which I have claimed is the basis of the *New Science* is the speech of the *sophos*. Vico's *sapienza poetica*, the thought of imaginative universals, of mythic *fantasia*,

[52]Grassi, "Rhetoric and Philosophy," 214.

is reflected on the level of recollective memory as a kind of *sapienza critica* in which Vico shows us the *archai* upon which the human world is based. The speech of Vico's *New Science* bursts forth out of the rational night and shows us the origin of humanity. Our attention is directed to a way of reading the signs of human thought and activity so that we can see their inner form, so that we can see their *storia ideale eterna*. In his *Study Methods* and in his oration "On the Heroic Mind" Vico identifies wisdom with the whole.[53] What we are presented with in the *New Science* is the whole. In Vico's work we are presented not with a new theory of knowledge, but with a new science of wisdom. By this I mean we are presented with a way of speaking about the *archai*, of recollecting and articulating in language the common sense of humanity.

Vico is ordinarily thought of as a philosopher of time. His philosophy is traditionally interpreted as a philosophy of history. In such interpretation his thought is identified with his conception of *corsi* and *ricorsi*, with a theory of cycles of history. My contention is that Vico is above all a philosopher of place, not time.

A nation is a place, a locus in which the ideal eternal history takes place. Etymologically a nation is a "birth," that which comes from a common origin. A *nazione* involves the common life of a people, a common system of institutions. Fisch distinguishes several related senses of the term *nazione* for Vico; in its broad sense this term designates the entire ontogenetic pattern of activity in the human world: "There is not only an original and individual birth for each system [of institutions] but a continual birth of new institutions within it, a continual transformation of old institutions, and even a rebirth of the nation after death."[54] The nation as birth and death requires a geography, a place.

---

[53]*Study Methods,* p. 77. "On the Heroic Mind," trans. Elizabeth Sewell and Anthony C. Sirignano, in *Vico and Contemporary Thought,* ed. Giorgio Tagliacozzo, Michael Mooney, and Donald Phillip Verene (Atlantic Highlands, N.J.: Humanities Press, 1979), pt. 2, pp. 239–40.

[54]Fisch, Introduction, *New Science,* par. B1.

Like the primordial flux of sensation in which each sensation cancels the last, and in which every facial expression is a different face, the primordial forest that covered the earth at the beginning of gentile humanity is without locus or place. The forest is continuous without place for habitation. In the frontispiece of the *New Science* objects are depicted in a clearing in the forest. The globe on which the female figure of metaphysic is standing has a belt around it containing the signs of the zodiac Virgo and Leo. Vico says that Leo "signifies that our Science in its beginnings contemplates first the Hercules that every ancient gentile nation boasts as its founder, and that it contemplates him in his greatest labor. This was the slaying of the lion which, vomiting flame, set fire to the Nemean forest, and adorned with whose skin Hercules was raised to the stars."[55]

In the first *New Science* Vico uses Hercules as a basis for his discussion of the nature of a poetic character.[56] Each nation has its Hercules, as each also has its Jove. They are elements of the common mental vocabulary which are expressed in different names in different languages. Jove is the first place or *topos* from which to think. Hercules through his work signifies the first place in which to act.[57] Before the appearance of Jove in consciousness, thought wanders from one sensation to another. In their actions, in their mode of living, the first men originally wander in the great forest from one life struggle to another. Juno, the wife of Jove, is associated with marriage. The fear of Jove leads the first humans to control their bodies. This fear also leads them to copulate away from the sight of Jove, in caves, and this leads them to marriage. Marriage causes them "to remain in one place with their women [*con le loro donne a star fermi*]."[58] Marriage begins the human sense of place but human society

---

[55] *New Science*, §3.

[56] *Scienza nuova prima*, bk. 3, ch. 5.

[57] See Grassi's remarks on the connection of common sense and work in Vico: "The Priority of Common Sense and Imagination: Vico's Philosophical Relevance Today," in *Vico and Contemporary Thought*, pt. 1, pp. 174–75.

[58] *New Science*, §524.

does not begin until Hercules clears the great forests for cultivation. Juno imposes the great labors on Hercules.[59]

When Hercules clears a place for founding human society, a connection is made between the centerpoint he has established on earth and the sky. Hercules was raised to the stars. The taming of nature by Hercules' work makes possible the human world of culture and at the same time this relationship between nature and culture establishes a relationship to the divine. Only when this threefold set of relationships has been established can there be a *nation*. When there is place for a nation, a "birth," there begins the ideal eternal history of its life. Physical, mental, and social place arise in a common process. They make each other possible. In Vico's view the origin of the human world is neither materialistically based nor based in the idea. Both factors of the human world arise as codeterminations of the human and remain such throughout the course of the ideal eternal history of a nation.

Vico says that time or the reckoning of time begins with the labor of Hercules.[60] Reckoning of time begins with the cultivation of the fields. It does not begin with the apprehension of the sky as Jove. Time reckoning begins only when a physical distinction is made between nature and culture. The appearance of the divine in the form of Jove begins the process of creating place or *topos* for mind, but it is not sufficient for the beginning of time for gentile humanity. Time requires that the opposition between nature and culture be added to that between sky and earth.

This suggests a way to understand how Vico can place the ancient Hebrews outside the principles of ideal eternal history. Vico insists that the *New Science* of the common nature of nations applies only to gentile nations and not to the Hebrews. Fisch points out that this distinction is not clearly and consistently drawn between the Hebrew-Christian tradition and the gentile nations, and that it disappears in the second cycle of ages of

[59]*New Science*, §514.
[60]*New Science*, §§3–4.

Christian Europe as described in the *New Science*.[61] The Hebrews have no Hercules. Their society is not built on labor as the means for establishing culture in the face of nature. Their history is sacred history and not ideal eternal history because it is the direct manifestation of God. The divine is not reached through the intermediate step of the auspices. The practice of divination is necessary for the gentile peoples as a type of spiritual labor that gives purpose to the physical labor of the cultivation of the fields and the building of cities. For the gentile peoples the divine can be approached only indirectly through reading the signs of the divine in nature. Once the place of culture is established in relation to the place of nature, the access to the place of the divine is altered. Vico says a principal difference between the Hebrews and the gentile nations is the prohibition of divination among the Hebrews.[62]

The Hebrew-Christian nation can be seen as an example of providence as simple place which does not take temporal form as ideal eternal history. For the gentile nations providence appears as time acting against place. In the stages of the ideal eternal history, each new stage is achieved by a redefinition of the sense of place which becomes less and less definite in relation to the divine, to the sky. In the first age, place is determined as the clearing and the altar, the *loci* of physical and spiritual work. In the heroic age a new sense of place is developed in the form of the cities. Attention to the sky is offset with horizontal vision. The city is a nearly self-contained reality. In the age of men place becomes indefinite. Place and property are the subject of abstract definition by governments and laws. The nation becomes more and more a temporal sequence whose movement appears historically self-generated rather than charted in terms of the movements of the divine in the sky. Absolute idealism, which is a philosophy of time, reflects on human institutions from this third perspective and fails to understand their real origin in the primitive sense of place.

[61]Fisch, Introduction, *New Science*, par. F7.
[62]*New Science*, §§167–68.

Human society and human thought begin in a sense of place, and our understanding of them ultimately requires a type of thought that is itself based on a sense of place. I have claimed that Vico's *New Science* is a process of recollection, of recollective *fantasia*. This is a kind of memory whereby things are ordered "by a constant and uninterrupted order of causes and effects present in every nation, through three kinds of natures."[63] This memory that proceeds in terms of an order of causes and effects (*ordine di cagioni e d'effetti*) must itself be embodied in a kind of archaic speech that calls up for us the images on which human society rests. It is an art of topics, except these topics are not arbitrarily chosen. They are the topics out of which humanity originally constitutes itself in its sensory acts of ordering the world.

In this sense Vico's *New Science* is in many respects like the fascinating memory theater of Giulio Camillo (c. 1480–1544). Camillo, known as the "divine Camillo," was one of the most famous thinkers of the sixteenth century, but he was all but forgotten after the eighteenth century. The importance of his work has been revived in our day by attention from Paolo Rossi, F. Secret, E. Garin and, most especially, by Frances Yates's discussion of his views in *The Art of Memory*.[64] Is there a sense in which Vico's *New Science* is a work of memory places? Is it a work of *topoi* for philosophical memory?

Camillo's major work is limited to the theater and to *L'idea del Theatro* (1550), his small book explaining its parts, a copy of which exists in the national library in Florence.[65] I do not intend my remarks to add to the interpretation of Camillo, but to see him as a key to viewing Vico's work as an art of memory. It is quite possible that Vico's work can be placed within the tradition

---

[63]*New Science*, §915; see also §1020.

[64]Frances A. Yates, *The Art of Memory* (Chicago: The University of Chicago Press, 1966), chs. 6–7. Regarding the work of others on Camillo see, ibid., p. 130, note 4.

[65]*L'idea del Theatro dell'eccellen. M. Giulio Camillo*, ed. Lodovico Domenichi (Florence: Appresso Lorenzo Torrentino, 1550). Camillo's book is eighty-seven pages in length.

of memory systems developing from such figures as Giordano Bruno, Tommaso Campanella, and Robert Fludd, but this is beyond my concern. I wish to place the idea of a theater of memory beside Vico's *New Science* and ask what this juxtaposition suggests.

The art of memory is classically based on the notion of place. It originates from the incident related by Cicero, in which Simonides was able to identify the bodies of guests killed by the collapse of a roof at a banquet. Simonides, who escaped death by having been called from the hall before its collapse, was able to identify the bodies of the other guests for their relatives by recalling the place at which each had been seated. This suggested to Simonides the possibility of an art of memory based on associating images with places. By associating certain images with a series of places the orator can move through the places and call up the images as he moves through the points of his speech. Yates says: "The art of memory is like an inner writing. Those who know the letters of the alphabet can write down what is dictated to them and read out what they have written. Likewise those who have learned mnemonics can set in places what they have heard and deliver it from memory."[66]

Topoi were frequently rooms or scenes, architectural spaces selected by the orator and formed as images with which to associate certain thoughts to order his speech. The orator's memory goes to the image of each place and brings forth the next point required in the speech. These places are a kind of "inner writing," an inner architecture from which the speech is constructed. *Topoi,* pursued in this way, are aids to the weakness of memory.

Camillo's system of memory differs from this classical conception of memory aids. His system is a system of first causes. Camillo's theater of memory, which was an actual place, a building large enough for at least two persons to enter, was a micro-

[66]*Art of Memory,* pp. 6–7.

cosm of the universe. Yates, whose work contains a diagrammatic reconstruction of the theater, states: "It is because he believes in the divinity of man that the divine Camillo makes his stupendous claim of being able to remember the universe by looking down upon it from above, from first causes, as though he were God. In this atmosphere, the relationship between man, the microcosm, and the world, the macrocosm, takes on a new significance. The microcosm can fully understand and fully remember the macrocosm, can hold it within his divine *mens* or memory."[67] The philosophical presuppositions of Camillo's system are, as Yates says, derived from the hermetic tradition, especially the philosophy of Giordano Bruno. Camillo mentions *Mercurio Trimegisto* (Thrice-great Hermes) in the first pages of the *Idea del Theatro*.

Camillo's theater is not the presentation of aids to the weakness of memory to be used for the preparation of speeches. The theater captures the true speech of the world or, more precisely, the basis of such speech. The world appears in the theater as a place constructed of its own essential places, each reduced and set within the real order of things. Here the *mens* can be tuned to acquire the divine wisdom otherwise hidden in ancient texts. The divine Camillo begins the *Idea del Theatro* with the sentence: "The most ancient and wisest writers have always had the habit of entrusting to their writings the secrets of God under obscure veils, so that they are not understood except by those (as Christ says) who have ears to hear, namely who by God are chosen to grasp his most sacred mysteries."[68]

The theater orients the inner senses to the inner writing of the mind and the world. Camillo says that the theater is ordered with such facility that scholars are made spectators (*che facciamo*

[67]Ibid., pp. 147–48.

[68]The original is: "I piu antichi, & piu saui scrittori hanno sempre hauuto in costume di raccomandare à loro scritti i secreti di Dio sotto oscuri uelami, accio che non siano intesi se non da coloro, i quali (come dice Christo) hanno orecchie da udire, cio è che da Dio sono eletti ad intendere i suoi santissimi misteri" (*L'idea del Theatro*, p. 7).

gli studiosi come spettatori).[69] In the theater the scholar is placed in an immediate relationship to the divine order. He finds himself on the theater's stage, and the eternal places, their symbols and emblems, are spread out before him, all arranged in seven rows running up on seven levels. The scholar is spectator, but a spectator whose position is reversed to assume the perspective of the actor. The memory images or mute language of the real are a waiting audience that faces whoever enters. On entering the theater of Camillo, as on opening Vico's *New Science,* the scholar is placed in a world of fundamental images that he cannot understand.

The experience resembles the original speech which Grassi describes, in which one is placed suddenly in the actor's position in relation to thought. Thought appears not as an instrument for making observations, but as something that speaks. One is not in the position of forming hypotheses and evaluating evidence. The theater is the notion of an entrance into an original place where one sees "as though he were God." One's memory is suddenly put into motion. The abruptness and surprise that must have been experienced by the individual who entered the stage of Camillo's theater is like that experienced when one suddenly finds oneself on the stage of Vico's *New Science,* when one becomes the reader of whom Vico speaks, who can experience the divine pleasure and use the frontispiece as the aid to his memory and imagination. Camillo performed a special labor of Hercules. He constructed the universe as an actual place. His theater is a clearing within the universe, a place within its place.

Vico's *New Science* is not a system of eternal places of all reality. Vico's system is a system of memory for all of human reality. It is a system of cultural memory that can be used by the individual to remember the human. The relation of microcosm to macrocosm describes the relation between the *New Science* and the totality of human action and thought. The knowledge of the *New Science* is governed by the *verum-factum* principle. Only what

[69]Ibid., p. 14.

is made by the human can be known by the human. The human memory can be moved by Vico's science back to its origin but not actually back to an explicit knowledge of the ground of reality itself.

The human world is within the world. Because the world is not made by the human, the human has an external relationship to it. Recollective *fantasia* can produce only a knowledge of what *fantasia* has originally made and not a knowledge of what is made by the divine *mens*. In the frontispiece of the *New Science*, metaphysic is an agent reflecting the ray of the eye of God onto the course of nations, but this eye is also transcendent of their course. Camillo's theater is neo-Platonic, giving form to the places of all reality. Vico's *New Science* is a theater of wholly human wisdom. This human wisdom allows for contact with the eternal places through providence as manifest in the ideal eternal history of nations, as the illumination shining from behind the canvas of history.

When the *New Science* is meditated by the individual, the "inner writing" of the human world is taken up into the individual's memory. The *vocabolario mentale* that lies below the surface of any articulated language is apprehended as the *topoi* of which it is the representation. As an orator whose subject is humanity, the Vichian scientist can move from nation to nation, revealing in his speech the ideal eternal history of each. This speech allows us to situate ourselves in the world, to find our identity through an origin. This speech of place and origin is a direct narration of the necessity of things, of the causes of the human world.

Such narration is as much about the nature of narration as it is about the nature of its subject matter. Its subject matter is the self-constituting activity of humanity, and the understanding of this subject matter it produces is constituted in the process of its narration. Narration does not exist as a method independent of the narrative act. It is like the divine that makes through the word. By its nature no narration has a single meaning, any more than the human motion which it reflects has single meaning. The narrative allows us to preserve opposition ·which we are

191

otherwise in danger of losing to the flatness of the concept and conceptual criticism.

When we enter Vico's theater, we enter the *sensus communis* of the human race. The objects of Vico's frontispiece and his explanation of the significance of each place us immediately in the center, in the clearing he makes for us around which the oppositions of humanity can be arranged. Each of Vico's axioms is a recollective universal, a production of the bonding of the philological with the philosophical which can concretely affect the memory. His 114 axioms circulate before us, leading our memory to the "inner writing" of the human world, to its inner form. We are led back to the poetic wisdom, the *sapienza poetica* of the first humans, by a kind of *sapienza retorica,* an art of original philosophical speech in which the causes of humanity are narrated.

The divine Camillo intended to reveal the secret of his theater only to the King of France. Yates remarks that Torquato Tasso, whom Vico cites twice in the *New Science* and in other works, discusses at some length in one of his dialogues this secret of Camillo, "stating that Camillo was the first since Dante who showed that rhetoric is a kind of poetry."[70] Vico shows not only that rhetoric is a kind of poetry, but that it is a kind of philosophy. It is a kind of philosophy, a science of wisdom which builds its thoughts from the originating powers of speech in the image, which seeks the original places of the *sensus communis* of humanity and seeks to present them in a true narration.

---

[70]*Art of Memory,* p. 169. The work of Tasso is *La cavaletta overo de la poesia toscana, Dialoghi,* ed. Ezio Raimondi, 2 vols. (Florence: Sansoni, 1958), II, 661–63. The text states: ". . . 'l primo ch'ardisse di manifesta ⟨r⟩ le dopo Dante, il qual pose la retorica per genere de la poesia o per differenza ne la definizione, fu Giulio Camillo . . ." (pp. 661–62).

CHAPTER 7

Wisdom and Barbarism

In the conclusion to the *New Science* Vico describes the end of a people, their final barbarism when they dissolve from within. It is the most forceful passage in the *New Science* and compares in strength of language only to the well-known passage on the "night of thick darkness" which describes the first barbarism, the origin of human society.[1]

.Concerning the end of a people whose dissolute life is not stayed by a leader from within or who are not overcome by another people from without, Vico says:

> But if the peoples are rotting in that ultimate civil disease and cannot agree on a monarch from within, and are not conquered and preserved by better nations from without, then providence for their extreme ill has its extreme remedy at hand. For such peoples, like so many beasts, have fallen into the custom of each man think-ing only of his own private interests and have reached the extreme of delicacy, or better of pride, in which like wild animals they bristle and lash out at the slightest displeasure. Thus no matter how great the throng and press of their bodies, they live like wild beasts in a deep solitude of spirit and will, scarcely any two being able to agree since each follows his own pleasure or caprice. By reason of all this, providence decrees that, through obstinate factions and desperate

[1] *New Science*, §331.

193

civil wars, they shall turn their cities into forests and the forests into dens and lairs of men. In this way, through long centuries of barbarism, rust will consume the misbegotten subtleties of malicious ingenuities [*ingegni maliziosi*] that have turned them into beasts made more inhuman by the barbarism of reflection than the first men had been made by the barbarism of sense. For the latter displayed a generous savagery [*una fierezza generosa*], against which one could defend oneself or take flight or be on one's guard; but the former, with a vile savagery [*una fierezza vile*], under soft words and embraces, plots against the life and fortune of friends and intimates. Hence peoples who have reached this point of reflective malice [*riflessiva malizia*], when they receive this last remedy of providence and are thereby stunned and brutalized, are sensible no longer of comforts, delicacies, pleasures, and pomp, but only of the sheer necessities of life. And the few survivors in the midst of an abundance of the things necessary for life naturally become sociable and, returning to the primitive simplicity of the first world of peoples, are again religious, truthful, and faithful. Thus providence brings back among them the piety, faith, and truth which are the natural foundations of justice as well as the graces and beauties of the eternal order of God.[2]

There are two types of barbarism in Vico's view. There is a barbarism of the end as well as of the beginning. The barbarism of sense (*la barbarie del senso*) is the barbarism of the "thick darkness" of antiquity from which the society of the first men arises. The barbarism of reflection (*la barbarie della riflessione*) is that of Vico's third age. The "deep solitude of spirit and will" (*somma solitudine d'animi e di voleri*) of which Vico speaks is brought about by the overuse of the intellect in human affairs, such that society and the human spirit lose touch with the natural forms of imagination. The common perspective, the *sensus communis*, which constitutes the basis of human society and which is spontaneously attained through the powers of language and custom, is replaced by determinations of the intellect and reflectively devised means of social organization. *Ingegno* is now divorced from its original bond with *memoria* and *fantasia*. This barbarism of *in-*

---

[2]*New Science*, §1106. I have modified the translation of this passage for emphasis.

gegno is more confining and inhuman than the conditions of primitive life out of which society originally comes. There is a "night of thick darkness" (*densa notte di tenebre*) which lives within nations, within the course of their ideal eternal history. Societies are tragic. They begin, rise, and fall by a flaw of their own life.

The barbarism of reflection, which Vico also calls the barbarism of the intellect (*la barbarie degl'intelletti*),[3] is connected to the third age of ideal eternal history, the age of men who have forgotten the true meaning of the hero and lost the vitality of the life of the heroic cities. This third age is marked by a malicious ingenuity, a vile ferocity or savagery. This is a barbarism of reflection (*barbarie della riflessione*). It is a product of a reflective intellect that has reached the level of malice, a *riflessiva malizia*. In this ultimate period of Vico's third age, men are like those in the lowest level of Dante's *Inferno,* the final pit of treachery, those who violate humanity itself by poisoning the common confidences that are necessary for human society. They turn their *ingegno* into *insidia*: they plot "against the life and fortune of friends." *Ingegno* has been turned upside down. They live like "wild beasts," like the three beasts that block Dante's way to the *dilettoso monte* at the beginning of the *Divina commedia*—the *lonza, leone,* and *lupa.* They deal in lust, violent greed, and trickery, perversions that distort the faculties necessary to the *sensus communis* upon which truly human society depends. This third age is Vico's own. It is our age. What is the task of philosophical thought in such an age?

Vico connects the barbarism of sense with wisdom. The thought of the first men was that of poetic wisdom, *sapienza poetica*. It was poetic in the sense that the first men structured their world according to the principles of the poetic character or imaginative universal.[4] *Sapienza poetica*, used as the title of the second book of the *New Science*, designates the entire manner of thought and acting through which the human world originally

[3]*New Science,* §159.
[4]*New Science,* §381.

195

comes into being. It also refers to the way of thinking that is once again adopted by the survivors of a nation that has undergone total collapse as a result of the dissolute state Vico describes above.

To introduce his notion of poetic wisdom Vico makes some remarks on wisdom in general in Book II. He defines wisdom or *sapienza* as "the faculty which commands all the disciplines by which we acquire all the sciences and arts that make up humanity."[5] Vico goes on to claim that wisdom among the gentile peoples began with the Muse and that the Muse was a knowledge of good and evil based on divination; the nature of this point has been discussed previously. Wisdom begins in our comprehension of the world as gods, just as social order begins not in reflective judgments but in the fear that produces religion, and in the fear of the fathers, who derive their authority from control of the altars, the places of divination.

In the barbarism of reflection we lose touch with our ability to see the gods, to form the world with our imagination. We become so dissolute in our belief in the reality of the concept and its power to provide a basis for life that we lose all touch with the *sensus communis*. The humanity of a nation can, when progressed to so dissolute a level, be reinstated only by providence, which brings the actual course of the nation back to the original condition of the first men. In the collapse of a nation men must out of necessity to survive establish contact with the world through their senses. They can once again develop their powers of memory and imagination and learn to think like children. They can situate themselves in terms of a sense of the divine in nature.

I wish to consider the sense in which Vico's new science is a kind of wisdom in an age dominated by the barbarism of reflection. I take it as given that we live in such an age and that the particular modality of our barbarism is fixed in the phenomenon of technical procedure. The abstract concept when transformed into the technical procedure becomes the unifying element of all economic, social, and mental activities. Our ability

[5]*New Science*, §364.

to transform all human activity through technique replaces the *sensus communis* as the basis of social life. The form of barbarism of the present age and the fate of the present in the ideal eternal history is a problem in itself too large to be fully treated in this account. My aim is to suggest in general fashion what light Vico's conception of the decline of society and the intelligible universal may throw on contemporary consciousness and life.

In his introduction to *On the Study Methods of Our Time,* Elio Gianturco claims that "we live in a Cartesian world, a world of scientific research, technology, and gadgets, which invade and condition our lives." Gianturco's remark expresses the contemporary sense of the barbarism of which Vico speaks.[6] It suggests that the world of postindustrial states has a Cartesian mentality that is problem-oriented, progressive, and geometric. This is not to say that the ideas of Descartes have caused the world in which we live, nor that Descartes could have even imagined it, although his arguments are punctuated by such possibilities as machines that speak, and by such doubts as whether hats and cloaks seen in the street might conceal automata that move by springs, rather than covering humans.[7] Vico saw in Descartes' philosophy the opposite of his own thought. He saw in Descartes a position and, more deeply, a mentality with which he was fundamentally at odds. What Vico experienced as matters of intellectual dispute between the Cartesian position and his own have become life problems in our own age.

This point can be seen if Gianturco's remark is connected with an analysis of the technological character of contemporary society, such as that developed by the French thinker, Jacques Ellul.[8] In Ellul's view, the world of "scientific research, technology, and

[6]My remarks here follow in part my essay "Vico's Science of Imaginative Universals and the Philosophy of Symbolic Forms," in *Giambattista Vico's Science of Humanity,* ed. Giorgio Tagliacozzo and Donald Phillip Verene (Baltimore: The Johns Hopkins University Press, 1976), pp. 296–300.

[7]*The Philosophical Works of Descartes,* trans. Elizabeth S. Haldane and G. R. T. Ross, 2 vols. (Cambridge: Cambridge University Press, 1931), pp. 116 and 155.

[8]Originally in: *La technique ou l'enjeu du siècle* (Paris: Colin, 1954); *Propagandes* (Paris: Colin, 1962); and *L'illusion politique* (Paris: Laffont, 1965). Also, *Le système technicien* (Paris: Calmann-Lévy, 1977).

gadgets, which invade and condition our lives," functions according to a logic of its own. The world in which we live involves the transformation of all areas of human activity—productive, political, and psychological—into systems of order achieved through technique. The logic whereby all areas of life are made part of the single phenomenon of technique is based on the ever expanding application of a single principle, which Ellul calls "efficient ordering."[9] All aspects of life are increasingly turned into procedures. Through a process of selection of the most efficient means, technique becomes the medium of contemporary social life. Through technique all economic, political, and individual human activity is ordered into worked-out patterns and step-by-step processes, such that with every new structuring of a physical means or social relationship there occurs a heightened sense of improvement and a widening sense of the possibilities of application.[10] Each new technique opens up new possibilities of technical order.

The concept of contemporary society as technological does not imply that technique is present only in this society and not in earlier social forms. Technique, as a means of doing things, is present in all periods and types of human society, but contemporary society is distinguished by the fact that it is technological in its *form,* by the fact that the coherence of contemporary society is based on an "ensemble of means."[11] The "ensemble of means" becomes the replacement for the *sensus communis* as the basis of social order. In his remarks for the American edition of his first major work, which has as the English title *The Technological Society,* Ellul says that his purpose is to create an awareness of technological necessity. He says, "It is a call to the sleeper to awake."[12] It is a sleep like that of Vico's second barbarism, a sleep

[9]Jacques Ellul, *The Technological Society,* trans. John Wilkinson (New York: Knopf, 1964), p. 110.
[10]See Ellul's discussion of the "technical operation" and the "technical phenomenon," *Technological Society,* pp. 19–21.
[11]Ibid., p. 19.
[12]Ibid., p. xxxiii.

of the spirit and the will. The French title of this work is *La technique ou l'enjeu du siècle* (Technique or the "Stake" of the Century). *Enjeu,* a word associated with gaming tables, with money placed at hazard in games of chance, implies that all has been wagered by human society on one phenomenon—*technique.*

One is reminded of the wager of another French thinker, Pascal. In Pascal's argument the individual thinker in the deep solitude of his spirit and will can know nothing of the existence or non-existence of the Deity. He is in a position only to wager on the existence of God. Pascal says: "It forces me to wager, and I am not free [*on me force à parier, et je ne suis pas en liberté*]."[13] The technological citizens are in the position where they must stake all without any way to know the outcome or the ultimate value of the wager they have made. Like Pascal's wager, the technological society always offers a choice without choice.

In the view of Ellul and of others who have examined contemporary society from various perspectives,[14] value experience and humanistic and imaginative thought have little effect on contemporary social order. They stand out as thought forms of the past which are unconnected to and unnecessary for objective technological advance. In technological life such forms of thought come to serve, at most, as means for the "rhetorical" embellishment of society's advance. Ellul's account of technological society brings into full view the single fact that is felt by intellectual thinkers, artists, and ordinary citizens: the centrality of technique in all affairs of modern life. I wish to suggest that behind this central fact is the Cartesian model of mind. The way in

[13]Pascal, *Pensées,* ed. H. F. Stewart (London, 1950), I, 223.

[14]E.g., Herbert Marcuse states: "In the medium of technology, culture, politics, and the economy merge into an omnipresent system which swallows up or repulses all alternatives" (*One-Dimensional Man: Studies in the Ideology of Advanced Industrial Society* [Boston: Beacon Press, 1964], p. xvi). Karl Jaspers states: "In our epoch of the mass-order, of technique, of economics, when an attempt is made to render this inevitable institution absolute, there is a danger to the selfhood that the fundamental basis of the mind may be destroyed" (*Man in the Modern Age,* trans. Eden and Cedar Paul [Garden City, N.Y.: Doubleday Anchor Books, 1957, orig. pub. 1931], p. 123).

which the technological ordering of human society has come about as a historical development involves all the political, economic, physical, and psychological forces that have produced the modern world. If technological order is considered as it stands, it entails a particular mentality, a conception of knowledge and truth.

No clearer or more essential account of this mentality can be found than that way of thinking described by Descartes in the *Discourse on Method*. Here, at the very beginning of modern philosophical thought, is a prescription for the step-by-step transformation of experience into a determinate series of orders. Descartes' four principal rules—(1) to begin only with what can be taken as evidently true, (2) the division of initial difficulties into parts, (3) the movement from simple to complex, and (4) the achievement of completeness by continual review and enumeration—are intended as a means for the attainment of intellectual knowledge.[15] The implications of such passages from Descartes can now be understood more fully. The development of Western life since Descartes can be thought of as constituting the progressive transformation of this four-step formula for thought into a formula for the organization of action. Although machines were largely a matter of intellectual curiosity for Descartes and his age, the appearance of the machine as a means of production in the 1750s transformed the procedural ordering of experience from an ideal of intellectual thought to a physical and social reality. The phenomenon of technique, first realized in the machine, spread throughout modern life.

In technological life the certainty of action, the clarity of order which is achieved in the machine, is extended to all spheres of the human world by the rational dissection of the world in all its processes and their reformulation as procedures to be enacted. In the technological universe the first condition of Descartes' fourfold conception of rules—that of beginning with what is evidently true—is always fulfilled by the definiteness of order

---

[15]*Philosophical Works of Descartes*, p. 92.

that has been achieved by the previous applications of technique. Its endpoint is always fulfilled by the need to evaluate immediately each new technique, reviewing both its possibilities for improvement and for wider application within society.

In the technological world we experience as human agents what Descartes conceived we could experience only as seekers of intellectual truth. The difficulty Vico saw in Descartes' conception of knowledge and truth, constructed as it is on the basis of mathematical and scientific thought, lies in what it excludes, the result of which is, as Vico says, to "degrade all the other studies included in divine and human erudition."[16] What is widely felt in technological life is that the process of technological ordering, particularly the techniques of individual and social order, do not generate meaning. Technology never seems entirely human.

What Descartes originally excludes from knowledge in the construction of his method—the workings of the humanistic imagination—has continued to occupy its problematic position. There seems no viable place in the contemporary world for those forms of thought and feeling which have in the past provided Western man access to his own nature; they are the forms through which self-knowledge was thought possible—literature, rhetoric, the arts, history, ethics, and moral discourse. Traditional forms of self-knowledge occupy a place in technological life correspondent to that which they occupy in Descartes' conception of knowledge.

In the *Discourse on Method,* as mentioned in chapter two, Descartes presents the reading of fables and histories as the study of his youth. Although they broaden and stimulate the mind, fables make one imagine events that are not possible in reality, and histories exaggerate and distort the real events they describe. Descartes regards such forms of thought as potentially dangerous to the individual's reason. He says: "Those who regulate their conduct by examples which they derive from such a source, are liable to fall into the extravagances of knights-errant

---

[16]*Autobiography,* p. 113.

of Romance, and form projects beyond their power of performance."[17] Such extravagances have no place in the Cartesian conception of knowledge. They also have no place in the mentality of technological life. In technological life there is no room for men "to form projects beyond their power of performance [*a concevoir des desseins qui passent leurs forces*]."

For Descartes, "those who have the strongest power of reasoning, and who most skillfully arrange their thoughts in order to render them clear and intelligible, have the best power of persuasion even if they can but speak the language of Lower Brittany and have never learned Rhetoric."[18] Truth has no need of eloquence or rhetoric, and all the arts and activities of the mind that involve them can be replaced or superseded by a single piece of clear reasoning. Descartes grants humanistic forms of thought the respect due to those things experienced in youth, but he feels that they are not matters for adulthood and the mature concern for knowledge.

The humanities are at best ways of embellishing truths. They lack method and are not forms in which truth can be truly stated. Such embellishment, while it may in fact give pleasing form to truth, contains the danger of clouding the mind. Descartes' message is clear: the humanities are one thing, truth is another, and it is eloquent in itself. Descartes leads us into the deep solitude of which Vico speaks. The monologic separations within the mind and deep within the spirit are the signs of the fatigue and dispersion of energy that mark the end of a *corso*, although this end need not come suddenly. It may take centuries to complete.

Vico associates the intelligible universal with the third age of the ideal eternal history, the age of men. The intelligible universal is the Aristotelian notion of the concept formed by abstracting genera and species from the grouping of individual existents, discussed in the third chapter. This process of thought

---

[17]*Philosophical Works of Descartes*, p. 85.
[18]Ibid.

which abstracts the concept from the particular is characteristic of the third age in any *corso*. In our age the intelligible universal has produced the technical universal. In another sequence of history the power of the concept contained in the intelligible universal might develop itself in a different particular form. How is the mentality of technique connected to the intelligible universal? How can the barbarism of reflection as it has developed from Vico's century to the present age be understood?

To suggest the answer to this I wish to connect the technical concept with Cassirer's view of the scientific concept. I will pay particular attention to the view developed in his essay "The Influence of Language upon the Development of Scientific Thought"[19] and to his conception of the *Bedeutungsfunktion*—the conceptual or purely significative function of consciousness.[20] In this essay Cassirer is concerned with the shift from the Aristotelian conception of the physical world to that of Galileo. The fundamental category of Aristotle is that of substance, or being (*ousia*). The subject of the sentence reflects the substance, or substratum (*hypokeimenon*), to which the predicate refers. Physical nature is described in Aristotelian terms through substances or things and their qualities or properties.

Aristotle describes a physical thing much as Galileo does. A physical thing has in itself a principle of motion or rest such that "nature is a source or cause of being moved and of being at rest in that to which it belongs primarily, in virtue of itself and not in virtue of a concomitant attribute."[21] Aristotle describes motion and rest in terms of substance and qualities. Galileo describes them in terms of relations and quantities. The shift from Aristotelian and scholastic physics to Galilean physics depends upon replacing the symbols of language, with its subject and predicate

[19]Ernst Cassirer, "The Influence of Language upon the Development of Scientific Thought," *Journal of Philosophy*, 39 (1942), 309–27.

[20]Ernst Cassirer, *The Philosophy of Symbolic Forms*, 3 vols., trans. Ralph Manheim (New Haven: Yale University Press, 1957), III, pt. 3.

[21]*Physics*, trans. R. P. Hardie and R. K. Gaye, in *The Works of Aristotle*, ed. W. D. Ross, vol. 2 (Oxford: Clarendon Press, 1930), 192^b 21–23.

structure, with the symbols of mathematics, with its notational and calculative structure.

Cassirer points out that in Galileo's *Il saggiatore* (The Assayer), we first meet with the distinction between primary and secondary qualities. What Aristotelian thought regarded as the objective qualities of things—heat, cold, bitter, sweet, red, blue—are now regarded as only secondary characteristics of physical nature. For Galileo, Cassirer says, nature "is an open book legible to everyone. But to read this book we first have to learn the letters in which it is written. These letters are not the ordinary sense-data: the perceptions of heat and cold, of red or blue and so on. The book of nature is written in mathematical characters, in points, lines, surfaces, numbers. By this postulate Galileo removed the keystone of Aristotelian physics."[22]

The title of the *New Science* was inspired by Galileo's *Dialoghi delle Nuove Scienze* as well as by Bacon's *Novum Organum*.[23] With the shift from the Aristotelian intelligible universal to the universal of *fantasia*, Vico intends to read the book of humanity. In this way he can discover humanity's true character while Hobbes and the seventeenth-century natural-law theorists cannot because they are still bound to the intelligible universal. Their attachment to the concept as the key to human society leads them into the conceit of scholars. It prevents them from understanding how the world of the first men was different in form from ours. Vico's *vocabolario mentale,* his mental dictionary, contains the special letters of the book of humanity which we can learn to read by *fantasia*. Galileo's magnificent art of reading degenerates into the dominance of method and technological procedure, and Vico's art of reading the hieroglyphics of the *sensus communis* of humanity has its degenerate counterparts in historicism and the contemporary concern with methodology in the humanities.

This shift in the symbols in which the book of nature can be

---

[22]"The Influence of Language upon the Development of Scientific Thought," p. 316.

[23]Fisch, Introduction, *Autobiography,* p. 20.

read, which is accomplished in its most rudimentary form by Galileo, develops through the period of modern science to the level of the functional concept (*Funktionsbegriff*), which is, in Cassirer's view, the basis of modern physical science. The power to form functional concepts is characteristic of the *Bedeutungsfunktion* of consciousness which underlies the notational form of thought, the logical and mathematical systems of symbols that constitute modern science. Cassirer regards the propositional function as the fundamental model or elemental structure of this form of thinking. What interests Cassirer is the sense in which the propositional function $\phi(x)$ is composed of two logically dissimilar factors that are yet held together in a bond. The universal element ϕ can never be a member of the series represented by x, that is, $x_1, x_2, x_3, \ldots$ In like manner the particular elements of the series $x_1, x_2, x_3, \ldots$ can never be, within this particular structure, transformed into ϕ or the principle of the order of the series.[24] Cassirer's notion is absolutely simple, yet it is very telling for a theory of conceptual consciousness.

Underlying the thought of Aristotle, Galileo, and the notion of technique as the medium through which all physical and social activity is transformed into a means, there is a movement in which scientific consciousness develops itself toward an endpoint. In Aristotelian thought the concept is based on linguistic relationships. The mind moves between various individual entities; by comparison of their similarities and differences it discovers their kinds of properties. The individual entity and its essential and accidental properties are reflected in the subject-predicate structure of language. As the mind moves to higher and higher levels of specific and generic abstraction, the particular position of the individual entity is lost. At the highest level of abstraction the Aristotelian concept is unable to offer any structural determination of individual entities. The concept and the particular to which it ultimately refers are fundamentally split. Physical events can be spoken about only in terms of gener-

[24]*Philosophy of Symbolic Forms*, III, pt. 3, ch. 1.

al definitions. The universalizing power of the concept has no ability to connect with or follow the course of the physical event.

In the general form of scientific consciousness which is originally introduced through the thought of Galileo, the physical event is formed in terms of number. Numbers and their formulas can now be used to follow the particular event in its motions with other events. The motions of things can be calculated. The concept now has the power to adjust itself perfectly, at least in principle, to the observable actions of nature. The power of the concept and the knower is greatly increased. But on this level the concept is still *observational* and *calculational*. The particular x's of the series of x of the propositional function gain their physical meaning through their relation to observational reason. Once the meaning of the particular x's is in some sense observationally known and once their connection with the universal element ϕ has been determined, the concept can perform its work on the intellectual level. The concept does not wholly dominate the object in this process. Unlike the Aristotelian concept, the universal has the power to adjust itself determinately to the elements, but they are still independents to be investigated. Nature qua nature still means something and the individual elements cannot be completely drawn up into the knower's perspective.

What I wish to call the *technical concept* emerges from the *functional concept*. On the level of the functional concept nature is allowed to follow its course. Nature is an independent to which the concept must adjust. The technical concept takes up the notion that knowledge is power in its fullest sense. The technical concept does not bridge the relation between ϕ and (x) by the adjustment of ϕ to the series of observational independent particulars that become the x series. In the technical concept, reality is taken in hand from the side of the knower. The knower devises a *means* to accomplish the connection between the ϕ and the (x) of the functional concept. Through the power to grasp and develop the notion of *procedure,* the relation between the universal and the particular elements of this structure becomes wholly *active.* Through increased consciousness of the nature of procedure, the particular event is made to fit the law of the concept in a specific and workable fashion. As the thought-form of technique comes to be understood, all reality, physical and social, is transformed into the "ensemble of means" that actively and fully integrates the particular into an objective order. All powers of technique are brought to bear on the particular, a process that can be accomplished because of the *unicité* of technique. Once something is conceived it can actually be brought about in the field of action. The technical concept does not follow nature; it supersedes the reality of nature. Technology becomes the work of the gods without any need for their presence.

The technical concept is the development of the functional concept. The technical concept fulfills what the functional concept desires but cannot in itself accomplish. The functional concept is the movement of the knower fully in the direction of the particular. The technical concept is the realization of the possibility of actually moving the particular back toward the universal objectivity of the concept. The technical concept or procedure is the power to force the particular into the mold of the concept. The technical phenomenon can move the recalcitrant particular of the functional concept back in the direction of the determinant and massing power of the concept. Through technique the concept can tie the particular to itself. This sense of closure and perfect adjustment of all elements of experience is characteristic of technological consciousness and technological life.

This picture of contemporary society and thought as Cartesian and technological is a basis from which the barbarism of the contemporary age can be understood in Vichian terms, as a period within the third age of Vico's ideal eternal history. I wish to consider how wisdom is possible in a barbaric age regardless of the form the barbarism takes in a course of ideal eternal history. My aim is to connect *scienza* and Vico's *nuova arte critica,* described in chapter five, to *sapienza.* The key to this lies in the structure of *sapienza poetica,* in the barbarism of sense of the first men. What is the relation between wisdom and barbarism?

Vico says that "we must trace the beginnings of poetic wisdom to a crude metaphysics. From this, as from a trunk, there branch out from one limb logic, morals, economics, and politics, all poetic; and from another, physics, the mother of cosmography and astronomy, the latter of which gives their certainty to its two daughters, chronology and geography—all likewise poetic."[25] To describe the divisions of poetic mind Vico uses a basic symbol of mind itself, that of the *arbor scientiae*. Paolo Rossi in *Le sterminate antichità* notes that the tradition of using this image dates back to the tree of knowledge of Ramon Lull (1295), which is connected with the *ars reminiscendi,* and includes the later memory systems of Giulio Camillo and others who employ a theory of places for construction of a theater of the world.[26] Rossi also points to the use of this image in Bacon and Descartes. Giorgio Tagliacozzo has expanded Vico's tree to a comprehensive theory of contemporary human knowledge.[27] The differences between Vico's tree and Descartes' use of this image in the "Author's Letter" to the *Principles of Philosophy* are instructive.

Descartes says that "philosophy as a whole is like a tree whose roots are metaphysics, whose trunk is physics, and whose branches, which issue from this trunk, are all the other sciences. These reduce themselves to three principal ones, viz. medicine, mechanics and morals—I mean the highest and most perfect moral science which, presupposing a complete knowledge of the other sciences, is the last degree of wisdom."[28] In Vico's tree the trunk is metaphysics and physics is the first science of one branch. The other branch, beginning with poetic

[25]*New Science,* §367. Vico also uses the tree metaphor to describe as branches the origins of various social institutions of the first age (§18).
[26]Paolo Rossi, *Le sterminate antichità: Studi vichiani* (Pisa: Nistri-Lischi, 1969), pp. 190–94.
[27]Giorgio Tagliacozzo, "Epilogue," in *Giambattista Vico: An International Symposium,* ed. Giorgio Tagliacozzo and Hayden V. White (Baltimore: The Johns Hopkins University Press, 1969), esp. pp. 610–13; and Giorgio Tagliacozzo, "General Education as Unity of Knowledge: A Theory Based on Vichian Principles," in *Vico and Contemporary Thought,* ed. Giorgio Tagliacozzo, Michael Mooney, and Donald Phillip Verene (Atlantic Highlands, N.J.: Humanities Press, 1979), pt. 2, pp. 110–38.
[28]*Philosophical Works of Descartes,* p. 211.

logic, contains the poetic arts of humanity. In Descartes' tree knowledge moves in one upward direction from metaphysics through physics to morals, the highest science. Morals is to presuppose physics as its basis although, as pointed out in the preceding chapter, Descartes never developed such a highest science. Vico's tree is not based on such an upward growth but embodies the division between nature and culture. This division is initially reached from metaphysics formed through the activity of *fantasia*.

The "crude [*rozza*] metaphysics" that makes up the trunk of Vico's tree is centered in Jove as an imaginative universal. This formation of the divine as a thought by means of the power of *fantasia*, rather than by means of speculative reason, is the basis of poetic wisdom. This power of formation immediately takes two directions—one is the series of poetic arts of humanity and the other is the poetic sciences. This twofold direction fits with Vico's definition of wisdom as the faculty that commands the disciplines by which we acquire the arts and sciences. The power of the *universale fantastico*, once realized as the faculty of wisdom itself in the form of poetic metaphysics, develops into the formation of the human arts, the arts of culture, and the formation of nature. The poetic sciences are a mode of human experience, but they are that part of the mind directed to a knowledge of the natural object which cannot itself be made in the scientific act of making it intelligible. Poetic physics is itself an analogue of this twofold direction of metaphysics and of the whole of the tree itself. Vico describes poetic physics as directed toward both the formation of the cosmos of nature and the formation of the cosmos of the human body.[29]

Poetic metaphysics centered in the apprehension of Jove is not a single, unified act of mind. Jove immediately gives the first men access to nature through the split introduced between earth and sky, but at the same time Jove as the sky is seen as full of signs. Vico says: "They believed that Jove commanded by

[29]*New Science*, §§692f.

signs, that such signs were real words, and that nature was the language of Jove."[30] The power to read these signs was the basis of the first religion, the first basis of culture. Metaphysical thought itself is drawn out between these two poles. Vico says that "the first language in the first mute times of the nations must have begun with signs, whether gestures or physical objects, which had natural relations to the ideas [to be expressed]."[31]

Cassirer points out in *The Philosophy of Symbolic Forms* that when we take language back to the gesture we are faced with two semiotic acts, neither of which comes from the other. We find the mimetic gesture which actually imitates in a different medium what is meant, and the indicative gesture which points to the object.[32]

We find two phenomena: the body takes the world up into its own medium and mimetically presents something that is meant, such as folded hands for sleep or fluid movements for water, or the body sets itself off from the world by the pointing finger. Here the same gesture is used in each instance where anything is meant. Pointing is always the same gesture repeated on different objects. The pointing finger and the mimetic movement are both directions taken within the first mute language of Jove. Jove can be apprehended as nature, pointed at and affixed in the sky. He can also be read as a sign, imitated in a ritual of fearful shaking. In the mimetic gesture or ritual act Jove can be transferred as a meaning into a different medium. He is grasped as a metaphor.

Jove as mimetically apprehended yields the branch of the poetic arts of thought and humanity. Jove is imitated and embodied in the figures of the fathers who establish altars and families and offer centers of protection. The poetic arts of logic, morals, economics, and politics are the imitation of the divine who makes by knowing. They are forms achieved through the *verum-*

[30]*New Science,* §379.
[31]*New Science,* §401.
[32]Ernst Cassirer, *The Philosophy of Symbolic Forms,* I, ch. 2, sec. 1.

factum principle. Through *fantasia* as a kind of knowing the forms of human culture can be made and, once made, human life has intelligibility.

The poetic sciences of physics, cosmography, astronomy, chronology, and geography are Jove indicatively apprehended. The object of these sciences is nature, which is itself made directly by the divine and cannot be known by the human mind in terms of the *verum-factum* principle. The poetic sciences achieve their knowledge by using the body itself as a kind of pointing,[33] as a model for nature and as a model for mind.[34] The poetic sciences are indicative because they can give structure to nature. They can point out what nature is in terms of the human medium of the body, but they can never make nature truly intelligible because they are not the makers of the natural object as the human is the maker of the cultural object.

Through the poetic sciences the mind of the first men is active in defining and knowing the world as a place related to man. In the poetic arts man is active, making his existence into a place, forming the commonplaces of his *sensus communis*. The poetic sciences and arts are two polar activities of mind that make up the whole of mind in its original state. But there is no common element of unity in which they share. Mind is by nature a duality, but it is a whole in that each of its two branches reciprocally determines the nature of the other. Mind is this activity. Jove is not an internal principle of unity for mind because his appearance always has two aspects. Jove is manifest in two types of signs. He is not one sign any more than pointing is imitating.

Wisdom in Vico's view is the whole. He says in the *Study Methods* that the whole is the flower of wisdom[35] and he makes this association of the whole and wisdom in his late oration "On the Heroic Mind."[36] In what sense is poetic wisdom a whole? In the

[33]*New Science,* §691.

[34]*New Science,* §699.

[35]*Study Methods,* p. 77.

[36]"On the Heroic Mind," trans. Elizabeth Sewell and Anthony C. Sirignano, in *Vico and Contemporary Thought,* pt. 2, p. 239.

114th axiom, the last axiom, Vico speaks of the practice of wisdom in affairs of utility. He has in mind points in the law; he says: "Wisdom in its broad sense is nothing but the science of making such use of things as their nature dictates."[37] In another place he says that wisdom is "the faculty of making those uses of things which they have in their own nature, not those which opinion supposes them to have."[38]

Wisdom makes use of things according to their own nature. Poetic wisdom is wisdom formed through *fantasia*. As the origin of mind it shows that the nature of the mind is to move through opposite powers of the sign. The mind functions in terms of two branches. Wisdom, or *sapienza,* is the use of the mind in accordance with its own nature. The mind has within it both the image and the concept. The image is associated with the branch of poetic arts and the concept is associated with the branch of poetic sciences. The image is mimetic and forms its object in accordance with the *verum-factum* principle. The concept derives from the act of pointing and makes a knowledge of its object only externally.

Each of the three ages of the *storia ideale eterna* has its own mode of language. The first two ages, those of gods and heroes, are governed in form of thought by the *universale fantastico.* The third age, that of men, is governed by the intelligible universal, the *universale intelligibile* or *universale astratto.*[39] The languages of all three ages begin at the same time. Vico says: "To enter now upon the extremely difficult [question of the] way in which these three kinds of languages and letters were formed, we must establish this principle: that as gods, heroes, and men began at the same time (for they were, after all, men who imagined the gods and believed their own heroic nature to be a mixture of the divine and human natures), so these three languages began at the same time, each having its letters, which developed along with it."[40]

[37]*New Science,* §326.
[38]*New Science,* §706.
[39]*New Science,* e.g., §§1033 and 1040.
[40]*New Science,* §446.

The language of the gods was almost entirely mute; that of the heroes was a mixture of articulate sounds and mute; and the language of men is articulate and only slightly mute. In the language of men the use of the gesture and the body as a means of expression is greatly reduced. Vico describes each of the kinds of speech—mute, mute and articulate, and fully articulate—as directions immediately taken by consciousness from the original experience of Jove. Vico says articulate language began in onomatopoeia.[41] The first words for Jove were images of the sound of the thunder and lightning of Jove's body. Like the mute gesture such language had a natural relation to the object. Human words or human speech (*le voci umane*), that which develops finally into the language of the age of men, were formed as monosyllables. Vico says: "Human words were formed next from interjections, which are sounds articulated under the impetus of violent passions. In all languages these are monosyllables."[42]

The intelligible is based on the abstract word. In the axioms concerning imaginative universals Vico says that the Egyptians were unable to form the intelligible universal, the genus, civil wisdom or civil sage because they lacked the power of such abstract words. They formed this notion as the Thrice-great Hermes (*Mercurio Trimegisto*), that is, as a poetic character or imaginative universal.[43] The intelligible universal does not evolve from the imaginative universal but is a direct development of the expression of the primordial experience of Jove which has its beginning in the monosyllabic interjection. The interjection is a verbal pointing. It does not imitate as does the onomatopoetic utterance of the heroic expression. Although the intelligible or abstract universal is specifically connected with the Aristotelian theory of concept formation, in its more general sense it stands for that way of thinking that issues in something other than a figurative formation to what is sensed, in short, for cognitive or discursive thought.

[41]*New Science,* §447.
[42]*New Science,* §448.
[43]*New Science,* §209.

The mentality of the natural sciences as it develops to its full form in the age of men preserves the monosyllabic character of its origin. The abstract word as the direct embodiment of the concept is monosyllabic thought. It is a thought that strives for one meaning. It attempts to give univocal form to the multiplicity of experience. The language of the concept is always single-minded. The meaning of the event is not presented in its ambiguity, but planed out into a single constant sense. The monosyllabic interjection is like pointing; it calls attention to its object. It proclaims the existence of the object.

In the ages of gods and heroes the mind is guided by the imaginative universal, but the intelligible universal is already present in a rudimentary form. In the age of men the intelligible universal becomes dominant and the abstraction inherent in it becomes the flaw that creates the conditions of a nation's collapse. Vico says that poetic speech lasted a long time: "The poetic speech which our poetic logic has helped us to understand continued for a long time into the historical period, much as great and rapid rivers continue far into the sea, keeping sweet the waters borne on by the force of their flow."[44] The poetic or imaginative background of the life of a nation continues to supply thought with its creative powers even after the original mental energy of the mind has become dispersed into the abstraction of the intelligible universals.

The imaginative powers become tired in history. The language of the gods and heroes is forgotten, and men come to speak only one language, the language of literal meanings. Onomatopoeia is irrelevant to a language of conceptual truth, as is also the mute sign. Men lose their way and wander ignorant of the commonplaces of the *sensus communis*. Their language can no longer take them to the sense of the divine that is the origin of human society. They enter the "deep solitude of spirit and will." Under these inhuman and fatiguing conditions, they "grow dissolute in luxury, and finally go mad and waste their substance."[45]

---

[44]*New Science*, §412. See also §629.
[45]*New Science*, §241.

Literal language ultimately offers no guide for life, for human affairs, because it cuts us off from the sense of the two branches of mind that constitute the nature of mind. It cuts us off from wisdom. Vico shows that to believe in the reality of the concept is a form of madness. An exclusive attachment to conceptual analysis is a kind of dissoluteness of mind that is accompanied by a dissoluteness of life founded on wit and not on an apprehension of the necessities of the human condition. Forms of life and forms of thought, in Vico's view, go hand in hand.

In his theory of poetic wisdom Vico intended to show that human thought and human society did not arise from a rational, discursive mentality that concealed itself in fables but that the fables were themselves a kind of wisdom. As his conclusion to Book II of the *New Science* Vico says: "The theological poets were the sense and the philosophers the intellect of human wisdom."[46] Human wisdom requires that the language of sense be joined with the language of philosophy. Vico says that poetic sentences "are formed by feelings of passion and emotion, whereas philosophic sentences are formed by reflection and reasoning. The more the latter rise toward universals, the closer they approach the truth; the more the former descend to particulars, the more certain they become."[47] The *New Science* through its new art of criticism aims at the interconnection of these two tendencies. The barbarism of reflection occurs when we have only the abstraction of the purely philosophical proposition and the barbarism of sense occurs when we have only the pure poetic sentences of feeling which have not taken on the form of poetic wisdom.

Philosophical thought can become a science of wisdom rather than simply a science of the truth of the universal proposition only if it is able to join itself to the language of sense formed by *fantasia* in the fable. Philosophy must speak in accordance with the nature of that about which it desires wisdom. It must reflect the duality of mind in its speech. Poetic wisdom expresses this

[46]*New Science*, §779.
[47]*New Science*, §219.

215

nature of mind in its language. It can speak in the manner of both the poetic arts and the poetic sciences. It cannot speak in both their manners at once. Each is a way in which the original experience of Jove takes form. There is no principle of unity or absolute standpoint of mind that contains them as a single mode of symbolism. If we ask what the imaginative universal is, the answer can be understood in terms of its presence in the logic *or* the physics of the first men, in their politics *or* in their chronology and geography. There is no language of the imaginative universal in itself.

Vico's thought contains an original notion of philosophical speech, one that could be arrived at only by refusing to make the logical judgment the basis of mind. The basis of philosophical speech must be the judgment made "without reflection" that Vico associates with topics, the metaphor, and the imaginative universal, what I am calling by the general term—the image. The logical judgment has the category as its presupposition. The category preserves in the language of discursive thought the impetus of the original monosyllable out of which human language arises.

Categories are the determinant elements of the relations present in the structure of cognitive judgments. The thought of categories is thought that eliminates opposition between things and makes them into a network of relations. There are no categories of the imagination because the forms of imagination are not determinate judgments. Their unifications of universal and particular are not based on specifiable principles of relation. Categorical thought has no place for memory and the narrative. The category invites us to create ultimate singles, unequivocal grounds for thought and being. Memory and imagination allow us to treat opposition as a dramatic force. The category robs us of any actual sense of drama or time or place. The category is internally free of opposition and has validity for all times and places.[48]

[48]Donald Phillip Verene, "Categories and the Imagination," in *Categories: A Colloquium,* ed. Henry W. Johnstone, Jr. (University Park: published by Department of Philosophy, The Pennsylvania State University, 1978), pp. 185–207.

The mentality of the concept, the mentality that attempts to understand knowledge and reality through the logical judgment, bases its comprehension on the category. The category is thought to be the ultimate basis of our comprehension of knowing and being. There are no categories of the imagination because the imaginative universal is not a logical judgment, nor is it a kind of proto or incomplete version of such a judgment. We are so accustomed to thinking philosophically in terms of conceptuality that we look across experience and believe that there are categories of all forms of experience and of all of experience. The logic of imagination does not differ from the logic of the concept because it uses different categories but because it uses no categories at all. The belief that there are categories of the imagination is a conceit of the mind, a *boria,* which must be overcome because it blinds us to the sense in which the image is itself an original mode of thought.

The difference between Vico and absolute idealism, to which Croce connected Vico, is that in Vico's view wisdom is never mediation. The struggle to connect wisdom with mediation stems from an interest in the attempt to comprehend being as a progressive movement of categories. Wisdom involves a language that preserves opposition, that speaks of the two branches of the tree without an attempt to reduce them to a single basis in the trunk. Wisdom stems from an understanding of the image as the first and genuine thought. It regards the image as the guide to philosophical speech as it has been the original guide to human speech itself. The original sense of true narration in the *mythos* must be the guide to a true narration from the standpoint of recollective mind. Because it lacks this understanding of the myth, philosophical idealism can give us at most a wisdom of the concept.

Fantasia suggests a way of forming experience without categories; it suggests a language of oppositions that is not based on a logic of the category. The fable, unlike the category, is a language of oppositions, because in it the opposed forces of experience are preserved. Good and bad, large and small, light and dark, life and death are kept before the mind in the fable as active forces of existence. The fable, or *mythos*, is a true story because it does not relieve the presence of the positive and the negative. These poles are neither taken up into a common synthetic order nor resolved in a judgment that joins them on the basis of a common category.

The fable offers its own form of understanding. The image or metaphor that is the basis of the fable opens the mind to itself. It provides the clearing from which to see further the reality of the opposition. This clearing is a reflection in mind of the physical clearing and light established in the original forests by the labor of Hercules, from which sprang the first altars and later the cities in which the opposition of the divine and the human is first given form. The category would turn into one meaning what is always for the fable two meanings. The reduction of opposition is the aim of the mind when it goes in the direction of scientific understanding. In this aim it gives up interest in the whole. The fable's language of opposites is the guide to the thought that attempts a recollective understanding of the whole, that intends consciously to recapture what it can of the original power of *fantasia*.

In the language of the imaginative universal the bond between the universal and the particular is not dialectically developed. It is narrated. Its story of Jove is told, but not in a progressive fashion. The true narration of the ideal eternal history is tragic, unprogressive, and non-dialectical. Vico's *New Science* demonstrates the importance of a language that can preserve oppositions without resolution. In this sense it is a true language of humanity whose actual life is not that of the category. Vico's *New Science* contains no statement of categories. The axioms of the *New Science* remain memory aids that can be turned over in the mind and can direct vision to the oppositions in nations.

The whole which is the hallmark of wisdom exists within the poetic world of the first two ages. What is lost in the fatigue of history when the intelligible universal gains strength is not simply the prominence of the image. What is lost is the language that can speak in two ways at once, that can produce both the mute imitation and the monosyllabic interjection. This language that originally gives life to the whole is not monologic. It is dialogic, reflecting the opposition of the branches of the tree which themselves reflect the duality of mind.

The kind of bond that makes up the inner structure of the *universale fantastico* suggests the way in which philosophy can produce its understanding of the two branches of the mind—the arts and sciences. In the age of men the common context of the *universale fantastico* is gone. The original power of the *universale fantastico* to refract itself into the languages of both branches is lost. In the age of men the original power of *fantasia* is lost. It is narrowed to the one branch of the arts and the power of the monosyllable is separated out into its own form, that of the *universale intelligibile*. It becomes the basis from which the natural and especially the technical sciences are slowly generated as forms of understanding existing independent of *fantasia*. In the age of men the two branches no longer function within any common locus of mind. We may speak of imagination in science, but what we refer to is an activity directed by the concept and different from imagination as it directs life and shapes the wisdom of life.

What is lost in the third age of ideal eternal history is not an original unity of mind but the original dialogic character of mind embodied in *fantasia*. The barbarism of the third age comes about not by the elimination of *fantasia* but by narrowing it to art and the aesthetic. As art, *fantasia* can no longer become wise. It cannot become wise because as something apart it does not have access to the whole. As art, images are assigned their own independent reality or become images "of something," things that present in a secondary way a reality established by the concept. Barbarism is a failure of wisdom in the sense that mind loses its power to be dialogic. It loses its power of narration, its power to build a fable of itself in the languages of the mute, onomatopoetic, and monosyllabic sign. The imaginative universal and the intelligible universal become simply separate. There is no education of the whole. There is no wider sense of *fantasia* that can move between the two branches of mind and speak of the object in each of their distinctive ways.

In the age of men all mind becomes a specialist variation on the fundamental split that occurs in the original language of *fantasia*. Mind is taken into many monologic paths, many disciplines, where it wears itself out. Vico's new art of criticism is a pedagogical art of mind. By the *ars reminscendi* the mind can learn something of the language of the wisdom of *fantasia*. By these arts philosophy can develop a sense of language that brings *fantasia* to life as recollection. In so doing philosophy becomes the language of mind in its dual reality. Philosophical language as the language of recollective universals, of recollective *fantasia,* is the power to speak about both these branches of mind. But it has no principle of unity to offer beyond its speech, its narration of the differences of the branches.

This praxis can refresh mind in its last days of rust and misbegotten wit, but it does not thereby convert a negative into a positive. It will not itself stay the necessity of the end of a *corso* of ideal eternal history, any more than a knowledge of the cause of a tragic event will alter the actual condition itself. Yet this language of recollective *fantasia* carries its own justification. It allows us to attain a sense of the beyond in the face of the language of "malicious wits," to grasp the nature of the mind even in the "dens and lairs of men."

In his oration "On the Heroic Mind" Vico says that *sapientia* is what one obtains in a true education, an education of the whole.[49] Such education, he says, is a process of healing. The notion of wisdom as a whole for Vico is not the notion of unity. It is instead the notion of a language for the preservation of fundamental opposition. Thus philosophical speech comes from the branch of the image, the branch of the arts of humanity, but speaks of them only in relation to their opposite, the branch of the sciences, the life of the concept. This speech heals the

---

[49]"On the Heroic Mind," p. 233.

soul by stirring its memory. It heals us from the madness of the concept, the thick night of rationality, with its language of the single sense of meaning, its inability to speak without a specifiable principle of order.

The barbarism of reflection which is more inhuman than the barbarism of sense is not overcome by this new philosophical speech. Once poetic wisdom as the basis of society is gone, it is gone. The gods disappear with the disappearance of the language of the gods. Their presence as the basis of society is possible only through the providential order of the *storia ideale eterna*. In his discussion of poetic morals Vico says: "Above poetic heroism Plato raised his own philosophic heroism, placing the hero above man as well as beast; for the beast is the slave of his passions, and man, in the middle of the scale, struggles with his passions, while the hero at will commands his passions; and thus the heroic nature is midway between the human and the divine."[50] Plato was the first of Vico's four authors. Vico says in the *Autobiography* that Plato was prevented in his theory of commonwealths from formulating the ideal eternal history because he did not know of the fall of man.[51] The "long centuries of barbarism" and mental rust that precede the fall of a nation require philosophy as a means to remember the heroic place midway between the human and the divine. This memory does not cancel the fall of a nation, but it allows us to hear something of the language of the gods. We hear this not only as poetry, but as the necessary and true narration of the principles of humanity.

[50]*New Science*, §515.
[51]*Autobiography,* p. 122.

APPENDIX

Bibliographies of
Work on Vico

Benedetto Croce. *Bibliografia vichiana*. Rev. and enlg. by Fausto Nicolini. 2 vols. Naples: Ricciardi, 1947–48.

Elio Gianturco. *A Selective Bibliography of Vico Scholarship 1948–1968*. Supplement of *Forum Italicum*. Florence: Grafica Toscana, 1968. Lists many works that are not on Vico but in the opinion of its compiler are of Vichian nature.

Maria Donzelli. *Contributo alla bibliografia vichiana* (1948–1970). Naples: Guida, 1973. Lists works in various languages continuing from the terminating date of *Bibliografia vichiana*.

Giorgio Tagliacozzo. "Bibliography." In *Giambattista Vico: An International Symposium,* ed. by Giorgio Tagliacozzo and Hayden V. White, pp. 615–19. Baltimore: The Johns Hopkins University Press, 1969.

Molly Black Verene. "Critical Writings on Vico in English." In *Giambattista Vico's Science of Humanity,* ed. by Giorgio Tagliacozzo and Donald Phillip Verene, pp. 457–80. Baltimore: The Johns Hopkins University Press, 1976. Incorporates and expands the bibliography of *Giambattista Vico: An International Symposium* and includes a section о `works that cite Vico.

Molly Black Verene. "Critical Writings on Vico in English: A Supplement." *Social Research,* 43 (1976), 904–14. Extends the preceding bibliography.

Robert Crease. *Vico in English: A Bibliography of Writings by and about Giambattista Vico (1668–1744)*. Atlantic Highlands, N.J.: Humanities Press, 1978. A comprehensive bibliography done from the bibliographies of Giorgio Tagliacozzo and Molly Black Verene. Published for the Institute for Vico Studies, New York.

Bollettino del Centro di Studi Vichiani, vol. 1, 1971—. Published by the Centro di Studi Vichiani, Naples.

Index

225

INDEX

226

Library of Congress Cataloging in Publication Data

Verene, Donald Phillip, 1937–
  Vico's science of imagination.

  Includes index.
  1. Vico, Giovanni Battista, 1668–1774. I. Title.
B3583.V45   195   80-69828
ISBN 0-8014-1391-5   AACR1